01/03/00
50
ABH-3569

LITERARY MASTERPIECES

ISSN 1526-1522

LITERARY MASTERPIECES

Volume **3**

The Maltese Falcon

Richard Layman

A MANLY, INC. BOOK

GALE GROUP

Detroit
San Francisco
London
Boston
Woodbridge, CT

THE MALTESE FALCON

Matthew J. Bruccoli and Richard Layman, *Editorial Directors*

Copyright ©2000

The Gale Group

27500 Drake Road

Farmington Hills, MI 48331

ISBN 0-7876-3965-6

ISSN 1526-1522

Printed in the United States of America

10 9 8 7 6 5 4 3 2 1

For the Trailblazers

William Godschalk
William F. Nolan
Joe Gores
David Fechheimer
Don Herron

TABLE OF CONTENTS

A NOTE TO THE READER

Think of it this way: you are about to embark on a journey. This book is, among other things, designed to be at once a reservation and a round-trip ticket. The purpose of the journey, the goal and destination, is for you to experience, as fully and as deeply as you can, a masterpiece of literature. Reading a great work is not a passive experience. It will be demanding and, as you will see, well rewarded.

by George Garrett, Henry Hoyns Professor of Creative Writing, the University of Virginia

What is a masterpiece? The answer is easy if you are dealing with the great works of antiquity—for example the *Iliad* and *Odyssey* of Homer, the tragedies of Aeschylus, Sophocles, and Euripides—works that have endured for millenia and even outlasted their original language. Closer in time there are the accepted monuments of our languages and culture, such as the plays of Shakespeare, the *Divine Comedy* of Dante, and the comedies of Molière. But here and now we are dealing with work that is nearer to us in time, that speaks to and about persons, places, and things that we either know at first hand or at least know about. These works are accepted by critical consensus (and tested in the marketplace and in the classroom) as among the most original and influential works of their times. It remains for you to experience their power and originality.

There is much to be gained from close and careful study of a great book. You will always find much more than you expected to, than you are looking for. Whether we know it and admit it or not, we are one and all constantly being changed and shaped by what we read. One definition of a literary masterpiece is that it is a great work that can touch us most deeply. It can be, is, if you are wide awake and fully engaged, a profound experience. Lighthearted or deadly serious, it is about things that matter to us. The Gale Study Guides are intended to help you to enjoy and to enlarge your understanding of literature. By an intense focus, these Guides enhance the values you discover in reading enduring works. Discovery is always an important part of the process. With guidance you will see how personal discoveries can be made and, equally important, can be shared with others studying the same book. Our literary culture is, ideally, a community. This book is meant to serve as your introduction to that community.

From the earliest days of our history (until the here and now), readers have looked for pleasure and meaning in whatever they read. The two are inextricable in literature. Without pleasure, enjoyment, there can be no permanent meaning. Without value and significance, there is no real pleasure. Ideally, the close study of literary masterpieces—comedy or tragedy, past and present—will increase our pleasure and our sense of understanding not only of the individual work in and of itself but also of ourselves and the world we inhabit.

There is hard work involved. What you have labored to master you will value more highly. And reading is never exclusively a passive experience. You have to bring the whole of yourself to the experience. It becomes not a monologue, but a dialogue between you and the author. What you gain from the experience depends, in large part, on what you bring and can give back. But, as great voices have told us since the dawn of literature, it is well worth all the effort, indeed worth any effort.

We learn how powerful words can be. The language of great voices speaking to us across time and space, yet close as a whisper, matters enormously. Sooner or later, our buildings will crumble; our most intricate and elegant machines will cough and die and become rusty junk; and our grand monuments and memorials will lose all their magic and meaning. But we know that our words, our language, will last longer than we do, speaking of and for us, over centuries and millenia. Listening to great voices, reading their words and stories in the enduring works of literature, we are given a reward of inestimable value. We earn a share in their immortality.

You will meet some memorable characters, good and bad, and you are going to participate in unforgettable events. You will go to many places, among them the Africa of Chinua Achebe, the England of Virginia Woolf, the China of Maxine Hong Kingston. You can visit 1920s Paris with Ernest Hemingway, the magical Latin America of Gabriel García Márquez, the Mississippi of William Faulkner, the dark side of San Francisco with Dashiell Hammett. Gale Study Guides are good maps to the literary territory. Envision the journey as a kind of quest or pilgrimage, not without difficulty, that can change your understanding of life.

ACKNOWLEDGMENTS

This book was produced by Bruccoli Clark Layman, Inc. R. Bland Lawson is the series editor; senior editor Karen L. Rood was the in-house editor.

Production manager is Philip B. Dematteis.

Copyediting supervisor is Phyllis A. Avant. Senior copyeditor is Thom Harman. The copyediting staff includes Brenda Carol Blanton, James Denton, Worthy B. Evans, Melissa D. Hinton, William Tobias Mathes, and Jennifer S. Reid.

Indexing was done by Alex Snead and Cory McNair.

Layout and graphics supervisor is Janet E. Hill. Graphics staff includes Karla Corley Brown and Zoe R. Cook.

Photography editors are Charles Mims, Scott Nemzek, Alison Smith, and Paul Talbot. Digital photographic copy work was performed by Joseph M. Bruccoli and Zoe R. Cook.

Systems manager is Marie L. Parker.

Typesetting supervisor is Kathleen M. Flanagan. The typesetting staff includes Mark J. McEwan, Kimberly Kelly, and Patricia Flanagan Salisbury.

Special thanks to William P. Arney, Jane Gelfman, Joe Gores, Nicholas Layman, Josephine Hammett Marshall, Julie Rivette—and especially to Vince Emery.

Following is a list of the copyright holders who have granted us permission to reproduce material in this volume of Gale Study Guides to Great Literature. Every effort has been made to trace copyright holders, but if omissions have been made, please contact The Gale Group.

Bogart, Humphrey, Peter Lorre, Mary Astor, and Sidney Greenstreet in the film *The Maltese Falcon,* photograph. Corbis-Bettmann. Reproduced by permission.

Comic strip advertisement for Wildroot Cream Oil in *The Adventures of Sam Spade,* King Features, circa 1946.

Cover of *The Maltese Falcon.* Pocket Books, 1944. Collection of Richard Layman.

Dust jacket of *The Maltese Falcon.* By Dashiell Hammett. Alfred A. Knopf, 1930. Copyright 1930. Reproduced by permission of Alfred A. Knopf, Inc. Collection of Richard Layman.

891 Post Street, photograph. Collection of Richard Layman.

Flitcraft Compend 1929. Thomas Cooper Library, University of South Carolina.

Hammett, Dashiell, in New York, circa 1931. *New York Journal American* Archive. Reproduced by permission of Harry Ransom Humanities Research Center, University of Texas, Austin.

Hammett, Dashiell, 1933. Courtesy of Josephine Hammett Marshall.

Hammett, Dashiell, testifying before the McCarthy committee. *New York Journal American* Archive. Reproduced by permission of Harry Ransom Humanities Research Center, University of Texas, Austin.

Hammett, Josephine. Courtesy of Josephine Hammett Marshall.

Hammett, Josephine, and her two daughters, 1929. Courtesy of Josephine Hammett Marshall.

Last page of the fourth installment of *The Maltese Falcon,* in *Black Mask,* December 1929.

The Maltese Falcon, Movie lobby card. Collection of Richard Layman.

The Maltese Falcon comic book. Collection of Josephine Hammett Marshall.

Opening page of *The Maltese Falcon* in *Black Mask,* 1929.

Shaw, Joseph T., photograph.

Still from *Satan Met a Lady,* Warner Bros., 1936.

ABOUT DASHIELL HAMMETT

I n March 1928, just after Dashiell Hammett had submitted his first novel for publication, he wrote to his editor, Blanche Knopf, that unlike most moderately literate people, he took detective fiction seriously: "Some day somebody's going to make 'literature' out of it . . . and I'm selfish enough to have my hopes." Hammett wrote only five novels and sixty-eight published short stories in his twelve-year writing career, but it is generally acknowledged that his impact on detective fiction is unequaled in this century.

When Hammett began writing in 1922, there was an abundance of mystery writers who satisfied a growing hunger among American readers for stories of murder and intrigue. Even so, the mystery was written largely by untrained and unskilled writers or by professionals as a diversion from their serious work. It was commonly agreed that the sole purpose of the mystery was to present a problem, usually a murder, to provide the clues to its solution, and then, after a proper interval, to reveal the criminal and his method. There was little place for character development, because it was only a distraction from the description of the crime and the clues. The crime, it was felt, had to be unusual to be interesting, and therefore fictional murderers bore little resemblance to actual criminals, and the methods of crime in fiction often tested the reader's credulity. The setting was typically in a middle- or upper-class society, because there the crime was more shocking and more worthy of the attention of a detective, most often a brilliant amateur who solved crimes as a hobby.

Hammett's mysteries were different. He was the most accomplished of a school of writers that emerged in the early 1920s who were called hard-boiled. "Hammett took murder out of the Venetian vase and dropped it into the alley," Raymond Chandler explained. "Hammett wrote at first (and almost to the end) for people with a sharp, aggressive attitude to life. They were not afraid of the seamy side of things; they lived there. Violence did not dismay them; it was right down their street.

Dashiell Hammett, 1933

Hammett gave murder back to the kind of people that commit it for reasons, not just to provide a corpse; and with the means at hand, not hand wrought dueling pistols, curare, and tropical fish. He put these people down on paper as they were, and he made them talk and think in the language they customarily used for these purposes."[1] Hammett brought realism to mystery fiction and, by the time he wrote his last novel in 1933, he could boast, with the support of the literary establishment, that he had accomplished the goal he had expressed to Blanche Knopf five years earlier. He had written mysteries of lasting literary worth.

Samuel Dashiell Hammett was born on 27 May 1894 in St. Mary's County, Maryland, about sixty miles southeast of Washington, D.C. Richard Hammett, his father, was a justice of the peace and tended the family farm, called Hopewell and Aim, which was owned by Samuel Hammett, Richard's father. Until about 1900 two families lived in the three-story house on Hopewell and Aim: Samuel Hammett, his second wife, and their three young children; Richard, his wife, Annie, and their three children: Aronia Rebecca (called Reba) born 1893, Samuel Dashiell (called Da-shéel) born 1894, and Richard Thomas Jr. (called Dick) born 1896. Annie Hammett worked as a nurse when she was able, but poor health and the duties of motherhood kept her home much of the time. Richard Hammett was an ambitious man who suffered from bad luck and impatience. Dashiell Hammett told his daughter Josephine that Richard Hammett was a tobacco broker. He apparently also sought a political career in St. Mary's County by opportunistically switching parties, but such disloyalty was looked on with disfavor and, according to one family account, he was run "out of the county, more or less, on a rail." In 1900 the Hammetts moved to Philadelphia, where they stayed for about a year before they went to Baltimore and entered Dashiell in public school. In 1908, after his first semester of high school at Baltimore Polytechnic Institute, Dashiell Hammett quit school to help his father salvage a business enterprise, probably selling fresh seafood and produce door-to-door. When the business failed, Hammett took a succession of temporary jobs to help support the family. "I became the unsatisfactory and unsatisfied employee of various railroads, stock brokers, machine manufacturers, canners, and the like. Usually I was fired,"[2] he wrote later.

His instability ended in 1915, when, at the age of twenty-one, Hammett became an operative for Pinkerton's National Detective Agency. He worked at Pinkerton's until 1918, when he went into the army, and off and on for two years after his discharge in 1919. It was the longest-lasting job Hammett ever held and the most important in terms of his development as a writer. In 1915 Pinkerton's was the largest detective agency in the country, and its work was varied. During labor disputes of the time Pinkerton's operatives acquired a reputation as strike busters because they were often called on to enforce picket lines. They also hunted law-breakers, methodically and, according to their advertisements, tirelessly. As an operative, Hammett worked on a wide variety of cases. He broke strikes; he chased crooks; and he conducted surveillance. Hammett worked out of Pinkerton's Baltimore office, though his duties took him all over the Southeast. He boasted later in his life that as a Pinkerton he had once been hired to find a man who stole a Ferris wheel. On another occasion, he said, he had helped arrest a gang of blacks accused of stealing dynamite: "In the excitement I had a feeling something was wrong but I could not figure what it was till I happened to look down and saw this negro whittling away at my leg."[3]

His career was interrupted in June 1918 when he was inducted into the army. Though Hammett never got more than twenty miles from his home as a soldier, he left the service as a war casualty. He was stationed at Camp Meade, Maryland, in the ambulance corps and contracted Spanish Influenza during the worldwide epidemic that claimed more American lives than military action during World War I. His influenza developed into tuberculosis, and Hammett was given a medical discharge with a 25 percent disability rating in May 1919. His illness afflicted him permanently, and he was never again fit for an occupation that required physical labor—including work as a private detective.

Nonetheless, Hammett tried to resume his career at Pinkerton's, working as his health permitted. After a year of sporadic work in Baltimore, Hammett left in 1920 for Washington State, where he worked out of Pinkerton's Spokane office. He seems to have worked briefly in Montana at the Anaconda Copper Mines, where there had been labor troubles since before the war, and Pinkerton's had been hired to break the unions. The experience in Montana provided the material for Hammett's first novel, written seven years later.

Just over six months after his move west, Hammett's health deteriorated seriously, and he was hospitalized in the U.S. Public Health Service Hospital in Tacoma, Washington, fully disabled. He stayed there from 6 November 1920 to 21 February 1921, when he was transferred to another USPHS hospital near San Diego, where he stayed until 15 May. In Tacoma, Hammett fell in love with his nurse, a twenty-four-year-old named Josephine Dolan, whom he called Jose (pronounced with a long o). By early 1921, she was pregnant, and she went to Butte, Montana, to stay with her relatives while she and Hammett planned their future. Their marriage came on 7 July 1921, less than a month after Hammett was released from the hospital in San Diego, and they established a residence in San Francisco. Mary Jane Hammett was born three months later on 16 October.

The early days of Hammett's marriage were difficult ones. He had a family to support and little prospect of steady employment. He worked briefly for Pinkerton's in San Francisco and later bragged about his role in several big cases, including the Fatty Arbuckle rape-murder case and the Sonoma gold-specie theft in which $125,000 in gold coin was stolen from a freighter; but by the end of 1921, Hammett's Pinkerton days were over for good as worsening health caused him to be bedridden. Hammett had to find another occupation by which to support his family, and he chose writing.

HAMMETT ON LOAFING

I'm a two-fisted loafer. I can loaf longer and better than anybody I know. I did not acquire this genius. I was born with it. I quit school when I was thirteen because I wanted to loaf. I sold newspapers for a while, loafed, became a stevedore, loafed, worked in a machine shop, loafed, became a stock broker, loafed, went into the advertising business, loafed, tried hoboing in earnest, loafed, became a Pinkerton detective for seven years and went into the army.

Quoted in Joseph Harrington, "Hammett Solves Big Crime; Finds Ferris Wheel," *New York Evening Journal*, 28 [?] January 1934.

In February 1922 he took advantage of a rehabilitation program for disabled veterans and signed up for an eighteen-month vocational-training course in stenography. But he was too sick for regular employment. Now twenty-eight, and with only his veterans' disability checks to live on, Hammett needed money to pay the rent and buy groceries. He could write, and he had an abundance of interesting stories from his Pinkerton years. He decided to turn those resources to profit. Hammett began his writing career in October 1922 with a short publication in H. L. Mencken and George Jean Nathan's magazine *The Smart Set*. Before the end of the year he managed four more publications of short stories and brief articles, and in 1923, he had fourteen stories and two articles published. With the exception of five early publications in *The Smart Set* and a handful of stories in the 1930s, all Hammett's stories were published in detective-fiction pulps, primarily in *Black Mask*, the most notable of that group.

In 1922 there was a movement underway among certain *Black Mask* writers that transformed the detective story from fanciful, elaborate puzzles in fictional form to tough, realistic accounts of life in the criminal underworld. The movement was particularly well suited to Hammett, whose fiction was based primarily on his experience as a detective and his knowledge of criminal behavior. In October 1923 Hammett's story "Arson Plus" was published in *Black Mask*. It introduced the dominant character of his short fiction and marked the beginning of his development as the most accomplished of the hard-boiled writers in the so-called

Black Mask School. The character is the Continental Op, an unnamed operative—short, fat, and middle-aged—for the Continental Detective Agency. Hammett later said the Continental Op was based on his Pinkerton's supervisor in Baltimore, Jimmy Wright, and it is clear that the Continental Detective Agency is modeled after Pinkerton's, which had its Baltimore offices in the Continental Building.

The distinguishing characteristic of the Continental Op is his utter believability. Unlike the amateur supersleuths of the classic detective story or the invincible street fighters of the new hard-boiled fiction, Hammett's Op was neither a genius nor a ruffian. "I see in him a little man going forward day after day through mud and blood and death and deceit—as callous and brutal and cynical as necessary—towards a dim goal, with nothing to push or pull him towards it except that he's been hired to reach it," Hammett wrote.[4]

Twenty-one of Hammett's Op stories were published between October 1923 and March 1926 in addition to two related novelettes and two novels featuring the Op. By the time he had finished with that character, Hammett had established a standard against which all hard-boiled detective fiction is measured.

Like most hard-boiled fiction, Hammett's stories were dominated by the character of his detective, who is the first-person narrator. He is tough, cynical, and realistic—he is not possessed of any notion that he can eliminate evil from the world; he simply does the best he can to make his small part of it livable. The Op, like Hammett's other detectives, is a code hero. He lives according to a personal sense of right and wrong that for him transcends both civil and religious law. The plots of Hammett's stories are of secondary importance. Normally he used conventional plot devices of the classic mystery writers, revived by realistic characters (relative to other crime fiction of the time, at least) and a spare vernacular writing style. By the mid 1920s Hammett was a successful pulp-story writer. That means he had a story a month published, usually in *Black Mask*, had earned himself a reputation among the magazine's regular readers, and made perhaps $1,000 a year from his writing.

In May 1926 Hammett's second daughter, Josephine, was born, and again he faced the problem of stretching his income to support his family. In anticipation of his new family responsibilities, he decided to give up writing for advertising, an interest of his since he had left Pinkerton's. In March 1926 Hammett took a job at Samuels Jewelry Company in San Francisco as advertising manager. The money was good, and the prospects were bright—but short-lived. On 20 July 1926 Hammett collapsed at work from a lung hemorrhage and was not able to continue his job. Moreover, his condition was considered infectious by the Public Health Service nurses who visited him at home, and Hammett was required to take up residence away from his wife and daughters. They went to Montana to be with Jose Hammett's family, and Hammett stayed behind, convinced he was dying. Bedridden and lonesome, he returned to fiction.

Jose, Josephine, and Mary Hammett, circa 1928

In November 1926 there was a change of editors at *Black Mask*. Captain Joseph Thompson Shaw, a World War I bayonet instructor with a paucity of magazine experience, took over the editorial reins and determined to make *Black Mask* the best magazine of its kind. Largely through self-promotion, Shaw was later celebrated as the innovator at *Black Mask* of the hard-boiled form, though Hammett had already refined it by 1926. Shaw's real importance was not as an innovator, but as a promoter and an organizer. His first move after he took over *Black Mask* was to lure the best writers who had previously been published in the magazine back as regulars. Hammett was chief among his priorities.

In February 1927 Hammett's first story in eleven months appeared in *Black Mask*. It was his most ambitious to date, the first installment of a two-part, 35,000-word novelette consisting of "The Big Knock-Over" and "$106,000 Blood Money" (published in May 1927). Hammett had now firmly dedicated himself to a literary career. Probably with Shaw's help, he had become a reviewer of mystery novels for the *Saturday Review of Literature*, a position he held from January 1927 to October 1929.

More important, he began writing longer works, again almost certainly at Shaw's urging, and in November 1927 the first installment of Hammett's first novel was published in *Black Mask*. The novel, then known as "The Cleansing of Poisonville," was episodic in structure because it was written for serial publication. It appeared in four monthly segments, concluding in February 1928. That same month, Hammett sent the manuscript of his novel, unsolicited, to Alfred A. Knopf, Publishers. It caught the attention of Blanche Knopf, who was chief editor of the firm's mystery line, and by March Hammett's novel was accepted for book publication on the condition that he revise it extensively and change the title. *Red Harvest* was published by Knopf in February 1929.

In *Red Harvest* the Op narrates the story of his involvement with the mining town of Personville. He was hired by Donald Willsson, the son of Elihu Willsson, the town's wealthiest and most powerful man, to help in an investigation of corruption. When Donald is murdered before the Op meets him, Elihu Willsson hires the Op to find his son's murderer. During the course of his investigation, the Op has his fun "opening Poisonville up from Adam's apple to ankles,"[5] as he puts it. He discovers that there are four gang leaders who, working under Elihu Willsson's protection, control illegal activities, and the Op destroys them by setting them against each other. There are twenty-four murders in the novel (revised down from twenty-six in the serial version), most arranged by the Op. In the lawless environment of the town, "it's easier to have them killed off, easier and surer" (197), he explains. At the end of the novel, the Op has cleaned up Personville. All of the gang leaders are dead, and Elihu Willsson, whose irresponsible use of power had caused the town's corruption, lives on, though he is old and withered. The Op does not provide a system of order for the town. He leaves the rubble behind him.

When the novel was published, some reviewers found the violence excessive and repulsive, despite the fact that Hammett had accurately described an area of the Northwest at a time when, according to a *New York Times* report, murders were common occurrences.[6] Others saw real talent exhibited in Hammett's first novel. "It is doubtful if even Ernest Hemingway has ever written more effective dialogue," Herbert Asbury stated in *The Bookman*.[7] "We recommend this one without reservation. We gave it A plus before we'd finished the first chapter," was Walter R. Brooks's verdict in *Outlook and Independent*.[8]

Hammett did not need the encouragement of reviewers to go on. In February 1929, the same month that Knopf published *Red Harvest*, the last of four installments of his second novel, *The Dain Curse*, appeared in *Black Mask*, and he had substantially finished his third novel. *The Dain Curse* is generally considered to be Hammett's weakest novel—even he called it "a silly story"[9]—and much of the blame lies with his attempt to write for two markets at once. *Black Mask* wanted long works broken into episodes for serial publication; Knopf wanted integrated novels. In an attempt to please them both, Hammett wrote a rambling novel in which the intensity of the action rises and falls too often to sustain the reader's interest. When he was asked for revisions by Harry Block, who edited his work at Knopf under Blanche Knopf's supervision, Hammett resisted, making only the easiest changes. It was the summer of 1928, and he was working on *The Maltese Falcon*, a better book more worthy of his attention, Hammett thought.

The Dain Curse is about the Op's investigations centered on Gabrielle Leggett, a helpless girl victimized by corrupt and possessive villians. Gabrielle's family was broken up when she was five by her aunt, Alice Dain (who later became her stepmother). Both Dain sisters had been in love with the same man, and Alice's sister had married him. Determined to have her man, Alice tricked Gabrielle into shooting her mother. The plot failed when Gabrielle's father came home at the instant of the murder and determined to take the blame for the murder himself to protect his daughter. The present action begins in San Francisco some thirteen years later after Gabrielle's father has escaped from Devil's Island, assumed the name Leggett, and fled to the United States, where Alice Dain, who has raised Gabrielle, has found him and blackmailed him into marriage.

A REASON TO WRITE

When the Armistice came along, all I could boast was a pair of weak lungs contracted in the Ambulance Corps. I did some private detective work for Pinkerton's, but all the time I was getting sicker, and found myself shortly in a California hospital.

Then it was a case of turning to something to keep the butcher away from the door while I tried to bluff along the baker. So I rented a second-hand typewriter and pounded out my first novel. It was just a case of lucky breaks after that.

Dashiell Hammett, quoted in Henry Dan Piper, "Dashiel [*sic*] Hammett Flees Night Club Round Succumbing to Rustication in New Jersey," *Daily Princetonian*, 11 November 1936, pp. 1, 4.

A force as pernicious as Alice Dain was to Leggett now threatens Gabrielle. The evil writer Owen Fitzstephan, himself distantly related to the Dains, is in love with Gabrielle, who spurns him. He sets out to torment her and possess her. The Op intercedes and rescues Gabrielle from a series of dangers before he exposes Fitzstephan and accomplishes Gabrielle's spiritual awakening.

The reviewers were complimentary about Hammett's second novel and often enthusiastic about his talent as a writer. By August 1929, the month after its publication, *The Dain Curse* had gone into its third printing (indicating a respectable sale of about five thousand copies), and in January 1930 it became Hammett's first novel to be published in England.

The year 1929 was a turning point in Hammett's life. Hollywood moviemakers were beginning to take note of his work, and Hammett was beginning to realize that he could make big money from his writing. More important, in 1929 he completed work on *The Maltese Falcon,* the novel that many critics feel is his best and the book that earned Hammett permanent respect in literary circles. *The Maltese Falcon* was the first of Hammett's novels not written specifically for serial publication in *Black Mask*. Shaw did publish Hammett's third novel in five parts, but Hammett made no concession to his magazine audience this time. *The Maltese Falcon* is a tightly organized novel, not a long work patched out of related stories as *Red Harvest* and *The Dain Curse* had been.

The Maltese Falcon introduces a new detective, Sam Spade. Like the Continental Op, Spade lives by the detective's code, but his motives are more ambiguous than those of the Op. Spade does not work for a detective agency; he is a loner who keeps his own confidence and answers to no one but himself. Much of the success of the novel is due to the enigma of Spade's character and Hammett's skill at manipulating point of view in drawing Spade's characterization. Unlike most hard-boiled detective fiction, Hammett's included, *The Maltese Falcon* is narrated in the third person so that Spade can be described to the reader as are the other characters in the novel, so that Hammett can reveal information to the reader as the detective obtains it, and so that Spade's reaction to the evidence can be related objectively.

The reception of *The Maltese Falcon* was flattering for Hammett. Aside from rave notices about the novel as an exciting mystery, including Alexander Woollcott's claim that it was "the best detective story America has yet produced,"[10] Hammett was beginning to command respect as a mainstream writer. L. F. Nebel of the *St. Louis Post-Dispatch* wrote, "It seems a pity that this should be called a detective story. . . . Truly, it is a story about a detective, but it is so much about a detective that he becomes a character, and the sheer force of Hammett's hard, brittle writing lifts the book out of the general run of crime spasms and places it aloof and above as a brave chronicle of a hard-boiled man, unscrupulous, conscienceless, unique."[11] William Curtis in *Town & Country* went further: "I think Mr. Hammett has something quite as definitive to say, quite as decided an impetus to give the course of newness in the development of an American tongue, as any man writing."[12]

Sales were brisk—seven printings during the first year after publication—and there were serious inquiries from Hollywood about rights to Hammett's works. The money was beginning to come for Hammett; his health was better; and he had a girlfriend—a writer named Nell Martin. In October 1929 Hammett left San Francisco and went to live with Nell Martin in New York, where he was received as a literary celebrity. By that time his fourth novel, *The Glass Key,* was well underway.

The Glass Key was completed in February 1930 and published in four parts by *Black Mask* between March and June. Book publication by Knopf was in April 1931. In *The Glass Key* Hammett's experiment with the objective third-person point of view is carried a step further than in *The Maltese Falcon.* In his fourth novel, Hammett depersonalizes the narration to the point that the book's primary character, Ned Beaumont, is always referred to by his full name, removing any hint of narrative familiarity with him.

The Glass Key is not a detective novel, though it is Hammett's most hard-boiled work, and it utilizes the narrative elements of the detective novel. Ned Beaumont is a gambler and the chief assistant to his friend, political boss Paul Madvig. While arranging support for the inept Senator Henry, Madvig foolishly falls in love with the senator's daughter, Janet. After a meeting at Henry's house between Madvig and the senator, Henry's son is murdered, and suspicion falls on Madvig. Though he is at first able to resist the charges because of his political power, Janet Henry, who is repulsed by Madvig, is certain of his guilt and sets out to destroy him. During the course of her amateurish investigation, she encounters Beaumont, who is also trying to solve the murder because he realizes that Madvig is being damaged politically by the growing pressure for his indictment.

Janet Henry falls in love with Ned Beaumont and Beaumont with her, though he still feels loyalty to his friend Madvig. The novel ends as Beaumont exposes the senator as his son's murderer—saving Madvig from what is, by that time, sure prosecution—and leaves town with Janet, whom Madvig still loves.

The Glass Key is a complex novel about friendship and its responsibilities, about the corrupting nature of political power, and about the terrible aspect of knowledge—certain facts are painful to know (as when Janet Henry learns her father murdered her brother), but once they are revealed, they must be acted on. Thus, Janet Henry must react against the corruption her father represents. Similarly, Ned Beaumont has to face up to the knowledge of Paul Madvig's foolishness and his own affection for Janet Henry. The only responsible course of action for him is to leave the city where Madvig operates.

The Glass Key received even higher praise than *The Maltese Falcon* and sold about as well. Twenty thousand copies were sold by the end of the year, and Hammett was hailed again as one of the hottest authors in the country.

Since 1930, Hammett, who had left Nell Martin behind, had been in Hollywood writing original movie scripts and arranging to have his novels adapted into movies. In February 1930 *Roadhouse Nights,* based on *Red Harvest,* was released by Paramount, and by summer 1930 Hammett had signed a short-term contract to write original screenplays for that studio, which proved unfruitful for Paramount. Throughout the 1930s Hammett maintained what amounted to a dual residence in Hollywood and New York, spending roughly equal amounts of time on each coast. He was finished as a serious writer by 1931, when he became assured of a steady income from Hollywood. It was the era of hard-boiled detective films, and Hammett was acknowledged as the best of the tough mystery writers. Between 1930 and 1935 five movies were made from his works, and in 1934 he signed a generous contract with M-G-M that assured him, along with other earnings from previously published work, an income in excess of $100,000 a year. That spelled the ruin of a writer who had always written for money: now he did not need new sources of income, so he devoted himself to flamboyant living. He spent money lavishly; he displayed freely what Raymond Chandler called his "shocking capacity for liquor"; he took shameless advantage of the availability of starlets and harlots; and he exploited his position as a full-blown literary celebrity.

In 1930 or 1931 Hammett began a novel called "The Thin Man," but when his agent illegally sold serial rights to a magazine, Knopf, who had a contract for the novel, objected, and Hammett abandoned the project. In 1933 he wrote a new novel, again called *The Thin Man* (1934). Perhaps because Hammett felt he could not afford to spend much time on the novel because of its poor earning potential relative to screenwriting, *The Thin Man* is a facile work and, with the possible exception of *The Dain Curse,* it is his weakest. It was also his best-selling, and it includes wonderfully witty and well-crafted scenes.

Since the winter of 1930, Hammett had been keeping company with the woman who would be his steadiest companion for the rest of his life, Lillian Hellman, then a script reader at M-G-M attempting to become a playwright. Her spirit of self-indulgent independence matched his own, and together Hammett and Hellman spent everything he earned, living high. Hammett modeled his dissolute Nick and Nora Charles in *The Thin Man* on himself and Hellman, a fact made obvious by the novel's dust jacket, for which Hammett himself posed as the suave Nick Charles, and the dedication, "To Lillian."

The Thin Man is set during the week of Christmas 1932. Nick Charles has married rich and given up detective work to manage his wife's money. During a visit to New York, he becomes interested in the murder of an old acquaintance (the thin man of the title). In an alcoholic haze, between shopping trips and seemingly endless parties, Nick Charles conducts an unconventional investigation and solves the murder—a little too easily and a little too smugly.

The novel is an entertainment: casually structured, implausible, and impossibly flippant, but it is redeemed by the creation of the Charleses, a couple who transcended their literary origins. "Maybe there are better writers in the world," Hammett wrote Hellman in 1937, "but nobody ever invented a more insufferably smug pair of characters."[13] *The Thin Man* was filmed in 1934, with William Powell and Myrna Loy as the Charleses, and the movie was successful enough to warrant five sequels, the last of which appeared in 1947. Moreover, the characters were the subject of a radio series, *The Adventures of the Thin Man,* from 1941–1942; 1946–1950, and an NBC television series, starring Peter Lawford and called *The Thin Man,* in 1957 and 1958.

The Thin Man was published in an expurgated version in *Redbook* magazine in December 1933 and by Knopf in January 1934. It was Hammett's last novel. Reviewers were respectful, though most agreed that *The Thin Man* was not up to the standard set by *The Maltese Falcon* and *The Glass Key.* Hammett said twenty-three years later that *The Thin Man* had always bored him.[14]

When Hammett's career as a professional writer ended in 1934, he was forty years old, and he had twenty-seven years to live. He was supported well by his income from his literary works throughout the 1930s and 1940s. He continued to be a literary man—he was respected for his literary judgment, and he took an active interest in the career of his friend Lillian Hellman, whose first play, *Children's Hour* (1934), was developed from an idea suggested by Hammett. He always planned to write another novel, and on at least six occasions began work, but he rarely got beyond an outline and only in the case of "Tulip" in the early 1950s got as far as a partially finished draft.

From 1934 to 1937, Hammett was under contract to M-G-M as a screenwriter, but although he produced original stories for two of the Thin Man sequels, work highly regarded by producers, Hammett was chronically undependable. By 1937 he was more interested in politics. He joined the Communist Party and worked actively for a variety of leftist organizations. He was one of the founders of Equality Publishers, a short-lived enterprise dedicated to "an uncompromising fight against the enemies of humanity," a goal that characterized his political beliefs.

In 1942, although he was forty-eight, in uncertain health, and considered subversive, Hammett managed to join the U.S. Army. He was stationed in Alaska from 1943 until his discharge in 1945, and during much of that time he edited a camp newspaper called *The Adakian,* which he founded on the island of Adak. In 1943 Hammett took a screen credit from M-G-M for adapting Lillian Hellman's anti-Nazi play *Watch on the Rhine* into a screenplay, though his true contribution would be better described as transcription rather than adaptation. The movie is faithful to the play, and the additional dialogue included in the movie version was supplied by Hellman.

When Hammett left the army, he returned to New York, where he lived quietly and well, supported primarily by radio series based on characters from his works. Though Hammett had no hand in the scripts, he earned an average of $400 a week from each of the three long-running series: *The Adventures of the Thin Man, The Fat Man* (1946–1950), and *The Adventures of Sam Spade* (1946–1951). Less rewarding financially, but important to his reading audience, was the publication between 1944 and 1951 of nine paperback collections of his stories, edited by Ellery Queen. Nothing he had written since 1934 was included in these collections, and most of the stories date from the 1920s; yet, they sold well, giving evidence to the fact that Hammett's reputation had lost none of its luster because of his inactivity.

In the summer of 1950 Hammett's political concerns caused another turning point in his life. Since 1946 he had been national vice chairman and New York State chairman of the Civil Rights Congress, a humanitarian organization considered subversive by the federal government. He also served as chairman of a CRC bail-fund committee, which provided bail for jailed left-wing political activists. In July 1951 Hammett was called to testify before a U.S. District Court trying to determine the whereabouts of four Communists convicted under the Smith Act who had skipped bail put up by Hammett's CRC committee. He refused to testify and was sentenced to six months in prison for contempt of court.

When Hammett got out of jail in December 1951, having served five months of his sentence, he was without income. His radio series had all been canceled because of his political problems. Moreover, the Internal Revenue Service had placed a lien against Hammett's estate for unpaid taxes amounting, finally, to more than $160,000, including state taxes.

Hammett testifying before the McCarthy committee, which was seeking to learn who chose books by Communists for distribution by the State Department Overseas Library Program, 25 March 1953

Hammett had never saved; he was destitute in 1951, dependent on the kindness of his friends.

He spent the last nine years of his life as a recluse, living most of the time in the gatehouse cottage of a friendly doctor in Katonah, New York. He tried a last time in 1953 to write another novel; the result is the autobiographical fragment "Tulip," which ends with the words: "When you are tired you ought to rest, I think, and not try to fool your customers with colored bubbles."[15] Hammett had rested for a long time before his death of various ailments, including lung cancer, on 10 January 1961. He was buried in Arlington National Cemetery.

Although Hammett's career as a writer lasted only twelve years, his influence was profound. He not only infused mystery fiction with tough realism, he made the crime novel respectable by writing works that were not bound by the artificial structures of a form. It is inaccurate to say that his best works are fine mystery novels; they are fine novels—measured by any standard.[16]

NOTES

1. Raymond Chandler, "The Simple Art of Murder," *Atlantic Monthly* (December 1944): 57–58.

2. Dashiell Hammett, in "Three Favorites," *Black Mask* (November 1924): 128.

3. James H. S. Moynahan, "Dashiell Hammett Confesses," King Features Syndicate article that ran in subscribing newspapers on 30 May 1936.

4. "Dashiell Hammett, Author, Dies, Created Hard-Boiled Detectives," *New York Times,* 11 January 1961, p. 47.

5. *Red Harvest,* New York: Knopf, 1929, p. 81.

6. "Troops Go to Butte to Guard Workers," *New York Times,* 11 January 1920, VII: 7.

7. *Bookman* (29 March 1929): 62.

8. *Outlook and Independent,* 13 February 1929, p. 3.

9. Elizabeth Sanderson, "Ex-Detective Hammett," *Bookman* (January 1932): 518.

10. *New York Herald Tribune,* 11 August 1929, p. 11.

11. 21 March 1931 (from clipping file).

12. William Curtis, "Some Recent Books," *Town & Country* (15 February 1930).

13. Hammett to Lillian Hellman, 26 December 1937. Harry Ransom Humanities Research Center, University of Texas, Austin.

14. James Cooper, "Lean Years for the Thin Man," *Washington Daily News,* 11 March 1957.

15. "Tulip," in *The Big Knockover,* edited by Lillian Hellman (New York: Random House, 1966).

16. This chapter is a revised version of the Dashiell Hammett entry in *Concise American Dictionary of Literary Biography: The Age of Maturity, 1929–1941* (Detroit: Bruccoli Clark Layman / Gale Research, 1989).

ABOUT *THE MALTESE FALCON*

SIGNIFICANT PUBLICATIONS

Black Mask magazine September 1929–January 1930, in five parts—first publication.

New York: Knopf, 1929—first book publication, with minor revisions.

London: Knopf, 1930—first British edition.

New York: Modern Library, 1934—adds introduction by Hammett.

New York: Pocket Books, 1944—first paperback edition.

New York: Vintage, 1972—foul text, inexplicably altered by the publisher; to be avoided.

San Francisco: Arion Press, 1983—limited edition; San Francisco: North Point, 1984—illustrated with scenes from Spade's San Francisco.

New York: Vintage Crime / Black Lizard, 1992—commonly available contemporary paperback edition.

DEDICATION

The novel is dedicated "To Jose," Hammett's wife. Six months before the novel was published by Knopf, Hammett left San Francisco for New York, and his family moved to Los Angeles. The Hammetts did not live together again, though they were not divorced until 1937 (and even then the Mexican divorce may not have been legal).

SETTING

San Francisco.

CHRONOLOGY

The novel takes place during a six-day period between Wednesday and Monday, 5 to 10 December 1928. The time is established by mention in

The Maltese Falcon

By DASHIELL HAMMETT

Spade and Archer.

AMUEL SPADE'S jaw was long and bony, his chin a jutting V under the more flexible V of his mouth. His nostrils curved back to make another, smaller, V. His yellow-gray eyes were horizontal. The V motif was picked up again by thickish brows rising outward from twin creases above a hooked nose, and his pale brown hair grew down, from high, flat temples, in a point on his forehead. He looked rather pleasantly like a blond Satan.

He said to Effie Perine: "Yes, sweetheart?"

She was a lanky, sunburned girl whose tan dress of thin woolen stuff clung to her with an effect of dampness.

7

Opening page of the *Black Mask* version of Hammett's third novel the novel that *The Merchant of Venice,* starring George Arliss, is playing at the Geary Street Theatre, and by Spade's references to daily issues of the *San Francisco Call* newspaper. The play was staged at the Geary Theatre from 3 to 15 December 1928. In an endnote to the illustrated edition of the novel published first by the Arion Press and reprinted by North Point in 1984, Glenn Todd identifies the newspaper references:

> It is possible to pinpoint those five days by deduction from the Friday newspaper that Sam consulted for ship's arrivals, the first copy of which he found in a waste basket in Cairo's hotel room. Hammett stated that this issue had 38 pages. *The San Francisco Call and Post* for Friday, December 7, 1928 had 38 pages, but Friday's issue of December 14 also had 38 pages. However, the newspaper of the 7th holds suggestion and proof that it was the one Hammett gleaned for facts to use in *The Maltese Falcon*. On page four, a story appears, "S. F. SHIP SAFE AFTER FIGHTING FLAMES IN HOLD. The Steamer *Quinault* bound for San Francisco is afire at sea, carrying a general cargo and cotton"; it may be only a coincidental echo of the fire in *La Paloma* touched off by Wilmer, but the stories on page five, "4 COUNTRY BOYS PLEAD GUILTY TO BOGUS MONEY" and "S.F. MAN JUMPS FOR DEATH AFTER ROW WITH WIFE" must have been scrambled by Hammett to read "SUSPECT ARRESTED AS COUNTERFEITER" and "BAY AREA YOUTH SEEKS DEATH WITH BULLET." The subjects of counterfeit money and an unsuccessful suicide are too specific for coincidence. Further proof is added by the entry in the *Arrived Today,* column on page 35: "5:18 a.m.—Caddopeak from San Pedro." Sam's newspaper listed among its arrivals "8:07 a.m.—Caddopeak from San Pedro."[1]

DAY 1, WEDNESDAY, CHAPTER I: Brigid asks Spade and Archer to shadow Thursby, whom she is meeting at 8 P.M. that night.

DAY 2, THURSDAY, CHAPTERS II–IX: Begins at 2:05 A.M. with Spade receiving a phone call informing him of Archer's death the previous evening. Ends with Spade and Brigid in his apartment: "We've got all night ahead of us."[2]

DAY 3, FRIDAY, CHAPTERS X–XIII: "Beginning day had reduced night to a thin smokiness when Spade sat up" (90). Ends with Spade drugged in Gutman's suite.

DAY 4, SATURDAY, CHAPTERS XIV–XVII: "Spade, coming around the corner from the elevator at a few minutes past six in the morning, saw yellow light glowing through the frosted glass of his office-door" (131). Ends with chapter titled "Saturday Night." The last section begins "Midnight was a few minutes away when Spade reached his home" (170).

DAY 5, SUNDAY, CHAPTERS XVIII–XX: The night-long meeting in Spade's apartment among Spade, Gutman, Brigid, Cairo, and Wilmer begins when he enters at midnight. The chapter ends with the action after Spade calls Effie at home at 7 A.M. and asks her to bring him the falcon (200). He tells her "I'm sorry to spoil your day of rest" (201). He turns in Gutman, Cairo, Wilmer, and Brigid on Sunday morning.

DAY 6, MONDAY, CHAPTER XX, FINAL SECTION: "Effie Perine put down her newspaper and jumped out of Spade's chair when he came into the office at a little after nine o'clock Monday morning" (216). She asks if the newspaper accounts of him turning in Brigid are accurate.

CHARACTERS

SAM SPADE: "Samuel Spade's jaw was long and bony, his chin a jutting v under the more flexible v of his mouth. His nostrils curved back to make another, smaller, v. His yellow-grey eyes were horizontal. The v *motif* was picked up again by the thickish brows rising outward from twin creases above a hooked nose, and his pale brown hair grew down—from high flat temples—in a point on his forehead. He looked rather pleasantly like a blond satan" (3). "He was quite six feet tall. The steep rounded slope of his shoulders made his body seem almost conical—no broader than it was thick—and kept his freshly pressed grey coat from fitting very well" (4). "The smooth thickness of his arms, legs, and body, the sag of his big rounded shoulders, made his body like a bear's. It was like a shaved bear's: his chest was hairless. His skin was childishly soft and pink" (12).

Spade is the private detective who takes the case that leads him into pursuit of the Maltese falcon; he is the main character of the novel. Spade accepts a fee from both Brigid O'Shaughnessy and her rival Joel Cairo. He agrees to help her find her fictitious sister and later to protect her. He agrees to help Cairo find the falcon. Spade is suspected by various people of the murders of Miles Archer and Floyd Thursby. Though he is repeatedly described as having satanic features, Spade tells Brigid O'Shaughnessy at the end of the novel, "Don't be too sure I'm as crooked as I'm supposed to be. That kind of reputation might be good for business—bringing in high-priced jobs and making it easier to deal with the enemy" (215). When he finally comes into possession of what is apparently the jewel-encrusted statuette, a gathering of crooks convenes in his apartment, and he arranges their arrest.

Spade is the most complex character in the novel, not least of all because he is as skilled as Brigid in the art of deception. A central question in the novel is his motivation. Is he as corrupt as the other characters, or is he a moral standard? Some critics, applying the metaphor introduced by Raymond Chandler in *The Big Sleep* (1939), read the hard-boiled detective as a modern version of a chivalrous knight seeking after the Holy Grail. The conventions of courtly love pertain, requiring the knight to attain virtue before he can realize his ultimate goal. This reading suggests that Spade is on a quest for truth, and in order to find the identity of the falcon, he must resist temptation—specifically, sexual temptation—to maintain the purity his quest requires. Because the history of the Maltese falcon includes knights (although they are a few hundred years later than the knights identified with the quest for the Holy Grail), that reading has some appeal. Readers should guard against being blinded by that metaphor, however. Spade is a detective, not a knight, and while he may share some qualities with archetypal questors, he is a modern man, who operates according to modern rules that have little to do with chastity. Chief among those rules is that there is a cost for living in a place, anyplace—one must pay for the privilege. Just as the good Hospitallers of St. John on Malta were required to pay tribute to their king for the use of their land, Spade, also a good man, must pay a tribute to the powers of his city for the right to live there. The tribute he pays is in the form of a service. He does his part to rid the city of predators, specifically, in this case, Brigid. If he fails to turn her over, if he frees her to prey on others, he loses the rights to his city. If there is a moral lesson to *The Maltese Falcon*, it is that everyone has the obligation to protect the place where he lives from those who would spoil it. Failure to do that means that the crooks take over.

Sam Spade is tougher, smarter, and better motivated than any other character in the novel, but he is not perfect. He is careless enough to let the ineffectual Cairo get the drop on him. He is foolish enough to allow Gutman to drug his drink, after which Wilmer kicks him savagely. He falls for the deception involving Rhea Gutman. And he allows Brigid O'Shaughnessy to lead him into the trap in his apartment. He may feel that when a man's partner is murdered he has to do something about it, but such loyalty did not extend to infidelity with his partner's wife. Indeed, loyalty is not a quality associated with Spade. Like the other characters in the novel, he cannot be trusted. He is a loner. He does not invest in relationships.

BRIGID O'SHAUGHNESSY: Tall, lanky, rounded body, with dark red hair "her full lips more brightly red. White teeth glistened in the crescent her

SELZNICK ON HAMMETT

Hammett has recently created quite a stir in literary circles by his creation of two books for Knopf, *The Maltese Falcon* and *Red Harvest*. I believe that he is another Van Dine—indeed, that he possesses more originality than Van Dine, and might very well prove to be the creator of something new and startlingly original for us.

David O. Selznick, then assistant to Paramount studio chief B. P. Schulberg, in an 18 July 1930 memo to his boss in *Memo from David O. Selznick,* edited by Rudy Behlmer (New York: Viking, 1972), pp. 26-27.

timid smile made" (4). She is the beautiful, sexy redhead who presents herself as Miss Wonderly in the opening pages of the novel and fabricates a tale to engage the services of Spade and his partner, Miles Archer. When her story is shown to be false, she hires Spade to protect her from her enemies. Brigid O'Shaughnessy also uses the pseudonym Miss LeBlanc.

Brigid has only one attractive quality: She is beautiful, an object of sexual desire whose allure blinds men to danger. But under her enamel—her clothes and her makeup—she is as leaden and as false as the falcon Captain Jacobi brings to San Francisco, and she is as predatory as a real falcon. The effectiveness of the last chapter of the book depends on the reader believing that Spade is seriously tempted to let Brigid go free despite her many faults. Spade loves Brigid in a purely sensuous way, for the physical pleasure she offers. In Spade's apartment on the evening she spends the night with him Brigid tells Spade:

> "I know two men I'm afraid of and I've seen both of them tonight."
>
> "I can understand your being afraid of Cairo," Spade said. "He's out of your reach."
>
> "And you aren't?"
>
> "Not that way," he said and grinned. (87)

Brigid, Gutman, and Cairo love the falcon similarly—not for what it represents; not for what it is; but for the sensuous pleasure it can bring. The difference is that they are excited by money; Spade is excited by sex.

Brigid is an actress, an habitual liar, with no interest except for her own gratification. She presents herself in different guises, using different names and telling different stories. She uses her sexuality as a weapon with deadly effectiveness. It is a tribute to Spade's cunning that he is able to have a sexual relationship with her on his own terms and to resist it when she attempts at the end of the book to use it against him. For her part, there is no desire, only cold calculation. She teases Spade with sex until fear causes her to spend the night with him, because he is easier to manipulate when the sexual tension is high. There is a musical hint that she enjoyed their night together. After her bath, she comes out of the bathroom whistling *En Cuba* (92). It is the song Spade whistles as he is calling Effie Perine Sunday morning to ask her to bring him the falcon (200).[3]

Brigid feigns loyalty to Thursby, Gutman, Cairo, Kemidov, Jacobi, and to Spade at various points in the book, and she betrays them all.

MILES ARCHER: "He was of medium height, solidly built, wide in the shoulders, thick in the neck, with a jovial heavy-jawed red face and some grey in his close-trimmed hair. He was apparently as many years past forty as Spade was past thirty" (7). Randy partner in the detective agency Spade & Archer. He is murdered while shadowing Floyd Thursby, an associate of Brigid O'Shaughnessy. Archer and Spade have apparently been partners for a year or less. Spade tells Brigid that Archer "hadn't many brains" (208) and tells her he "was a son of a bitch. I found that out the first week we were in business together and I meant to kick him out as soon as the year was up" (213). Archer realizes his wife wants a divorce and attempts to make her jealous by suggesting that he has a date with Brigid the night of his death.

FLOYD THURSBY: "he's thirty-five years old, perhaps, and as tall as you [Spade; i.e., six feet], and either naturally dark or quite sunburned. His hair is dark too, and he has thick eyebrows. He talks in a rather loud, blustery, way and has a nervous, irritable, manner. He gives the impression of being—of violence." His eyes: "They're blue-grey and watery, though not in a weak way. And—oh, yes—he has a marked cleft in his chin." "Quite athletic. He's broad shouldered and carries himself erect, has what could be called a decidedly military carriage" (8–9). "He was a sucker for women" (207). Thursby is a Midwestern hoodlum who has worked as a strong-arm man for at least two gangs. He left the country after falling out of favor with Dixie Monahan, his last boss. In Constantinople he met Brigid and agreed to act as her bodyguard/enforcer. She did not trust him to travel with the falcon from Hong Kong to San Francisco, where he was murdered in Burritt Street.

EFFIE PERINE: "She was a lanky sunburned girl whose tan dress of thin woolen stuff clung to her with an effect of dampness. Her eyes were brown and playful in a shiny boyish face" (3). Sam Spade's secretary. She lovingly organizes his affairs, and he looks to her for solace. Effie seems to be a model caretaker for Spade, but though he treats her tenderly and caresses her like a lover, she is more like his kid sister. She says of Iva Archer, "she's a louse, but I'd be a louse too if it would give me a body like

Josephine Dolan Hammett, to whom
The Maltese Falcon is dedicated

hers" (27), implying that she lacks the physical attributes to attract Spade. Effie is innocent, loyal, and well motivated—all qualities that lead her to the unperceptive conclusion that Brigid is a helpless victim who needs Spade's protection. She is too nice and naive to do more than take orders from Spade.

LIEUTENANT DUNDY: "a compactly built man with a round head under short-cut grizzled hair and a square face behind a short-cut grizzled mustache. A five-dollar-gold-piece was pinned to his necktie and there was a small elaborate diamond-set secret-society-emblem on his lapel" (17). Dundy represents the worst side of the police. He is a conniving bully, dumb and misguided. He lacks the finesse to solve problems any way except by force.

DETECTIVE-SERGEANT TOM POLHAUS: "a barrel-bellied tall man with shrewd small eyes, a thick mouth, and carelessly shaven dark jowls" (14). Spade calls him "Tom" and his boss "Dundy," suggesting his relationship with them. Polhaus is well motivated. He shares information with Spade, indicating that he is more interested in solving a crime than in closing a case. Even though he is not entirely forthcoming with Spade, Polhaus earns Spade's respect. At the end of the book Spade turns Brigid over to Polhaus, who comes to his apartment with Dundy and two other detectives.

IVA ARCHER: "She was a blonde woman of a few more years than thirty. Her facial prettiness was perhaps five years past its best moment. Her body for all its sturdiness was finely modeled and exquisite" (24). Wife of Miles Archer and lover of Sam Spade. Iva needs attention. She is manipulative and vindictive. On the night of her husband's murder she follows him, thinking he has a date with another woman, and then she stays out until she thinks he should be home, intending to make him jealous. When she suspects Spade is having an affair with Brigid, she calls Archer's brother and the police to suggest that he might be involved. She pursues Spade relentlessly, waiting for him late at night outside his apartment, calling and coming by his office daily. She expects him to marry her.

SID WISE: "a small olive-skinned man with a tired oval face under thin dark hair dotted with dandruff" (41). Spade's attorney who also counsels Iva Archer and then betrays her client privilege by divulging what she told him to Spade.

JOEL CAIRO: "a small-boned dark man of medium height. His hair was black and smooth and very glossy. His features were Levantine. A square-cut ruby, its sides paralleled by four baguette diamonds, gleamed against the deep green of his cravat. His black coat, cut tight to narrow shoulders, flared a little over slightly plump hips. His trousers fitted his round legs more snugly than was the current fashion. The uppers of his patent-leather shoes were hidden by fawn spats. He held a black derby hat in a chamois-gloved hand and came towards Spade with short, mincing, bobbing steps. The fragrance of *chypre* came with him" (42). Brigid calls him Joe. He is one of the principal seekers after the Maltese falcon.

Cairo is a homosexual caricature. Weak but wily, he is in some ways a counterpart to Brigid though more compassionate and less deadly. When Gutman suspects that Kemidov has the falcon, Gutman sends both Brigid and Cairo to entice him into giving it up, covering all sexual bases. At the end of the book Cairo attempts to comfort the thug Wilmer by stroking his face, and when Gutman, Cairo, and Wilmer leave Spade's apartment at the end of the book, Wilmer kills Gutman but spares Cairo.

WILMER COOK: "An undersized youth of twenty or twenty-one in neat grey cap and overcoat" (52). "Seen at this scant distance, he seemed certainly less than twenty years old. His features were small, in keeping with his stature, and regular. His skin was very fair. The whiteness of his cheeks was as little blurred by any considerable growth of beard as by the glow of blood. His clothing was neither new nor of more than ordinary quality, but it, and his manner of wearing it, was marked by a hard masculine neatness" (93). He has "curling lashes" (173).

Spade despises Wilmer, seizing every opportunity to humiliate him. Spade refers to Wilmer in homosexual terms, as he characteristically does to a man he detests. (He refers to Dundy as "sweetheart" [19] and as Polhaus's "boy-friend" [20].) But there is an angry challenge to his encounters with Wilmer. He calls Wilmer a "gunsel" (110), hobo slang for a boy homosexual, and refers to him as Gutman's "punk" (180). There is scant indication of Wilmer's homosexuality other than Spade's insults. Recognizing the danger Wilmer represents, Spade proposes Wilmer as the fall guy in Chapter XVIII and baits him unmercifully. When Cairo whispers in Gutman's ear and Spade tells Wilmer they have decided to sacrifice him, Wilmer loses his temper and draws his gun on Spade. Gutman grabs Wilmer's gunhand, and Spade disarms him then slugs him in the jaw. As Wilmer lies, disarmed and hurt, on the couch, Cairo caresses him, puts his arm around Wilmer's shoulders, and whispers to him. Wilmer throws off Cairo's arm, punches him in the mouth, and warns him to stay away. Spade remarks that it is the "course of true love" (199).

LUKE: House detective at the Belvedere, Cairo's hotel. "He was a middle-aged man of medium height, round and sallow of face, compactly built, tidily dressed in dark clothes" (95).

CASPER GUTMAN: "The fat man was flabbily fat with bulbous pink cheeks and lips and chins and neck, with a great soft egg of a belly that was all his torso, and pendant cones for arms and legs. As he advanced to meet Spade all his bulbs rose and shook and fell separately with each step, in the manner of clustered soap-bubbles not yet released from the pipe through which they had been blown. His eyes, made small by fat puffs around them, were dark and sleek. Dark ringlets thinly covered his broad scalp. He wore a black cutaway coat, black vest, black satin Ascot tie holding a pinkish pearl, striped grey worsted trousers, and patent-leather shoes" (104). In San Francisco he takes a three-bedroom suite at the Alexandria Hotel, suite 12-C, where he stays with Wilmer and his daughter Rhea (see 161).

Gutman is the criminal mastermind of the novel. It is apparently he who learned of the falcon, and he has gone to extraordinary lengths in his attempts to procure it. He hired Brigid and Cairo to help him find it, and he keeps Wilmer as his bodyguard. Gutman is a man who directs others to do his bidding. His own resources are his intelligence and his wealth. He is thoroughly amoral and self-indulgent. Gutman presides over an unsavory group, including his daughter Rhea, Wilmer Cook, and sometimes Cairo and Brigid O'Shaughnessy. There is the suggestion that their depravity extends beyond ruthless greed.

BRYAN: District Attorney: "He was a blond man of medium stature, perhaps forty-five years old, with aggressive blue eyes behind black-ribboned nose-glasses, the over-large mouth of an orator, and a wide dimpled chin. . . . his voice was resonant with latent power" (144). "Bryan is like most district attorneys. He's more interested in how his record will look on paper than in anything else. He'd rather drop a doubtful case than try it and have it go against him. I don't know that he ever deliberately framed anybody he believed innocent, but I can't imagine him letting himself believe them innocent if he could scrape up, or twist into shape, proof of their guilt. To be sure of convicting one man he'll let half a dozen equally guilty accomplices go free—if trying to convict them all might confuse his case" (180).

THOMAS: Assistant District Attorney: "a sunburned stocky man of thirty in clothing and hair of a kindred unruliness" (144).

HEALY: DA Bryan's stenographer: "younger [than Thomas] and colorless" (144). He is called in by DA Bryan to record Spade's comments during the "informal" meeting regarding Spade's knowledge of Archer's and Thursby's murders.

CAPTAIN JACOBI: Skipper of *La Paloma*, a freighter that arrived in port at San Francisco from Hong Kong. Brigid asked Jacobi to bring the falcon to San Francisco for her: "he was nearly seven feet tall. A black overcoat cut long and straight and like a sheath, buttoned from throat to knees, exaggerated his leanness. His shoulders stuck out, high, thin, angular. His bony face—weather-coarsened, age-lined—was the color of wet sand and was wet with sweat on cheeks and chin. His eyes were dark and bloodshot and mad above lower lids that hung down to show pink inner membrane" (156).

In Hong Kong Brigid presumably seduced Jacobi. He is loyal to her to the death. Even after Wilmer shoots him in the chest, he makes his way to Spade's office before giving up the falcon, because that is what Brigid asked him to do.

RHEA GUTMAN: "a small fair-haired girl in a shimmering yellow dressing-gown—a small girl whose face was white and dim" (161). She is Casper Gutman's seventeen-year-old daughter, who disfigures herself with a stickpin and, apparently, is drugged in an effort to mislead Spade.

Rhea Gutman is a puzzling figure. As Joe Gores observes, "What is Gutman doing with a daughter?" Spade goes to Gutman's suite at the Alexandria after Gutman and company "persuade" Brigid, on finding her in her apartment at the Coronet with Captain Jacobi, to call Effie Perine. Rhea has apparently talked about Spade's visit with Brigid. Rhea tells Spade: "She said you'd come . . . were so long" (163). She tells Spade she was drugged with the same dope Gutman gave him in Chapter XIII, and the scratches below her left breast are convincing evidence

THE FORMULA FOR SUCCESS

His one big case involved film star Roscoe (Fatty) Arbuckle.

The work was too hard and in 1922 after five years he had to quit.

"I would have been fired anyway," he says, "except for the literary quality of my reports. . . ."

Mr. Hammett explains his success: "I found I could sell the stories easily when it became known I had been a Pinkerton man. People thought my stuff was authentic."

James Cooper, "Lean Years for the Thin Man," *Washington Daily News*, 11 March 1957.

that she has a compelling interest in staying awake. She seems devoted to Brigid, and she tells Spade her father, Wilmer, and Cairo are going to kill Brigid in Burlingame, about twenty-five miles south of San Francisco. Her purpose, whether she is aware of it or not, is to misdirect Spade while her father and the others try to locate Captain Jacobi, who has the falcon. Gutman and Cairo have reason to be angry with Brigid, after learning that she double-crossed them, but they would not kill her until they had the falcon in their possession. After Spade puts Rhea to bed and leaves, he asks that an ambulance be sent for her, but she is removed before medical personnel arrive.

At the beginning of Chapter XVIII, Spade confronts Gutman with the story of his encounter with Rhea:

> The looseness of his lower lip and the droop of his upper eyelids combined with the v's in his face to make his grin lewd as a satyr's. "That daughter of yours has a nice belly," he said, "too nice to be scratched up with pins."
>
> Gutman's smile was affable if a bit oily.
>
> The boy in the doorway took a short step forward, raising his pistol as far as his hip. Everybody in the room looked at him. In the dissimilar eyes with which Brigid O'Shaughnessy and Joel Cairo looked at him there was, oddly, something identically reproving. The boy blushed, drew back his advanced foot, straightened his legs, lowered the pistol and stood as he had stood before, looking under lashes that hid his eyes at Spade's chest. The blush was pale enough and lasted for only an instant, but it was startling on his face that habitually was so cold and composed. (173)

That Spade's leer causes such a response from Wilmer suggests the possibility that the boy is romantically linked with her.

FRANK: Dispatcher Spade calls to order a car to take him to Burlingame after he meets with Rhea Gutman.

THE CHAUFFEUR: "a thick-set youngish man with a plaid cap set askew above pale eyes and a tough cheery face" (165).

GIRL IN BURLINGAME: "A dark-haired girl of fourteen or fifteen" (167), who lives next door to the vacant house at 31 Ancho Avenue, the address Rhea Gutman gives Spade.

PAPA: "A plump red-faced man, bald-headed and heavily mustached" (168), who has the key to the vacant house on Ancho Avenue in Burlingame.

PHIL ARCHER: Miles Archer's brother, who, according to Iva Archer, believes Spade killed Miles.

HOFF AND O'GAR: Police detectives who question Effie Perine after Jacobi's murder.

CHARILAOS KONSTANTINIDES: Greek dealer who once owned the falcon; "the man who traced most of its history and who identified it as what it actually was" (126). He "re-enamelled the bird, apparently just as it is now" (126). Before his death was reported in the London *Times*, Gutman had visited him and forced information from him. Gutman says "I didn't believe he had told anybody but me" (127).

GENERAL KEMIDOV: Russian who had the Maltese falcon in Constantinople. When the falcon delivered by Jacobi is shown to be a fake, Gutman and Cairo assume immediately that Kemidov substituted the lead bird for the real falcon. The chapter in which the falcon is revealed to be false is called "The Russian's Hand," a phrase spoken by Gutman agreeing with Cairo that Kemidov fooled them.

THE PLOT

The Maltese Falcon is a third-person narrative about a case investigated by the private detective Sam Spade. It is told in twenty chapters that proceed chronologically.

CHAPTER I, "SPADE & ARCHER": The novel begins with the appearance of a strikingly attractive woman in Spade's office. Introduced by his secretary, Effie Perine, she gives her name as Miss Wonderly and asks his assistance in locating her missing sister, who is keeping company with a man named Floyd Thursby. By shadowing Thursby, a detective can find the whereabouts of her sister, she hopes. She warns that Thursby is dangerous. Midway through the interview, Spade's partner, Miles Archer, comes in and displays his obvious lust for Miss Wonderly. Spade takes the case for $200, and when Miss Wonderly asks if Spade or Archer can do the shadow work themselves, Miles Archer eagerly volunteers.

CHAPTER II, "DEATH IN THE FOG": That night, Archer is murdered on the job. Spade's friend, police detective Tom Polhaus, calls to inform him and offer him the opportunity to examine the crime scene. After investigating, Spade calls Effie Perine, asks her to inform Archer's wife, Iva, of the murder, then returns home. In less than an hour, he is visited by Polhaus and his boss, Lieutenant Dundy. They inform him that Thursby was killed in front of his hotel thirty-five minutes after Spade left the crime scene, and Dundy insinuates that they suspect Spade of committing the murder.

CHAPTER III, "THREE WOMEN": The next morning when Spade arrives at his office, Effie Perine warns him that Iva Archer is waiting for him. When he goes into his office, Iva hugs him and asks if he killed Miles. He responds with dismay but does not deny it. He kisses her and sends her home. When she leaves, Spade tells Effie Perine of Iva's suspicion. Effie asks if he plans to marry Iva and tells him Iva has cause to expect it after the way he played around with her. Spade responds there was nothing serious in his dalliance. Effie tells him that when she went to Iva's house to tell her of Miles's murder, Iva had just arrived home. She wonders whether Iva killed Miles. Spade rejects the idea and asks her to have Archer's name taken off the door of their office.

That morning Spade goes to Miss Wonderly's hotel and learns that she has checked out after a two-day stay. She was seen only with a tall dark man in his mid thirties. She left a phony forwarding address. When he returns to his office, Effie tells him Dundy came by to look for his guns and that she sent him away. Also, Miss Wonderly called and asked him to visit at her hotel, the Coronet, where she is registered under an assumed name.

CHAPTER IV, "THE BLACK BIRD": It is still morning when Spade visits Wonderly at the Coronet. She confesses that her real name is Brigid O'Shaughnessy and that the story she had told him the day before was false. She says she had met Thursby, a gambler's bodyguard, in Hong Kong and that he had taken advantage of her, following her to San Francisco. She went to Spade initially to find out more about Thursby, and now she is afraid that she is in danger from whomever killed him. She assures Spade that Thursby killed Archer and says she does not know who killed Thursby. But she fears for her life, and she does not want the police involved. Spade agrees to help her and asks how much money she has. She says $500, and he agrees to take the job for that. When she hands the money over, she gives him only $400, telling him she has to keep some to live on. He tells her to hock her jewelry, takes her last $100, and gives her back $25.

After leaving Brigid's hotel, Spade visits his lawyer, Sid Wise, to ask whether he can withhold information from a coroner. Wise says Spade can try. Late that afternoon, when Spade returns to his office, a homosexual named Joel Cairo comes in and offers to pay him $5,000 if he can recover a lost ornamental figure of a bird. When Spade's secretary leaves for the night, Cairo pulls a gun on Spade, intending to search the office for the falcon.

CHAPTER V, "THE LEVANTINE": As he is being searched for weapons, Spade easily disarms Cairo and knocks him out. While Cairo is unconscious, Spade searches his pockets, finding, among other items, a ticket to that evening's performance at the Geary Theatre. When he comes to, Cairo renews his offer and pays Spade a $200 retainer to find the bird so it can be returned to its owner, whom Cairo represents and refuses to identify. When questioned about proof of ownership of the bird, Cairo says there is no firm evidence, but that the person he is working for has the best claim. Spade asks about his man's daughter, guessing apparently that Cairo is working for Brigid's father. Cairo excitedly says that man is not the owner, seeming to think Spade is referring to Gutman, and asks if that man is in San Francisco. Spade suggests they tell one another what they know, but Cairo objects. Spade agrees to help and returns Cairo's gun. Cairo turns the gun on Spade and searches his office, which Spade, in amusement, allows.

CHAPTER VI, "THE UNDERSIZED SHADOW": Spade drinks in his office alone for half an hour after Cairo leaves then goes to a cigar store and to dinner. He notices he is being followed by a small, twenty-year-old man. After dinner, he goes to the Geary Theatre to find Cairo. When Cairo appears, Spade asks who the shadow is. Cairo denies knowing, on his word of honor. Spade says he may have to hurt the kid. Cairo says okay. Spade then goes to his apartment, which has been searched.

Out again at about 9:30 P.M., Spade goes to Brigid's hotel. She is beautifully dressed and eager for news about Spade's investigation into who is after her. She acts seductively, and he reacts coldly. He tells her he has met Cairo and agreed to find the falcon for $5,000. She protests, saying he promised to help her. He reminds her she did not mention the falcon when she hired him. She offers him her body if he will help her; he says he will think about it. She says she wants to meet Cairo, and Spade offers to set up a meeting at his apartment after Cairo gets out of the theater.

As Spade and Brigid go into Spade's apartment building, he sees Iva Archer waiting in a car. They go inside, and Spade asks Brigid to wait while he goes back outside to talk to Iva. She is jealous and accuses him of pretending to love her. She wants to come inside, but he refuses. When

THE FEMME FATALE

Mr. Hammett was always placing distraction in the way of his heroes, usually in the persons of young women. It was typical enough of his detectives to spend a lavish evening in the company of one, neglecting no favor, and then to ransack her purse for the ultimate clue.

"Dashiell Hammett, Author, Dies: Created Hard-Boiled Detectives," *New York Times*, 11 January 1961, p. 47.

he sends her away, she leaves angrily. He goes inside to his apartment with Brigid.

CHAPTER VII, "G IN THE AIR": Spade and Brigid are in his living room, which doubles as a bedroom when the wall-bed unit is down. Spade immediately starts carefully telling a story about a case he worked on, involving a real-estate salesman in Tacoma named Flitcraft, who had abruptly disappeared in 1922. Spade was hired by Mrs. Flitcraft to locate her husband. Flitcraft was well off, had two young sons, and had set up a golf game half an hour before he vanished. Halfway through the story, Cairo calls. Spade invites him to his apartment then continues his story. Spade found Flitcraft in 1927 in Spokane living under the name Charles Pierce, remarried to a woman much like his first wife, and with a young son. He had a good business selling cars. When confronted, Flitcraft told Spade that on the afternoon of his disappearance, he was walking down the street beside a building under construction when a beam fell near him and chipped a piece of concrete on the sidewalk, which hit his face. He still had the small scar. Flitcraft realized that despite his well-ordered life, he could be destroyed by a random occurrence. He was out of step with the random order of the universe, so he decided to act randomly. He left Tacoma that afternoon and wandered around the Northwest for a while before settling into another well-ordered life. "He adjusted himself to beams falling, and then no more of them fell, and he adjusted himself to them not falling" (64). Brigid responds distractedly and begins to assess her position in the meeting with Cairo. She tells Spade she trusts him, and he dismisses her, promising to let her handle Cairo as she pleases.

Cairo arrives excitedly, saying he had come in good faith and Spade had tricked him. He saw the undersized shadow outside Spade's apartment. When Spade says the man has been following him, Brigid, too, becomes agitated and wants to know whether the man had followed Spade to her apartment. Spade says no. Brigid and Cairo then greet one another as old acquaintances, and she immediately seeks to confirm his offer of $5,000 for the falcon, asking if he has the money with him. He says no, but that he can have it by 10:30 the next morning. Brigid then says she does not have the falcon but will within a week. It is where Thursby hid it, she says. She asks Cairo who he is buying the bird for. He says its owner—he went back to him. Cairo then asks Brigid why she is willing to sell the falcon. She says because she is afraid that what happened to Thursby will happen to her. Answering Cairo's question about Thursby's death, Brigid traces the letter G in the air with her finger. Cairo then asks who might be aligned with G—suggesting by subtly pointing a finger that Spade might be an ally. He also suggests the undersized shadow. Brigid responds with a catty remark about Cairo being unable to make a boy in Constantinople, and he reciprocates. She jumps up to slap him, and Spade breaks them up. He slaps Cairo and disarms him, after which Brigid picks up the gun. Then, when Cairo attempts to spit on him, Spade hits him in the mouth, cutting his lip, just as the doorbell rings. No one knows who it is. Spade shuts the door to the room and tells Cairo and Brigid to keep quiet.

Lieutenant Dundy and Tom Polhaus are at the door. Spade will not let them in. They say that there is a rumor that Spade and Iva Archer were having an affair. Spade denies it. Dundy implies that the police suspect Spade of having set up Archer's murder. Spade makes fun of the accusation, saying they should not try to hang more than one murder on him at a time. Dundy calls Spade a liar for denying an affair with Iva Archer. They want to come in, presumably thinking Iva is inside. Spade refuses, and just as they are leaving, Cairo yells out for help. Dundy and Polhaus go inside.

CHAPTER VIII, "HORSE FEATHERS": When Dundy and Polhaus get inside Spade's apartment, they find Cairo bleeding, holding a gun on Brigid. Dundy disarms Cairo and asks what happened. Cairo tells one implausible story as Brigid batters him despite Dundy's efforts to control her. Brigid tells another version of what happened. Then Spade makes up two tales. He says he hired Brigid as an operative and that they were trying to find out what Cairo was after when he visited Spade's office earlier in the day. When Dundy says he is going to arrest everyone, Spade says they all decided to play a joke on the police by faking a dispute. That is their story and they will tell it to the newspapers, who will print it, he insists, making the police look foolish. In exasperation Dundy punches Spade, and Polhaus intercedes to keep Spade from hitting back. Dundy wants Cairo's and Brigid's addresses. Spade refuses to give Brigid's, saying she can be reached through him. Cairo leaves with the police, but, at Spade's request, Polhaus makes him leave his gun behind.

CHAPTER IX, "BRIGID": Spade is furious when the police leave because Dundy hit him, and he could not hit back. He composes himself, then rationalizes that if he had hit Dundy, then they would have ended up at the police station with their goofy story. He puts his arm around Brigid and asks her to tell him her story. She teases him, asking if he has to have

Dust jacket for the first edition of Hammett's third novel

his arm around her, and he withdraws it. It is 2:50 A.M. She says she has to go home. He says not until she tells the story, and besides, maybe the shadow is still outside. She asks him to check. He does.

Spade goes outside and finds no sign of the shadow. He goes back to Brigid and tells her the boy is still there. He makes breakfast and they sit down, she with a gun beside her. He presses her to tell the story. She tells him he is one of two people she is afraid of—Spade guesses Cairo is the other. Then she proceeds to tell him that she is after a black figure of a bird. In Marmora, an island off the coast of Constantinople (now Istanbul), Thursby and Cairo offered her money to try, presumably by offering sex, to get the falcon from the Russian Kemidov, who had it. They got the bird. They learned that Cairo meant to desert them, so she and Thursby double-crossed him first and sailed for San Francisco. Thursby said he would pay her when he sold the falcon, but she did not believe him and hired Spade to try to learn where Thursby had hidden the bird. Then, she says, she intended to bargain with Thursby. Spade calls her a liar, and she admits that she is. Some, but not much of her story is true, she says. Spade laughs and says they will try again. She embraces him and they kiss passionately.

CHAPTER X, "THE BELVEDERE DIVAN": Spade awakens in the morning with Brigid sleeping at his side. He gets out of bed and goes to her apartment, which he searches thoroughly. Before he leaves, he scars the window frame to make it appear someone broke in. On the way home, he stops at the grocery and buys breakfast food. When he enters the apartment, Brigid is startled and has her hand under the pillow, where she has kept a gun. He tells her he went out to see if the boy were still there and that he is gone. They eat breakfast, and he asks her to tell him the story about the bird again. She refuses.

When they leave, the boy is nowhere to be seen. Spade takes her to her apartment and drops her off, then goes to Cairo's hotel, where he finds the shadow waiting in the lobby. Spade approaches the boy and asks where the fairy is. The boy says he does not know what Spade is talking about. Spade insults him, establishes that he is from New York, and the boy spits out an insult and a threat. Spade calls over the house detective and has the boy thrown out of the hotel. The house detective tells Spade that Cairo has been at the hotel for four days, since the previous Monday, and says he will keep an eye on him.

At 11:21 A.M. Cairo comes in from the street, his head bandaged. Spade speculates he has spent the night at the police station being questioned. Spade explains that when Cairo picks a fight with Brigid, he has to take her side: She knows where the bird is; they do not. Cairo says he did not tell the police anything, and Spade leaves him to rest up.

When Spade gets back to his office, Effie Perine is on the phone with Iva Archer, telling her Spade is not in. It is the third time she has called. Brigid has been waiting for him since just after 9 A.M. Polhaus called, and so did G, who said he would call back. Brigid is upset because her apartment had been searched. Spade shows her a copy of the early-afternoon edition of the paper, reporting a burglar in an apartment house on Sutter Street. He says that is where he shook the shadow. The boy went into apartments with women's names, looking for Brigid. She protests that the break-ins occurred about the time Spade said the boy was outside his apartment. He responds that maybe he has an accomplice. Brigid is afraid to go back to her apartment. Spade asks Effie Perine to let Brigid stay at her place with her and her mother. Effie, who trusts Brigid, agrees. Spade sends Effie home, and says he will have Brigid follow in a taxi. It is about noon.

CHAPTER XI, "THE FAT MAN": When Spade returns to his office, the phone is ringing. It is Gutman, who sets up a meeting in fifteen minutes. When he hangs up, Iva Archer walks in. She tells him she sent the policemen to his apartment, telling them they would find something about Miles's murder there, because she was jealous. Miles's brother, Phil, was suspicious of Spade, because he knew Iva loved him. He was planning to go to the police, and Iva went to Spade's apartment to warn him. When he brushed her off, she called the police herself in anger. Spade tells her she should talk to his attorney, Sid Wise, and be truthful. Iva lies about being at home the night of Miles's murder, and Spade calls her on it. Iva says Effie Perine was trying to make her look bad because Effie dislikes her. Spade kisses Iva and sends her to Wise's.

At Gutman's suite in the Alexandria Hotel, Spade is met by the undersized shadow. Enormously fat, Gutman shows Spade to a sitting room, fixes him a drink, and gives him a cigar. Gutman is solicitous toward Spade, who wants to talk about the bird. Gutman is surprised that Spade does not know what the falcon is, and refuses to tell him, allowing that maybe even Cairo and Brigid do not know. Spade says he assumes Brigid is lying to him when she disavows knowledge. Spade says he knows where the falcon is and tells Gutman he has until 5:30 to make up his mind whether to cooperate with Spade or not. He throws his glass against a table, causing the boy to come into the room. Spade warns Gutman to keep the boy away from him, saying he will kill him if necessary. When Spade leaves, the boy curses him.

CHAPTER XII, "MERRY-GO-ROUND": When Spade leaves Gutman's suite, he goes to Sid Wise's office and asks him what Iva said. Wise tells Spade that the night of his murder, Miles Archer came home and told Iva he had to meet a woman at the St. Mark Hotel. She was suspicious and decided to shadow him. She followed him until she was convinced he was shadowing a man and a woman—the woman she later saw with Spade. Iva went to Spade's apartment between 9:30 and 10:00 and again at midnight, spending the time between visits at a movie. He was not there either time. Then she went for something to eat and home, hoping to find Miles there and to make him jealous. When he was not there, she went back to Spade's, at about 2:00 A.M. He was not there, so she went home, arriving just before Effie showed up with news of Miles's murder. Spade says he neither believes nor disbelieves the story, but that it ought to stand up.

When Spade goes back to his office, Effie is waiting with the news that Brigid did not show up at her mother's house. Spade is furious. He says he put her in her cab, rode with her for a way, and rechecked to make sure she was not being followed. He vows to find her and apologizes to Effie for being harsh.

Spade goes to the taxi stand where he took Brigid and finds the cabbie, who tells him Brigid wanted a paper. He stopped, and she got a copy of the *Call*. Then she told him she wanted to go to the Ferry Building. He took her there, and she paid him off.

Spade buys a copy of the *Call* and reads it, without finding a clue about her interest. Then he goes to Brigid's apartment at the Coronet. The dress she wore the night before is there, but her jewelry is gone.

When Spade returns to his office, Gutman's boy is waiting, saying Gutman wants to see Spade. The boy's hands are in his coat pockets, obviously holding guns. Spade insults the boy, then falls silent. In the corridor to Gutman's suite, Spade turns on the boy and takes his guns away. He knocks on Gutman's door with the boy's guns in his own pockets.

CHAPTER XIII, "THE EMPEROR'S GIFT": Gutman opens the door, and Spade hands him the boy's guns. They sit. Gutman serves scotch and cigars, and Spade asks about the falcon. Gutman proceeds to give a careful four-hundred-year history of the solid gold, jewel-encrusted bird, first prepared as a tribute to King Charles V of Spain by the Hospitallers of St. John for use of the Island of Malta. "He was giving it to them, but not unless they used it, and they couldn't give or sell it to anybody else" (123). In the twentieth century the falcon was owned by a Greek dealer, who was reported murdered when his shop, where the falcon was kept, was looted. Then it went to a Russian named Kemidov. Gutman sent agents, presumably Cairo and Brigid, to procure the falcon from him. Spade reiterates that Brigid has the bird and that he can deliver it within a couple of days. Gutman offers Spade $50,000 payable half now and half when he gets to New York or, in the alternative, one-fourth of what he is able to sell it for—a minimum of half a million dollars, he calculates. As Gutman concludes the offer, Spade realizes that his drink has been drugged. As he tries to make his way toward the door, the boy, Wilmer, appears, trips him, and kicks him in the temple. Spade sleeps.

CHAPTER XIV, "LA PALOMA": Just after 6:00 A.M., Saturday, Spade comes stealthily into his office when he sees a light shining. Inside, he finds Effie, asleep at her desk, waiting for him to return. He does not know what caused the bruise on the right side of his head, and he speculates that Gutman drugged him because he said it would take a couple of days to get the falcon; Gutman thought maybe he could find it himself before Spade woke up. She tells him the district attorney called and wants to see him. He asks her to check the history Gutman gave of the falcon with her cousin, a university history professor in Berkeley.

After breakfast, Spade goes to Brigid's apartment at the Coronet. Nothing has changed. Then he goes to Gutman's suite at the Alexandria Hotel. No one in the party, which includes Gutman, Wilmer Cook, and Gutman's seventeen-year-old daughter Rhea, is in. Then Spade goes to the Belvedere, Cairo's hotel, and finds he has been out all night.

AN INTERVIEW WITH THE AUTHOR'S SISTER

In North Carolina, a sister who passes up night-time television's movie reruns to reread English literature classics, and other people in Baltimore and elsewhere, wonder whether anybody from the early days still has first-hand Hammett stories worth writing down; and especially, whether an old-file drawer somewhere still contains any of his detective-agency case reports, written in language that ensured his job even if somebody did make off with the object to be guarded, that falcon supposed to have been fashioned out of gold and jewels by the Knights of Malta.

James H. Bready, "Books and Authors," *Baltimore Sun,* 8 May 1966.

Spade asks Luke, the hotel detective, to let him search Cairo's room. He says he is working for Cairo, and he does not trust some of his associates, such as Wilmer. Luke asks if one of them killed Archer. Spade says Thursby did, and, according to the police, he killed Thursby. In Cairo's room Spade finds nothing remarkable, except for a copy of the previous day's *Call* in the wastebasket. A piece has been torn from the shipping-news column. Spade asks Luke to call him when Cairo comes back. Then Spade leaves.

He goes to the business office of the *Call* and finds that the missing piece from Cairo's paper announces the arrival of six ships; one, *La Paloma,* is from Hong Kong. Back in his office, he calls to find where *La Paloma* is docked. He calls Tom Polhaus and invites him to lunch. He calls Mr. Bryan, the DA, and makes an appointment for 2:30 that afternoon. He calls Sid Wise to ask him to call at 4:00 in case there is trouble with the DA.

Effie comes back to say that her cousin verified that Gutman's story sounds accurate. She has soot on her nose. When Spade comments, she says that on the ferry back from Berkeley they passed a burning boat being towed from the pier. It was *La Paloma.*

CHAPTER XV, "EVERY CRACKPOT": Spade and Polhaus meet for a pickled pigs' feet lunch at the States Hof Brau. Polhaus tries to smooth over the last meeting among Spade, Dundy, and Polhaus. He says Dundy was wrong and knows it. Spade does not accept the apology easily. Polhaus says the police are sure Thursby killed Archer. A bellhop at Thursby's hotel saw a Webly-Fosbery automatic revolver in Thursby's room. The gun is not made any longer, and it is the gun Archer was shot with. Polhaus tells Spade what the police know about Thursby: He was a gunman in St. Louis for the Egan mob. He left there for New York and had a series of scrapes with the law, including a stretch in the federal prison at Joliet for pistol-whipping a woman. He took up with Dixie Monahan in Chicago and became his bodyguard until Monahan got in trouble with the mobs. Then Thursby left Chicago. Polhaus also says that Cairo was not questioned all night, but for fewer than a couple of hours. Spade says he has to leave for his appointment with the DA. Polhaus asks him not to mention that they have talked.

Spade goes to DA Bryan's office, and Bryan calls in an assistant DA and a stenographer. He then says the meeting is informal and asks Spade who killed Thursby. Spade refuses to guess. Bryan says he thinks the key to solving the murder is knowing who hired Spade. Spade refuses to say. Bryan goes on to say that he thinks Thursby was killed because of

Lobby card for the 1941 movie made from *The Maltese Falcon*

his association with Chicago gambler Dixie Monahan, who left town owing more than $200,000. Spade says it is his understanding that Thursby got rid of Monahan in the Orient. Bryan then says that either Thursby was killed by Chicago gamblers whom Monahan had cheated; by friends of Monahan because they thought he had killed the gambler; or by enemies of Monahan who killed Thursby after he had killed his boss. Bryan accuses Spade of, either knowingly or not, aiding the person who killed Thursby by helping the murderer find his victim. Spade says that his only option is to catch all the murderers himself, because the police have no idea about the crime. He storms out saying he will not attend any more informal talks; that he will respond only to a subpoena.

CHAPTER XVI, "THE THIRD MURDER": Spade goes into a hotel and calls Gutman and Cairo. Neither answers. Then he goes to his office, where he sees a theater owner who wants Spade to help him catch employees stealing from him. At about 3:45 Sid Wise calls to find out how the meeting with Bryan went. Spade tells him. Effie comes in and begins soothing Spade's head. She wants him to find Brigid. He tells her Brigid went to the boat and that he did not check after he learned it burned because he had appointments with Polhaus and Bryan. Effie gets very agitated, accusing Spade of abandoning Brigid because she did not go to Mrs. Perine's, as she was supposed to. Effie badgers Spade until he agrees to go to the dock to investigate. He goes, and she says she will wait for his return.

Spade returns to his office at 5:20. Effie tells him that while he was gone Luke called from the Belvedere to say that Cairo had returned. He rushes out, telling Effie he will let her know what happened when he gets back.

At 5:30 Spade arrives at the Belvedere to find that Cairo has checked out without leaving a forwarding address. He left his empty trunk in his room.

Back in his office, Spade tells Effie what he learned. On the previous day, Friday, Brigid went straight to the *La Paloma* pier from the Ferry Building. The captain, Jacobi, was not in, and she waited for his return at 4:00 P.M. They were together until mealtime, after which Gutman, Cairo, and Wilmer showed up. At 11:00 they had a fight, and a gun went off, apparently shot in the air. They all left together at midnight, and the captain has not been back to the ship. The fire was discovered late Saturday morning in the hold. As Spade is finishing his story, a seven-foot-tall man walks in, asks for Spade, and collapses. He is holding a package larger than a football. Spade checks the fallen man and finds that he is dead from half-a-dozen gunshot wounds. He unwraps the package; it is the falcon. Effie answers the phone and becomes frantic. It is Brigid, at the Alexandria, in danger. She implores Spade to go to her aid, but he is more concerned with the dead man, whom he suspects is Captain Jacobi. After he rewraps the falcon, Spade gives in to Effie's badgering and leaves for the Alexandria, but first he tells her to call the police and tell them everything as it happened, except about the falcon. She is to tell the police that he got a phone call and had to leave. She is not to give any information about the dead man's identity.

CHAPTER XVII, "SATURDAY NIGHT": Spade goes to the street and hails a taxi to the Pickwick Stage terminal. He checks the bird at the parcel station and mails the claim check to M. F. Holland at a post office box in San Francisco. Then he takes another taxi to the Alexandria. In Gutman's suite he finds a small fair girl heavily drugged. After working to arouse her, he learns she is Rhea Gutman, Casper Gutman's daughter. She has scratched and pricked herself with a three-inch-long pin to stay awake until he arrived. She tells him Wilmer, Cairo, and her father took Brigid to Burlingame, on the west shore of the San Francisco Bay, and says the words "kill her." She pleads with Spade not to call a doctor because her father will murder her. She says she is doing this for Brigid, and that she will be okay in the morning. Spade puts her to bed and leaves.

He goes to a telephone and calls the emergency hospital to report the girl, leaving a false name for himself. Then he calls a man named Frank to have a car meet him at John's Grill. When they get to the address Rhea gave Spade, they find an empty house.

The driver takes Spade back to the Alexandria. At the desk, he asks if the Gutmans are in. The desk clerk says no, but that a curious thing happened: someone called to report a sick girl, but no one was there. Spade calls Effie Perine at home and says he will be out in twenty minutes.

Spade tells Effie he ran into a plant. He asks if she is sure it was Brigid's voice on the phone, and Effie says she is sure. She tells him that Wilmer showed up after the police and that he stood in the corridor for a while then left. He asks if the body was in fact Jacobi, and she says it was. He leaves.

A few minutes before midnight he arrives at his apartment, and Brigid runs up to him on the street. She is panting and says she has been waiting for him. When they get into his apartment, a light goes on, and Gutman greets him; Cairo and Wilmer are there with pistols. Gutman says they should talk.

CHAPTER XVIII, "THE FALL-GUY": Spade and Brigid go into his living room and sit down on the sofa together, he with his arm around her, Wilmer and Cairo holding guns. Spade tells Gutman his daughter has a "nice belly," too nice to be scratched with pins. Wilmer stirs, but he is stared back into place by Brigid and Cairo. Gutman replies that Rhea's injuries served their purpose. Spade asks when Gutman is ready to make his first payment on the falcon. Gutman takes from his pocket an envelope containing ten $1,000 bills and hands it to Spade. He explains that it is less than they had agreed to before, but then things have changed. Spade counts the money, and puts the envelope on the sofa. He says that before they can go any further, they need a fall-guy, someone to hand over to the police and blame for the three murders—Archer, Thursby, and Jacobi. Cairo protests that Thursby undoubtedly killed Archer. Spade says the police have to be given someone to pin the crimes on. He explains that they will overlook details and even other suspects if they have a solid case against one person. He suggests Wilmer. Gutman at first laughs, then takes him more seriously before refusing. Wilmer becomes agitated and threatens to kill Spade, who is secure knowing that they will not harm him because only he knows where the falcon is. Then Spade sug-

ROSS MACDONALD ON HAMMETT

Probably Hammett intended the ultimate worthlessness of the black bird to be more than a bad joke on his protagonist. I see it as a symbol of a lost tradition. It represents religion and the great cultures of the Mediterranean past which are inaccessible to Spade. Its loss sets a final seal on the inadequacy and superficiality of Spade's life. If only his struggle for self-awareness were more fully realized, his guilt not left unspoken, the stakes for which he struggles not so arbitrarily lost from the beginning, Sam Spade could have been an indigenous tragic figure. As it is, this novel has astonishing imaginative energy after one-third of a century. It can still express contemporary truth, and comes close to tragedy, if there can be such a thing as deadpan tragedy.

Ross Macdonald, "The Scene of the Crime," in *Inward Journey,* edited by Ralph B. Sipper (Santa Barbara: Cordelia Editions, 1984), pp. 30–31.

gests Cairo as the fall-guy. Cairo asks angrily why not give the police Spade or Brigid. Spade says he is willing to discuss giving the police Brigid, if they can rig a case against her. Cairo moves behind Gutman and begins whispering in his ear. Spade bets Wilmer they are discussing how to give him up. He tells Gutman not to worry about the guns Cairo and Wilmer are carrying because he has experience taking their weapons away from them. With that, Wilmer jumps up and holds his gun out. Gutman grabs his gun hand, and Cairo grabs his other arm. Spade hits him in the face twice, and Wilmer collapses. Cairo then attacks Spade ineffectively, and Spade knocks him away, telling him to stop before he gets hurt. Cairo caresses Wilmer tenderly, and Spade collects the guns. Cairo agrees to give up Wilmer.

CHAPTER XIX, "THE RUSSIAN'S HAND": Cairo sits beside Wilmer on the sofa rubbing his face and wrists. When pressed—told that if he does not agree they will give him up with Wilmer—Cairo agrees to go along. It is 2:00 A.M., and Spade says he cannot produce the falcon until daybreak—as late as 8:00 A.M. Gutman looks at the sofa and asks where the envelope with the money is. Brigid says she has it. They agree to stay in the apartment to keep watch on each other until the bird is delivered. Spade wants to fix the details of the story implicating Wilmer. He asks when he shot Thursby. After some protest, Gutman attests that they knew Thursby was a killer and that he was Brigid's accomplice. They knew that she would not tell Thursby more than he needed to know. They did not realize then that she had given Jacobi the falcon to transport while she and Thursby took a faster boat from Hong Kong. Wilmer brought Thursby to Gutman, and when they could not get information from him, Wilmer followed Thursby back to his hotel and killed him, to deprive Brigid of protection. Cairo later saw the notice of *La Paloma* landing in San Francisco, and, having seen Brigid talking to Captain Jacobi in Hong Kong, assumed correctly that he had the falcon. Cairo, Gutman, and Wilmer went to the pier and found Jacobi and Brigid together. While Wilmer searched the vessel, starting the fire, Gutman arranged to buy the bird, taking receipt at his hotel. When they did not show at Gutman's, he sent Wilmer to find them. He went to Brigid's hotel-room door and heard the noise of a window being raised inside. He rushed to the fire escape and caught Jacobi with the falcon under his arm. Wilmer shot him six times, but Jacobi got away as a policeman came near. They forced Brigid to tell them that she had asked Jacobi to take the falcon to Spade. They made her call him to Gutman's suite, where he found Rhea, in an attempt to divert him from Jacobi.

As they pass the time, Spade asks Brigid to make breakfast for them. Before she goes into the kitchen, Gutman asks her to give him the envelope with the money. She does, and he counts it, finding only nine bills. Spade looks at Brigid who shakes her head no. Spade says he will find out what happened. He takes Brigid into the bathroom, leaves the door open, and tells her to undress. She does so, telling him he is killing something between them. He searches her clothes as she stands naked and finds nothing. Then he closes the door and goes to Gutman, who admits he palmed the bill. Brigid comes out of the bathroom dressed and begins to make breakfast.

While Brigid is in the kitchen, Gutman asks Spade if he means to share the money with her. Gutman warns Spade to be careful if she is unhappy with the split. Cairo, meanwhile, is trying to comfort Wilmer, who gets annoyed and punches Cairo in the mouth. Spade refers to the incident as "the course of true love" (199). Spade asks Gutman for more money, but Gutman refuses. When Brigid serves breakfast, they all eat, except for Wilmer.

At 7:00 A.M. Spade calls Effie Perine, tells her how to find the bird, and asks her to bring it to him. Fifty minutes later she arrives, gives Spade the package, and leaves. Gutman unwraps it and with a penknife shaves away the enamel first on the base, then on the head. It is lead, a fake. Brigid swears it is the bird she got from Kemidov. Cairo angrily screams that Gutman tipped off Kemidov to the bird's value by trying to buy it from him. He says Kemidov hired him to go looking for the bird after it was stolen. Gutman admits that it is the Russian's hand at work. Gutman says he has been trying to find the falcon for seventeen years. He will not give up now. He plans to go to Constantinople, and Cairo eagerly agrees to go along. Spade notices that Wilmer is gone. Gutman asks for his money back. When Spade objects, Gutman pulls a gun on him. Spade gives Gutman the money, keeping $1,000 for his trouble. Gutman invites Spade to join him in the continuing search for the real falcon and, when Spade refuses, suggests that any legal difficulty that comes to any of them will involve Spade and Brigid. Spade acknowledges that, and Gutman departs, leaving the false bird with Spade.

CHAPTER XX, "IF THEY HANG YOU": Spade stands staring at the door for five minutes before he picks up the phone and calls Tom Polhaus to report that Wilmer killed Thursby and Jacobi, that Gutman and Cairo are accomplices, and that they have just left his apartment, presumably on the way to Gutman's suite, planning a hasty departure. He warns Polhaus that Wilmer is dangerous. Spade then turns to Brigid, telling her the men will talk when apprehended and that their own situation is precarious.

She tells him that Gutman sent her to Constantinople and that she met Cairo there. She asked him to help her get the bird from Kemidov, and they planned to keep it for themselves. Then she became suspicious of Cairo and enlisted Thursby to help her. She got the bird, framed Cairo with a bad-check charge so he was detained in Constantinople, and went with Thursby to Hong Kong. She then became suspicious of Thursby and enlisted Jacobi to take the bird to San Francisco on *La Paloma* while she and Thursby took a faster boat. She lies to Spade that she came to him for protection, because she was fearful that Gutman, who was in New York, would find out what she had done and would get to San Francisco before the falcon did. Spade challenges her, saying she wanted to get rid of Thursby. She admits that she told Thursby he was being shadowed by Archer, and then begins another lie. Spade calls her, saying Archer was too experienced to be led into a blind alley to be shot by Thursby. At length she admits that she killed Archer, and then begins to lie again. He stops her. She wanted someone following Thursby who knew her, so she could lure him into the alley and kill him. She had already rented her hotel room at the Coronet before she hired Spade and Archer. Her plan was that Thursby would attack the shadow and that one of them would be killed. If it were Thursby, then she was rid of him. If it were Archer, then Thursby could be set up for his murder. When Thursby did not confront Archer, she lured Archer into the alley and killed him with a gun she had taken from Thursby earlier in the day. When she learned that Thursby had been killed, she knew that Gutman was in town, and she needed a protector, so she went back to Spade.

He tells her that he is going to turn her in. One of them will have to take the blame. He points out that she has been playing him for a sap. At Gutman's insistence, she led him on a wild goose chase to Burlingame; she came to his apartment with Gutman, Cairo, and Wilmer and met him outside without letting him know they were waiting for him; she was hugging him when they went inside to keep him from going for a gun when they surprised him. He says Gutman did not take her away with him because he thought she could convince Spade not to turn them in. He says he thinks he loves her, and she says she loves him, but he says he cannot trust her. She has double-crossed every man she has come in contact with and killed Archer in cold blood. She asks him then just to let her go. He refuses, pointing out that he has to turn her in to keep from taking the blame for Archer's murder himself. He warns Brigid not to think he is as crooked as he seems to be. She makes one more plea in the name of love, and he repeats that he will not play the sap for her. When the doorbell rings, she is in his arms.

Dundy, Polhaus, and two other detectives come in, and Spade turns over Brigid to Polhaus for Archer's murder. He gives them Cairo's and Wilmer's guns, the fake falcon, and the $1,000 he took from Gutman's envelope. Polhaus tells him that they arrested Cairo and Wilmer, who had just finished killing Gutman when the police arrived.

On Monday morning Spade enters his office and finds Effie reading the paper. He tells her the news stories are accurate and kids her about her intuition that Brigid was innocent. She cannot believe he turned over Brigid to the police. He tries to put his arm around her, and she resists him. She does not want him to touch her. They hear the outer office doorknob rattle. Effie goes out to see who it is. She comes back in and says it is Iva Archer. Spade shivers and says "send her in."

NOTES

1. Glenn Todd, "On the Photographs" in Dashiell Hammett, *The Maltese Falcon* (San Francisco: North Point Press, 1984), p. 281. Todd has misstated the number of days covered by the novel. It begins on Wednesday and ends on Monday. Most scholars, including Layman, have made a similar error.

2. *The Maltese Falcon* (New York: Vintage/Black Lizard,1992), p. 89. Page references are to this commonly available edition. Quotations have been checked against the first edition. Subsequent references are noted parenthetically in the text.

3. "En Cuba," by Eduardo Sanchez de Fuentes, was originally published in 1906 under the title "Tu (You) Habanera." It was republished by Jerome H. Remick & Co. in 1928 as "En Cuba." The lyrics, translated from the original Spanish, are

> In Cuba,
> fairest Island of pines and of palms,
> With their fragrance o'er laden,
> For embraced she has been in Dame Nature's fond arms
> and endow'd with her charms;
> In Cuba,
> 'Neath her sky so azure and serene,
> Dwells my beautiful maiden,
> Of the flowers that bloom in that garden so green,
> My brunette, you're the queen.

On flaming altar
has your heart been enshrin'd
In fires beatified
It is ever confined.
Nor heav'n did falter
In your eyes to infuse
All the light of the sun and the night
And the sky's brightest hues.

The palm trees,
Where they cluster in redolent glade,
In the soft breezes swaying,
Gently fan your dark tresses so freely displayed
As you lie in their shade.

The palm trees,
Like all nature, pay homage to you—
Hear the words they are saying
While you lie in their shadow 'neath Heaven's bright blue—
For they worship you too!

Your charms, transcending
All the beauties of earth,
To me are sanctified
As all treasures of worth;
Your sweetness blending
With the nectar of Heav'n
Nature's balm and the isle's soothing calm—
For to Cuba you're giv'n!

THE EVOLUTION OF *THE MALTESE FALCON*

In the case of *The Maltese Falcon,* as with all of Hammett's fiction, there is spotty evidence of the evolution of the work. There is no known manuscript, typescript, proof copy, or outline. A careful reader of all of Hammett's publications will find many similarities among characters and plots in *The Maltese Falcon* and earlier works. The reader may draw conclusions about how the novel evolved, but the validity of such conclusions is limited by the soundness of the reader's judgment. The evidence can easily be misconstrued, and readers should take Sam Spade's example, being always wary of assuming too much from too little evidence.

The similarities between Hammett's earlier works and *The Maltese Falcon* are significant in at least two major ways. First, they suggest how Hammett operated as a writer—how he developed and shaped literary ideas; how he combined characters and plots; how he tested the fictional elements of his novel in short works before settling on final versions. Second, they can provide insights into Hammett's intentions as a writer. As Hammett hones a character such as Brigid O'Shaughnessy into finished form, he expresses attitudes that may provide more information about his fictional intent than is available in the novel alone. Readers should use such information with extreme care, however, to amplify evidence in the novel rather than to supply new evidence. That so little of Hammett's prepublication writing is available suggests that he had no interest in having his writing process scrutinized. Nonetheless, the process by which a writer creates a masterpiece is always fascinating and instructive insofar as it can be reconstructed.

WRITING THE WORK

Hammett wrote only once about the composition of *The Maltese Falcon.* In the 1934 introduction to the Modern Library edition of the novel:

Joseph Shaw, editor of the *Black Mask* from November 1926 until November 1936

If this book had been written with the help of an outline or notes or even a clearly defined plot-idea in my head I might now be able to say how it came to be written and why it took the shape it did, but all I can remember about its invention is that somewhere I had read of the peculiar rental agreement between Charles V and the Order of the Hospital of St. John of Jerusalem, that in a short story called THE WHOSIS KID I had failed to make the most of a situation I liked, that in another called THE GUTTING OF COUFFIGNAL I had been equally unfortunate with an equally promising dénouement, and that I thought I might have better luck with these two failures if I combined them with the Maltese lease in a longer story.

I can remember more clearly where I got most of my characters.

Wilmer, the boy gun-man, was picked up in Stockton, California, where I had gone hunting a window-smasher who had robbed a San Jose jewelry store. Wilmer's original was not my window-smasher, unfortunately, but he was a fair pick-up. He was a neat small smooth-faced quiet boy of perhaps twenty-one. He said he was only seventeen, but that was probably an attempt to draw a reform school instead of a penitentiary sentence. He also said his father was a lieutenant of police in New York, which may or may not have been true, and he was serenely proud of the name the local newspapers gave him—The Midget Bandit. He had robbed a Stockton filling station the previous week. In Los Angeles a day or two later, reading a Stockton newspaper—there must be criminals who subscribe to clipping services—he had been annoyed by the description the filling-station proprietor had given of him and by the proprietor's statement of what he would do to that little runt if he ever laid eyes on him again. So The Midget Bandit had stolen an automobile and returned to Stockton to, in his words, stick that guy up again and see what he wanted to do about it.

Brigid O'Shaughnessy had two originals, one an artist, the other a woman who came to Pinkerton's San Francisco office to hire an operative to discharge her housekeeper, but neither of these women was a criminal.

Dundy's prototype I worked with in a North Carolina railroad yard; Cairo's I picked up on a forgery charge in Pasco, Washington, in 1920; Polhaus's was a former captain of detectives; I used to buy books from Iva's in Spokane; Effie's once asked me to go into the narcotic smuggling business with her in San Diego; Gutman's was suspected—foolishly, as most people were—of being a German secret agent in Washington, D.C., in the early days of the war, and I never remember shadowing a man who bored me as much.

Spade had no original. He is a dream man in the sense that he is what most of the private detectives I worked with would like to have been and what quite a few of them in their cockier moments thought they approached. For your private detective does not—or did not ten years ago when he was my colleague—want to be an erudite solver of riddles in the Sherlock Holmes manner; he wants to be a hard and shifty fellow, able to take care of himself in any situation, able to get the best of anybody he comes in contact with, whether criminal, innocent by-stander or client.

DASHIELL HAMMETT.

New York, January 24, 1934.[1]

Hammett began experimenting with the characters and plot situations that he used in *The Maltese Falcon* in his earliest pulp stories. In a November 1923 story in *Action Stories,* "Laughing Masks," Hammett created a femme fatale named Romaine, who anticipates Brigid O'Shaughnessy. She is victimized by a greedy Russian aristocrat named Kapaloff, who lost his property in the Bolshevik Revolution and then killed her father to gain control of his estate. The detective, Phil Truax, falls in love with the beautiful Romaine and saves her from those attempting to victimize her. In *The Maltese Falcon* Brigid and the others in search of the falcon are apparently outwitted by Kemidov, the greedy Russian general living in Constantinople who apparently has possession of the falcon. The relationship between Phil Truax and Romaine anticipates the attraction between Spade and Brigid O'Shaughnessy.

In "It," published in *Black Mask* the same month, a character hires the Op to investigate a crime he himself committed as a ploy to throw the police off his trail, a tactic similar to Brigid's when she first hires Spade to follow Thursby.

"The House in Turk Street" (*Black Mask,* 15 April 1924) foreshadows the essentials of the plot and the main characters in *The Maltese Falcon.* A Chinese criminal mastermind named Tai heads a gang that includes a gunman named Hook and a beautiful redhaired temptress

"Make it all right? he asked. "Or shall I carry you up?"

She shook her head against his shoulder.

"I'll be—all right—when I—get where—I can—sit down."

They rode up to Spade's floor in the elevator, and went around to his apartment. She left his arm, and stood beside him, panting, both hands to her breast, while he unlocked his door. He switched on the passageway light. They went in.

He shut the door, and with his arm around her again half-carried her toward the living-room. When they were within a step of the living-room door, the living-room light went on.

The girl cried out and clung to Spade.

Just inside the living-room door, fat Gutman stood smiling benevolently at them.

The undersized youth Gutman had called Wilmer came out of the kitchen behind them. Black pistols were gigantic in his small hands.

Cairo came out of the bathroom. He too had a pistol.

Gutman said:

"Well, sir, we're all here, as you can see. Now let's come in and sit down and be comfortable and talk."

(Concluded In January Issue)

To our readers:

I read this story just as you have read it—instalment by instalment. When I got this far I was as uncertain as you are how the story comes out, or who killed Archer and Thursby. I had ideas, of course, just as you probably have. It wasn't until, practically speaking, the very last word of the last instalment (the instalment you will read next—in the January issue) that I knew the answer; and it took me completely by surprise.

As a matter of fact, when I finished reading the last instalment I was breathless and almost overwhelmed. In all of my experience I have never read a story as intense, as gripping or as powerful as this last instalment. It is a magnificent piece of writing: with all the earnestness of which I am capable I tell you not to miss it.

THE EDITOR.

STATEMENT OF THE OWNERSHIP, MANAGEMENT, CIRCULATION, ETC., REQUIRED BY THE ACT OF CONGRESS OF AUGUST 24, 1912, OF BLACK MASK, PUBLISHED MONTHLY AT NEW YORK, N. Y., FOR OCTOBER 1, 1929. State of New York, County of New York, ss. Before me, a Notary Public in and for the State and county aforesaid, personally appeared Joseph T. Shaw, who, having been duly sworn according to law, deposes and says that he is the Editor of Black Mask, and the following is to the best of his knowledge and belief, a true statement of the ownership, management, etc., of the aforesaid publication for the date shown in the above caption, required by the Act of August 24, 1912, embodied in section 443, Postal Laws and Regulations printed on the reverse of this form, to wit: 1. That the names and addresses of the publisher, editor, managing editor, and business manager are: Publisher, Pro-Distributors Publishing Co., Inc., 578 Madison Ave., New York City; Editor, Joseph T. Shaw, 578 Madison Ave., New York City; Managing Editor, Joseph T. Shaw, 578 Madison Ave., New York City; Business Manager, A. W. Sutton, 578 Madison Ave., New York City. 2. That the owners are Pro-Distributors Publishing Co., Inc., 578 Madison Ave., New York City; E. F. Warner, 578 Madison Ave., New York City; Perkins-Goodwin Co., 551 Fifth Avenue, New York City. Stockholders of Perkins-Goodwin Company are: legatees under will of E. F. Crowe, Louis Calder, F. W. Westlake (estate), John Atkins, S. Goldman, W. F. Anders, J. A. Brady, C. T. Rue, Wm. H. Donaldson, all of 551 Fifth Avenue, New York City. 3. That the known bondholders, mortgagees, and security holders owning or holding 1 per cent or more of total amount of bonds, mortgages, or other securities are: None. 4. That the two paragraphs next above, giving the names of the owners, stockholders, and security holders, if any, contain not only the list of stockholders and security holders as they appear upon the books of the company, but also in cases where the stockholders or security holders appear upon the books of the company as trustee or in any other fiduciary relation, the name of the person or corporation for whom such trustee is acting, is given; also that the said two paragraphs contain statements embracing affiant's full knowledge and belief as to the circumstances and conditions under which stockholders and security holders who do not appear upon the books of the company as trustee, hold stock and securities in a capacity other than that of a bona fide owner; and this affiant has no reason to believe that any other person, association, or corporation has any interest direct or indirect in the said stock, bonds or other securities than as so stated by him. (Signed) JOSEPH T. SHAW, Editor. Sworn to and subscribed before me this 27th day of September, 1929. [Seal] A. W. Sutton. (My commission expires March 30, 1930.)

Last page of the fourth installment of *The Maltese Falcon* in the December 1929 issue of *Black Mask*, with Joseph Shaw's enthusiastic assessment named Elvira. Tai is the prototype for Gutman; Hook suggests Wilmer; and Elvira is one of the long line of Hammett's femmes fatales. Tai and his gang have stolen $100,000, using Elvira to seduce a bank messenger. The three attempt to double-cross one another, as well as other members of the gang, and the Op gains the upper hand by finding and hiding the money. At the end of the story Elvira escapes. She reappears in "The Girl with the Silver Eyes" (*Black Mask,* June 1924), now calling herself Jeanne Delano. At the end of the story the Op has Elvira in custody and she makes an appeal for freedom, Hammett's first developed attempt at the scene in which his detective resists the lustful appeal of a beautiful murderess:

> "Little fat detective whose name I don't know"—her voice had a tired huskiness in it, and a tired mockery—"you think I am playing a part, don't you? You think I am pleading for liberty. Perhaps I am. I certainly would take it if it were offered me. But—men have thought me beautiful, and I have played with them. Women are like that. Men have loved me and, doing what I liked with them, I have found men contemptible. And then comes this fat detective whose name I don't know, and he acts as if I were a hag—an old squaw. Can I help then being piqued into some sort of feeling for him? Women are like that. Am I so homely that any man has a right to look at me without even interest. Am I ugly?"

> I shook my head. "You're quite pretty," I said, struggling to keep my voice as casual as the words.

> "You beast!" she spat, and then her smile grew gentle again. "And yet it is because of that attitude that I sit here and turn myself inside out for you. If you were to take me in your arms and hold me close to the chest that I am already leaning against, and if you were to tell me that there is no jail ahead for me just now, I would be glad, of course. But, though for a while you might hold me, you would then be only one of the men with which I am familiar: men who love and are used and are succeeded by other men. But because you do none of these things, because you are a wooden block of a man, I find myself wanting you. Would I tell you this, little fat detective, If I were playing a game?"

> I grunted noncommittally, and forcibly restrained my tongue from running out to moisten my dry lips.

"I'm going to this jail tonight if you are the same hard man who has goaded me into whining love into his uncaring ears, but before that, can't I have one whole-hearted assurance that you think me more than 'quite pretty'? or at least a hint that if I were not a prisoner your pulse might beat a little faster when I touch you? I'm going to this jail for a long while—perhaps to the gallows. Can't I take my vanity there not quite in tatters to keep me company? Can't you do some slight thing to keep me from the after-thought of having bleated all this out to a man who was simply bored?"

Her lids had come down half over the silver-gray eyes, her head had tilted back so far that a little pulse showed throbbing in her white throat; her lips were motionless over slightly parted teeth, as the last word had left them. My fingers went deep into the soft white flesh of her shoulders. Her head went further back, her eyes closed, one hand came up to my shoulder.

"You're beautiful as hell!" I shouted crazily into her face, and flung her against the door.[2]

The Op recovers his senses, calls her a liar, and drives her to a police station.

In "Who Killed Bob Teal" (*True Detective Stories,* November 1924), the title character is a detective hired by a man involved in a land options swindle to shadow his partner. The man who hired the detective kills him and frames his partner for the crime. The plot and the motivation of the characters are similar to the circumstances of Miles Archer's murder.

"The Golden Horseshoe" (*Black Mask,* November 1924) suggests the Flitcraft anecdote Spade tells Brigid in Chapter VII. In the story, a woman named Ashcroft hires the Op to find her missing husband, who left, despondent, and after three years wrote that he was addicted to drugs and needed a monthly allowance to get himself in shape to return.

FROM HAMMETT'S PROSPECTUS

I am against people who push other people around and it's quieter with a knife. I am against Freud and Deceit and Abbott and Costello and the Articles of War and $50,000 officers. I am for people who are kind and courageous and honest and willing to bet on the second front. I do not believe that all mankind's problems are being solved but what do you expect in 50 years? I am in dead earnest about this. Dead. I am an American and I prefer democracy to any other form of government including Hammet-ism. Shut up.

From *The Adakian,* 27 May 1944, p. 1, the special DH at 50 Birthday Issue.

The Op finds that the man committed suicide just after he left, and his body was discovered by a crook, who has been extorting money.

In "The Whosis Kid" (*Black Mask*, March 1925), a beautiful woman named Inez Almad seduces a jewelry-store employee into stealing precious stones and faking a robbery ostensibly committed by Inez's accomplices, The Whosis Kid and Edouard Maurois. The accomplices assume Inez will double-cross the employee and keep the stones for them. She, in turn, makes separate deals with each of them to meet in distant cities to split the stones two ways. She meets neither accomplice and goes to San Francisco alone with the loot. The Kid and Maurois catch up with her in San Francisco and are both killed in a climactic gun battle. In the end everyone who teamed with Inez is killed. She is as dangerous, as cold-blooded, and as calculating as Brigid O'Shaughnessy.

"The Gutting of Couffignal" (*Black Mask*, December 1925) recounts the case in which a gang of Russian aristocrats, exiled after the Bolshevik Revolution of 1917, who determine to replenish their coffers by looting a residential island in San Pablo Bay near San Francisco. At the end of the story, one of the leaders of the assault, Princess Zhukouski, offers the Op first money and then sex to let her and her accomplices go free. In a second version of the speech at the end of "The Girl with the Silver Eyes," published eighteen months earlier, Hammett has the Op explain why he will not, cannot, do what she asks, focusing this time not on the temptress's speech but on the Op's response:

> "I like being a detective, like the work. And liking work makes you want to do it as well as you can. Otherwise there'd be no sense to it. That's the fix I am in. I don't know anything else, don't enjoy anything else, don't want to know or enjoy anything else. You can't weigh that against any sum of money. Money is good stuff. I haven't anything against it. But in the past eighteen years I've been getting my fun out of chasing crooks and tackling puzzles, my satisfaction out of catching crooks and solving riddles. It's the only kind of sport I know anything about, and I can't imagine a pleasanter future than twenty-some years more of it. I'm not going to blow that up!
>
> . . . You think I'm a man and you're a woman. That's wrong. I'm a manhunter and you're something that has been running in front of me. There's nothing human about it. You might just as well expect a hound to play tiddly-winks with the fox he's caught."[3]

In 1925 Hammett began a novel called "The Secret Emperor," about a Jew who realized he could not be elected president and determined to control the presidency by blackmailing a viable candidate. The Jew's name is Gutman, and he seems a study, at least, for the bulbous villain of *The Maltese Falcon*.

In "The Main Death" (*Black Mask,* June 1927) the Op is hired by an effeminate, aged antiques dealer named Gungen to reclaim money stolen from his assistant, Jeffrey Main, after the sale of a gold tiara. The Op learns that Main was killed by associates of the Gungens' maid after an adulterous liaison with Mrs. Gungen. The Op returns the money but refuses to disclose evidence of the young Enid Gungen's affair to her husband. Gungen's profession, his misplaced values on things rather than people, Enid Gungen's charged sexuality, and the Op's attitude toward his client all suggest fictional elements of *The Maltese Falcon,* which Hammett was already mulling over in his mind.

All of these precursors to characters and plot situations in *The Maltese Falcon* show how complex the writing process was. Before Hammett began writing his novel, he had been mulling over the material he would use in it for more than five years. He had tested his ideas, refined his descriptions, and developed his writing skills with the diligence of a craftsman. Equally important, because sometimes craftsmen go unrecognized, he was developing the professional credentials that would allow him to get his novel published. And just as critical, because sometimes life's circumstances do not allow the opportunity for creativity, Hammett had the time and the encouragement to write. Before 1928 *The Maltese Falcon* would not have been possible. All the pieces had not yet come together.

On 20 March 1928 Hammett wrote to Blanche Knopf, responding to her suggestions for revising his first novel *Red Harvest.* He told her another book was on the way to her—*The Dain Curse.* "Then I want to try adapting the stream-of-consciousness method, conveniently modified, to a detective story, carrying the reader along with the detective, showing him everything as it is found, giving him the detective's conclusions as they are reached, letting the solution break on both of them together. I don't know whether I've made that very clear, but it's something altogether different from the method employed in POISONVILLE, for instance, where, though the reader goes along with the detective, he seldom sees deeper into the detective's mind than dialogue and action let him. If I can manage it, I want to do this one without any regard for magazines' thou-shalts and thou-shalt-nots. I hope to get it finished by late summer, in time to do another—a plot I've been waiting to get at for two

Too Many Have Lived

A mystery story com-
plete in this issue by
the author of A MAN CALLED SPADE

DASHIELL HAMMETT

THE man's tie was as orange as a sunset. He was a large man, tall and meaty, without soft-ness. The dark hair parted in the middle, flattened to his scalp, his firm, full cheeks, the clothes that fit him with noticeable snugness, even the small, pink ears flat against the sides of

The green-eyed man lowered his voice, but there was no other change in his mien: "In a way I do. For instance, if you found him and fixed it so he stayed away for good, it might be worth more money to me."

"You mean even if he didn't want to stay away?"

Opening of a Sam Spade story in *The American Magazine,* April 1932

years—before 1928 is dead."[4] While *The Maltese Falcon* is far from a stream-of-consciousness novel, it seems in all other respects to be the book Hammett described to Mrs. Knopf. He came close to his deadline. The *Black Mask* began publishing the serialization of the novel in the September 1929 issue, which was on the newsstands in mid August. On Sunday, 16 June 1929, Hammett wrote to Harry Block, his editor at Knopf: "I started THE MALTESE FALCON on its way to you by express last Friday, the fourteenth. I'm fairly confident that it is by far the best thing I've done so far, and I hope you'll think so too."[5]

REVISING THE WORK

There are no known prepublication texts of *The Maltese Falcon,* but there are two published versions of the novel. The first is the *Black Mask* publication in five parts. Hammett's editor at *Black Mask* was Joseph Shaw, and there is no evidence that Shaw did not simply print what Hammett submitted, particularly after the success of *Red Harvest* and *The Dain Curse,* except that Shaw objected to curses and sacrilegious epithets. In the book Spade tells Brigid "I hope to Christ they don't hang you, precious, by that sweet neck."[6] In the magazine, it is "I hope to _____ they don't hang you."[7] In the book, Spade calls Miles a "son of a bitch" (213). In the magazine, he is a "____ ____ __ _____."[8]

Hammett's editors at Knopf, however, took an active interest in his first two novels, firmly recommending plot alterations, deletion of characters, stylistic refinements, and changes in title. *The Maltese Falcon* was a different matter. In a June 1929 letter to Harry Block, Hammett asked him to "go a little easy on the editing."[9] He

admits that his punctuation may be a bit unorthodox, but he asks for latitude in making his own decisions about it. Block responded by asking that Hammett omit some of the racier parts of the novel. Hammett refused. In a 14 July 1929 letter to Block, Hammett wrote: "I'm glad you like THE MALTESE FALCON. I'm sorry you think the to-bed and the homosexual parts of it should be changed. I should like to leave them as they are, especially since you say they 'would be all right perhaps in an ordinary novel.' It seems to me that the only thing that can be said against their use in a detective novel is that nobody has tried it yet. I'd like to try it."[10]

The best evidence indicates that Block granted Hammett's wish and that there was little editorial intervention in the book publication of the novel. The Knopf copyeditors seem to have combined paragraphs and fiddled with Hammett's use of commas, taking out many they judged to be superfluous by house style, substituting dashes for commas in many instances, and adding necessary punctuation occasionally.

What Hammett himself did, however, was substantive. He revised the *Black Mask* version heavily before the novel was published by Knopf. A collation of the magazine text with the novel text shows the care Hammett took with his writing. He went over every sentence in the book scrupulously after the magazine publication, sharpening the meaning, reordering words to get the rhythm of his sentences right, and substituting words.

When he first described Brigid in the magazine, "She was tall. She was pliantly slender. Her erect, high-breasted body, her long legs, her narrow hands and feet, had nowhere any angularity."[11] In the book, "She was tall and pliantly slender, without angularity anywhere. Her body was erect and high breasted, her legs long, her hands and feet narrow" (4). In the magazine, when Spade explained to Brigid what will happen that evening, he said, "Well, that should be easily enough managed. It's simply a matter of having a man at the hotel this evening to shadow him away when he leaves, and to keep on shadowing him till he leads us to your sister. If she comes with him, so much the better."[12]

In the book, he says:

"We shouldn't have any trouble with it. It's simply a matter of having a man at the hotel this evening to shadow him away when he leaves, and shadow him until he leads us to your sister. If she comes with him, and you persuade her to return with you, so much the better. Otherwise—if she doesn't want to leave him after we've found her—well, we'll find a way of managing that." (7)

Hammett frequently added sentences and paragraphs to sharpen his points. In Spade's dramatic speech to Brigid at the end of the book, explaining why he will not let her go free, Hammett added this passage that did not appear in the magazine:

He took her by the shoulders and bent her back, leaning over her. "If that doesn't mean anything to you forget it and we'll make it this: I won't because all of me wants to—wants to say to hell with the consequences and do it—and because—God damn you—you've counted on that with me the same as you counted on that with the others." He took his hands from her shoulders and let them fall to his sides. (215)

The revision process for *The Maltese Falcon* apparently took at least six months. On Friday, 14 June 1929, he mailed the typescript to Knopf, and there was another round of copyediting-type revisions, regarding such matters as punctuation and changing Hammett's use of the word "till" to "until," that could not have lasted more than about fourteen weeks. By 1 November 1929 Knopf had to have the book in production to meet the printer's schedule.

NOTES

1. Introduction to *The Maltese Falcon* (New York: Modern Library, 1934), pp. vii–ix.

2. In Dashiell Hammett, *The Continental Op*, edited by Steven Marcus (New York: Random House, 1974), pp. 157–158.

3. *The Big Knockover,* edited by Lillian Hellman (New York: Random House, 1966), pp. 28–29.

4. Dashiell Hammett to Blanche Knopf, 20 March 1928. Harry Ransom Humanities Research Center, University of Texas, Austin.

5. Dashiell Hammett to Harry Block, 16 June 1929. Harry Ransom Humanities Research Center, University of Texas, Austin.

6. *The Maltese Falcon* (New York: Vintage/Black Lizard, 1992), p. 211. Page references are to this commonly available editon. Quotations have been checked against the first edition. Subsequent references are noted parenthetically in the text.

7. *Black Mask* (January 1930): 51.

8. *Black Mask* (January 1930): 52.

9. Dashiell Hammett to Harry Block, June 1929. Harry Ransom Humanities Research Center, University of Texas, Austin.

10. Dashiell Hammett to Harry Block, 14 July 1929. Harry Ransom Humanities Research Center, University of Texas, Austin.

11. *Black Mask* (September 1929): 8.

12. *Black Mask* (September 1929): 10.

THE MALTESE FALCON ANALYZED

SETTING

The setting of *The Maltese Falcon* is integral to the plot. "This is my city,"[1] Spade tells Gutman. To Hammett researcher and San Francisco private detective David Fechheimer, "The City is not just a setting for the novel; it is a character, flowing between the dialogue like fog."[2] San Francisco shapes Spade, and he reflects the character of the city. The physical setting is precise. Hammett set the novel where he lived, and he placed Spade in the apartment where he wrote the novel. First Fritz Lieber, in his article "Stalking Sam Spade" (*California Living,* 13 January 1974), then Joe Gores in "A Foggy Night" (*City of San Francisco,* 4 November 1975) outlined the geography of *The Maltese Falcon.* Gores presents a careful argument based on clues in the novel for placing Spade's apartment at 891 Post Street. He identifies Spade's office at 111 Sutter Street. He says that the Coronet Hotel, where Brigid lived, was the Cathedral Apartments at 1201 California Street. The St. Mark, where Brigid and Thursby stay at the beginning of the novel, is probably the St. Francis on Union Square. The Belvedere, Cairo's hotel, is the Bellevue at 505 Geary, one block from the Geary Theatre, where he sees *The Merchant of Venice.* The Alexandria, Gutman's hotel, is probably the Drake. The restaurants Hammett mentions in the novel are all real. Indeed, John's Grill, where Spade eats while waiting for the car to take him to Burlingame, is the present-day headquarters of the Dashiell Hammett Fan Club. Burritt Street is marked with a plaque that announces "ON APPROXIMATELY THIS SPOT MILES ARCHER, PARTNER OF SAM SPADE, WAS DONE IN BY BRIGID O'SHAUGHNESSY." Hammett aficionado Don Herron began conducting tours of Hammett's San Francisco in about 1977, and he has built on Gores's research, publishing a pictorial guide to Hammett's city.[3]

The key place in the novel is 891 Post Street, at the corner of Hyde, Hammett's home from late 1926 until fall 1929 and the building where Spade lives, apparently in the same fourth-floor apartment. Kept as

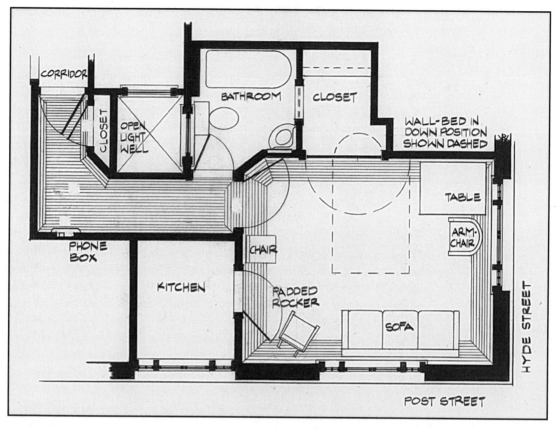

Architect William Arney's floor plan of apartment 401, 891 Post Street, Hammett's residence while writing *The Maltese Falcon* and the model for Spade's apartment

a shrine of sorts by Hammett fan and architect William Arney, the apartment meets the specifications laid out in the novel. It consists of one large sitting room that doubles as a bedroom, with a fold-down Murphy bed. The entrance to the apartment is through a winding corridor that has a telephone box near the bathroom door and a closet just inside the front door. There is a kitchen off the sitting room and a bathroom off the corridor. There is a three-story drop from the sitting-room windows, in the corner apartment, which fronts Hyde Street and Post. Chapter II, the end of Chapter VI, Chapters VII–IX, parts of Chapter X, and the end of Chapter XVII through all but the very end of Chapter XX are set there. The layout of the apartment is precisely described, and an accurate image of it is important to a visual understanding of the action. A reliable map of San Francisco and Bill Arney's floor plan of the apartment are useful aides to have at hand when reading the book.

A city is more than streets and buildings, though, and it is the spirit of San Francisco that seems to define Spade. He is a man who minds his own business and expects as much freedom as he can justify. He is unorthodox and unpredictable. He has a healthy suspicion of and disdain for authority; yet, he acknowledges that there is a cost associated with living in his city, and he pays his tribute responsibly. *The Maltese Falcon* is a western novel, as reliable a guide to the spirit of the city as any ever written.

PLOT

There are two structural considerations that affect the way the plot of *The Maltese Falcon* unfolds. First, Hammett told Blanche Knopf that with *The Maltese Falcon* he was writing a story in which the reader learns the facts of the case and can react to them just as the detective does. He said that his Op stories did not allow him to portray the reactions of the detective as he wished. His solution to the problem was to switch from a first-person narration, which he used in all the Op stories and in his first two novels, to a third-person narration. The narrative voice he chose is that of an objective reporter who sees and knows what Sam Spade knows. The narrator perceives the action as Spade does but without Spade's sensibility, and at the same time the narrator observes Spade. The reader learns how Spade acts, speaks, and looks—but not, except by observation, how he feels or what he thinks.

The second key to the structure of the novel comes from a comment Hammett made to Knopf editor Harry Block. He told Block he thought the novel could be adapted to a stage drama and asked for recommendations about a collaborator. Clearly, Hammett visualized each scene of the novel with extraordinary care. His sharply focused descriptions of the characters and their actions are a primary reason for the success of the novel. Because Hammett restricted himself to describing how people look, how they act, and what happens to them—refraining from describing thoughts that cannot be deduced from appearances—the novel is strikingly visual. It contains nothing that cannot be shown or heard or smelled, and the order of presentation of the material is determined by how it comes to Spade. *The Maltese Falcon* was written a year after the first sound feature movie, *The Jazz Singer,* was released. It is particularly remarkable, then, that the novel has such a cinematic structure, proceeding in an orderly fashion from scene to scene described with unusual attention to visual detail, relying on dialogue for the exposition of the plot and the development of character, and displaying an accomplished talent for dramatic scene making. Those qualities account in large part for the success of John Huston's 1941 movie from the book. Humphrey Bogart as Spade, Mary Astor as Brigid, Sidney Greenstreet as Gutman, Peter Lorre as Cairo, and Elisha Cook Jr. as Wilmer have come to be identified with the characters of the novel, even though they are sometimes physically dissimilar.

Hammett's interest in staged drama, whether in play or movie form, predated his relationship with Lillian Hellman by nearly two years. Her first play, *The Children's Hour* (1934), was written from a story idea given her by Hammett, and he worked closely with her as she was developing the script. Hammett's lifetime interest in staged drama seems to have begun with *The Maltese Falcon*. Unlike his first two novels, his last three have similar dramatic structures, generally observing the dramatic strictures that demand unity of time, place, and action. To accommodate the practicalities of staging, plays typically take place over a short period of time, in a limited number of places, and with action that can be acted out in a theater.

CHARACTERS

The Maltese Falcon is a complicated story told in a simple manner. The complexity results from the difficulty of knowing what or whom to believe. Often characters in the novel lie about who they are, what they know, and what they want. Sometimes characters draw false conclusions, which they act on as if they were the truth. Other times characters are simply unaware of information that would affect their perception of the truth. In key scenes characters follow their intuitions, which mislead them. The central challenge to the reader, as to Sam Spade, is to separate the truth from the deception and to deduce the plot as accurately as possible from the best information available.

No one in *The Maltese Falcon* is reliable. Brigid lies from the opening page of the novel until the end. She lies repeatedly to Spade; she frames Cairo in Constantinople; she seductively murders Archer; she double-crosses Thursby; she misrepresents herself to Effie; and she betrays her partnership with Gutman. The others lack her skill but not her disregard for the truth. Cairo withholds key information from Spade about the falcon. Gutman, Cairo, and Brigid (under duress) use Rhea Gutman to arrange a dramatic lie calculated to send Spade on a wild-goose chase to Burlingame. Polhaus and Dundy try to get information

THE BRITISH VIEW OF HAMMETT

The history of Mr. Dashiell Hammett's life has been, in its way, as strange and unexpected as the histories he writes of other people's lives. A Pinkerton's man to begin with, he found his health so much injured by war service that his return to his old profession did not last long. But, fortunately for him and for great numbers of readers, he found at the same time that he could write, and that so well that very shortly it became apparent that there was no further need for him to trouble himself about anything else.

From the introduction to the serialized version of The Maltese Falcon, The Evening Standard *(London), 3 January 1933.*

from Spade by lying about their suspicions of him. District Attorney Bryan lies to Spade about the purpose of his interrogation.

Intentional deceit is not the only way characters are misled. Iva Archer misconstrues Spade's actions and spreads information that leads the police and Miles Archer's brother, Phil, to false conclusions. Effie Perine, with the best of intentions, believes in her intuition that Brigid is innocent. The problem, of course, is that she lacks the facts and the experience to provide a solid foundation for her judgment.

One way to read the novel is to consider how different characters interpret the same information and why their interpretations are different. Miles Archer's murder is a good example. Effie assumes he was murdered by Thursby, a dangerous man who threatens Brigid O'Shaughnessy (though Effie then thinks Brigid is named Wonderly). Iva Archer and Phil Archer think Spade murdered his partner so he could marry Iva. The police think maybe Spade did it but more likely Thursby did, and Spade killed him in retaliation. All are wrong, and all base their conclusions on different sets of information: Effie relies on her feminine intuition; Iva Archer trusts a desperate love; Phil Archer has Iva's confession of her affair with Spade; the police are motivated by their dislike for Spade and by Phil Archer's tip.

The most striking deception of the novel is the Maltese falcon itself. For various reasons, characters in the novel believe in the falcon and take extraordinary risks to obtain it, only to find that the falcon is a fake. Yet, the evidence that the real falcon exists is not wholly convincing, especially within this context of lies. Though his story has the ring of truth, Gutman's account of the falcon's history is, if he is to be believed, based largely on information he forced from a Greek dealer who apparently once owned the falcon. Parts of Gutman's report of his investigation into the whereabouts of the bird are highly speculative. The lease agreement between Charles V of Spain and the Hospitallers of St. John that Gutman explains is roughly accurate historically, though in reality it is almost certain that the knights of Malta gave the king a real bird and not a jeweled one (the fact outside the fictional bounds of the novel). According to Gutman, the real falcon was enameled over as a disguise in about

1840. Between that time and 1911, it was "kicked around Paris for seventy years by private owners and dealers too stupid to see what it was under the skin" (126). Then Charilaos Konstantinides found it and re-enameled it. Three months after Gutman "made him confess" (127), Gutman claims to have read in the London *Times* that Konstantinides's shop was robbed and he was murdered. Gutman went to Paris the next day and learned the bird was gone; it did not reappear for seventeen years. Gutman does not account for that period except to say that he traced the bird to Kemidov, a Russian general living in a Constantinople suburb. Gutman tried to buy the falcon, without betraying its worth, and Kemidov refused him. Brigid was successful in getting the fake falcon from Kemidov. Spade asks her what she was hired to do to get the falcon from Kemidov: "'Oh, but that's not important,' she objected, 'and wouldn't help you'—she smiled impudently—'and is certainly none of your business'" (87). Brigid tells Spade that the falcon is made of "'Porcelain or black stone. I don't know. I've never touched it. I've only seen it once, for a few minutes. Floyd showed it to me when we'd first got hold of it.'" Spade responds, "'You are a liar'" (88). Indeed the entire story is pieced together from the accounts of known liars blinded by greed and intent on manipulating others for personal benefit.

The question of ownership of the falcon is raised twice in connection with Cairo. In Chapter IV, Cairo says that he is acting "on behalf of the figure's rightful owner" (43). In Chapter V, Spade asks what proof he has that his man is the owner. Cairo responds, "Very little, unfortunately. There is this, though: nobody else can give you any authentic evidence of ownership at all. And if you know as much about the affair as I suppose—or I should not be here—you know that the means by which it was taken from him shows that his right to it was more valid than anyone else's—certainly more valid than Thursby's." Spade takes a guess about Brigid's relationship with the falcon's owner and asks "What about his daughter?" Cairo reacts excitedly, thinking Spade means Gutman, and says "*He* is not the owner!" (50). In Chapter VII, Brigid O'Shaughnessy asks Cairo for whom he is buying the falcon.

"For its owner."

Surprise illuminated the girl's face. "So you went back to him?"

"Naturally I did."

She laughed softly in her throat and said: "I should have liked to have seen that."

891 Post Street. Hammett's apartment is at the upper right corner.

Cairo shrugged. "That was the logical development." (67–68)

Just after that exchange, when Cairo asks what happened to Thursby, Brigid traces a G in the air.

At the end of the novel, when the falcon is shown to be fake and Brigid swears it is the one she got from Kemidov, "Joel Cairo thrust himself between Spade and Gutman and began to emit words in a shrill spluttering stream: 'That's it! That's it! It was the Russian! I should have known! What a fool we thought him, and what fools he made of us!' . . . 'You and your stupid attempt to buy it from him! You fat fool! You let him know it was valuable and he found out how valuable and made a duplicate for us! No wonder we had so little trouble stealing it! No wonder he was so willing to send me off around the world looking for it. You imbecile! You bloated idiot!'" (202).

Brigid's remarks imply that Cairo's relationship with Kemidov was more complex than hers. After the two of them, working for Gutman, stole the falcon from Kemidov, Cairo offered his services to Kemidov again, apparently on his own. The relationship is telling. Cairo is shown, like the rest of the falcon hunters, to be utterly without loyalty. And Kemidov is shown to be wiser than any of them, ridding himself of Brigid (and initially Cairo) by allowing her to steal a fake falcon, and ridding himself of Cairo on his return by hiring him to chase after it.

Within this context a good investigator might question Gutman's account and ask a series of key questions: When was the fake falcon introduced? When Gutman forced Konstantinides to "confess," why did he not force him to give up the falcon? Assuming Konstantinides was really murdered, who did it? How did Kemidov get the falcon, especially if he did not know what it was? More to the point, does the falcon Gutman describes exist? According to Gutman, the "real" falcon was enameled to hide its identity in the mid-nineteenth century. He trusts that Konstantinides knew the real thing and had it re-enameled. Kemidov, Gutman says, was ignorant of what he had, knowing only that it was valuable. Konstantinides is the last person to have identified the enameled falcon as the real object. So the reader is in the position of trusting Gutman's account, in which that most unreliable source admits that he trusts the account of a dealer described as being equally untrustworthy. That is a lot of trust to give in a situation where no one is trustworthy. And that is the profound irony of the novel. People have paid the ultimate price in search of something that is not only illusive; it may, in fact, be an illusion conjured up from the depths of their greed.

Another problem for the reader is what to believe about the relationship between Spade and Brigid. At the end of the novel he tells her he thinks he loves her, and she professes her love for him. They consummate their relationship sexually in the early hours of Friday morning, about a day and a half after they meet, and Spade protects Brigid from Gutman and Cairo and from the police in Chapter VIII. But can they really be in love? She repeatedly demonstrates her disregard for him and his safety. By the end of the novel, he knows: 1) that Brigid murdered Archer and would have tried to kill him instead on Wednesday night had he been shadowing Thursby; 2) that on Saturday she called Effie Perine with a lie calculated to mislead him while she and Gutman tried to find Jacobi and that they sent Wilmer to Spade's office with bad intentions; 3) that she was waiting outside his apartment Sunday night to lead him inside, where Gutman, Cairo, and Wilmer were lying in wait; and 4) that she embraced him just before the three men showed themselves to keep him from pulling a gun.

In the scene in which he turns over the falcon to Gutman on Sunday, Spade demonstrates how little he trusts Brigid. When Gutman says some of the money is missing, Spade assumes that Brigid is the thief,

FOR THE RECORD

Professionally, I am and have been an author for about the past 25 years. My writings have consisted mainly of fiction in the mystery or detective story field. I have lectured on and have also been a critic and reviewer of literature in those fields. During the year 1926 as well as during the years of 1930 and 1931 I was engaged and served in the latter capacities for the Saturday Review of Literature and the New York Evening Post respectively. Prior to 1929 when I wrote the mystery detective story entitled "The Maltese Falcon" I had written a number of detective stories and two novels entitled "Red Harvest" and "The Dain Curse." These writings were published and well received.

"The Maltese Falcon" . . . was translated and published in Denmark, Spain, France, England, Germany, Hungary, Sweden, and Portugal, as well as in English on the Continent. Other American editions besides Knopf's were put out by Grosset and Dunlap, McClure, The Modern Library, and Pocket Books. It was included in "The Hammett Omnibus" which has been published by Grosset and Dunlap, the World Publishing Company, and Pocket Books. Serializations have appeared in foreign newspapers and American magazines.

Affadavit of Dashiell Hammett, U.S. District Court, Southern District of New York, 20 September 1948, regarding a suit by Warner Bros. for copyright infringement.

despite her denial. He forces her to strip naked in the bathroom with the door open, and then after she dresses sends her to make breakfast for everyone. It is a humiliating scene, for which he shows no regret. "Can't you see that if you make me you'll—you'll be killing something?" (196) she warns him without effect. He does not act like a man in love, and yet in the powerful last scene Hammett augmented Spade's speech to elaborate on his feeling toward her. He tells her he will not let her go free "because all of me wants to—wants to say to hell with the consequences and do it" (215). Spade refuses because he says he will not play the sap for her. He will not allow her to use him as she has used the others. Brigid's sexual allure is powerful, all the more so because she is such a skillful actress—another way to say she is an accomplished liar. Spade finds her very attractive. But then so did Thursby, Miles Archer, Jacobi—all of whom die for her—and presumably Kemidov. Spade recognizes the difference between lust and love, and he understands the danger of saying to hell with the consequences. Consequences are paramount in Spade's world, where doing a job is the point, not how one does it. Spade's disappointment at the end of the novel is in recognizing that Brigid is as false—and as falsely attractive—as the falcon.

Spade obviously tells Brigid the Flitcraft story to make a point. Like Charles Sanders Peirce, the philosopher whose name he takes, Flitcraft believes, or at least acts, in accordance with conditional logic: if A happens, then B is the reaction. If, on the other hand, C happens, D is the reaction. Peirce combined philosophy and the mathematics of logic to develop theories of how the human mind operates. He believed that there are mathematical models to illustrate patterns of thought, but the models vary according to circumstances and individuals. Flitcraft lived a well-ordered life and had a loving family. He felt in control, but the moral of the parable Spade tells is that there are factors in one's life that are beyond control. What Flitcraft recognizes when the beam falls is a mathematical problem. His life is organized according to strict rules: Noon = lunch; 4 P.M. = golf; job = money; car = Packard; wife + children = life in suburbs. There was no provision in these equations for falling beams. Flitcraft recognized that the algebra of his life was faulty when it was shown that, through no fault of his own and by virtue of an occurrence over which he could not possibly have control, the rules by which he ordered his life were invalidated. The question he faced was how to react. How could he most effectively rearrange his life to minimize the damage that would be caused by his sudden death. He concluded that the best solution would be to isolate himself and his family emotionally from such effects. He realized that the form of his family's devotion to each other, the inflexibility of the patterns of their lives, left them vulnerable. So he cut the ties that ordered his life. He could love his family without depending on their daily presence. When Spade finds Flitcraft, he has reconstructed an ordered life much like the one he left behind, with one difference. Now he accepts the notion of random occurrence. He is in step with his surroundings—comfortable in times of harmony; unpredictable in times of chaos; shielded at all times, insofar as is possible, by his emotional reserve and by his refusal to form hard attachments to people or things. Just as one can love art without owning it, Flitcraft finds he can love people, specifically his family, without controlling them.

Another way to view the Flitcraft parable is to consider the falling beam as a metaphor for some traumatic event. If, for example, Flitcraft were walking down the street and he met a beautiful woman and fell in love with her, left his family for her, and settled down again to a well-ordered life, the parable would not seem so odd, and yet the circumstances would not be so different. Or if Flitcraft went to the doctor, found that he had cancer, and left his family well provided for to seek some private solace, recovered, and resumed his life in another city, the story would fit into what we regard as understandable, if not exactly normal, patterns of behavior.

So why does Spade tell Brigid the Flitcraft story at the beginning of Chapter VII? By that point in the novel, Spade has been surprised by several unexpected occurrences—by several falling beams. He has been surprised twice by Brigid's lies about her identity; he is being followed for no apparent reason by Wilmer Cook; Cairo has attempted to hire him, pulled a gun on him, searched his office, and then hired him again to find the mysterious bird that Brigid is seeking as well. Moreover, Spade is stunned by his attraction to Brigid, whom he knows to be a deceiver. Now it is clear to Spade that Brigid O'Shaughnessy is lying to him again about her relationship with Cairo, while attempting to seduce him. Spade's reaction is to tell a parable that demonstrates his attitude. Like Flitcraft, he does not order his life according to rigid equations. He reacts to circumstances, and he can accommodate the unexpected because he has no rigid attachments. Nor is any possible with her, even if they should happen to fall in love. Brigid O'Shaughnessy's reaction is uncomprehending. She is too busy conniving, planning the meeting with Cairo, to ponder the implications of Spade's parable. Wily and smart as Brigid is, she would be unlikely to understand Spade's meaning in the best of circumstances. She is not an intellectual. She has not, as he has, thought about right and wrong, her function in society, and how best to organize her life. She is reckless and dangerous because she herself is as unpredictable as a falling beam.

Hammett was fond of the Flitcraft parable. He told it later in his life without reference to the novel. Clearly the story had a special meaning for him, and it can be viewed as his way of explaining his attempts to deal with the falling beams in his own life.

At the end of the novel Spade is left back where he started, with only minor differences. He has made $775 for his work since the previous Wednesday—$575 from Brigid, and $200 as a retainer from Cairo (about half the annual salary for a public-school teacher at the time). He also takes a $1,000-bill from the envelope containing the money that Gutman intended as payment for delivery of the falcon—for his "time and expenses," he says. But Spade hands that money over to the police as proof that he was never in collusion with Gutman. Knowing that after being arrested the fat man would try to implicate him, Spade arranged that $1,000 to be the sign of his innocence. Returning the money is insurance that his story will not be challenged. He has lost a partner whom he held in contempt and planned to get rid of within the month in any event. He is left with the problem of Iva Archer, who loves him and whom he does not want to hurt. He is left with the privileges of his city, having paid his dues for the right to live there.

THE THEMES AND HAMMETT'S LIFE

The Maltese Falcon is a work of fiction, not autobiography. Hammett certainly drew on his life experiences for the novel, though. Spade is a believable detective because Hammett knew from firsthand experience what a detective's work entailed. As his introduction to the Modern Library publication of the novel explains, he drew on real-life models for some of his characters. He named at least one character, Tom Polhaus, for a childhood friend in Baltimore. The novel certainly indicates Hammett's frame of mind in 1928 when he was writing the novel. But it is dangerous to confuse the novel with his life.

If there is a conclusion about Hammett's beliefs that can be drawn from the novel, it derives from the major themes of the book: the difficulty of knowing the truth and the necessity of self-reliance. Hammett was a student of philosophy. He had read Immanuel Kant as a teenager, and he had a sophisticated understanding of the major Western world philosophers. He was taken with the European thinkers who questioned the nature of perception and who challenged the notion of a god-ordered universe. *The Maltese Falcon* is influenced by those ideas, which Hammett believed in. The challenge for Spade in the book is to make up the rules as he goes along; to decide for himself, without outside guidance, what he believes and what he believes in. He is defining who he is. That is the simplest statement of the philosophy of existentialism that had its roots in the mid-nineteenth century and flourished in the United States from the 1930s until the 1960s.

Judging from what is known of Hammett's life, it is the problem he seems to have faced himself. At the time the novel was published, he, like Flitcraft, left his family to begin a life for himself elsewhere. Like Flitcraft, he did not stop loving his wife and daughters; he simply came to terms with the fact that there were falling beams—like fame, for example, or illness—that he could not predict or control. Like Sam Spade, Hammett had to decide what he valued. He seems to have steered a middle course: love without possession.

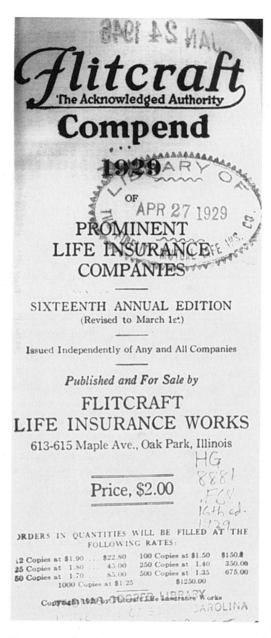

Front cover for the insurance industry resource that provided the name for one of Hammett's most discussed characters

Hammett's books reflect his personality, and an important element of his fiction is its wit. He is widely credited for fooling his editors, who complained about the homosexuality in *The Maltese Falcon,* by using the word *gunsel* to refer to Wilmer Cook. People ignorant of its meaning assumed then that the word meant gunman instead of homosexual kid. That misconception has continued with such persistence that the word has come to take on the meaning of gunman by virtue of common usage. Naming his obese villain Gutman is not a coincidence. The name of Captain Jacobi's boat, on which he delivers the false falcon, is *La Paloma,* Spanish for pigeon or dove, and, when applied to a woman, having the connotation of prostitute, a reference to the two "birds" of the novel, the lead one and Brigid. "La Paloma" is also the name of a classic love song by Sebastiá Yradier (1809–1865). Joel Cairo offers to retain Spade in a chapter named "The Levantine." The title refers to Cairo's Greek nationality (see p. 47), his sexual orientation—he has sex the "Greek way," that is, anally; and it puns on the slang use of *levant* to indicate a person who incurs debts with the intention of running off when they come due. In the Flitcraft parable Spade took the name of the man who fears falling beams from actuarial tables used by insurance agencies and has Flitcraft change his name to Charles Pierce, after the mathematician-logician Charles Sanders Peirce, who studied the logic of probability. The most interesting naming pun in the novel was suggested by Don Herron. In 1912, Michael M. O'Shaughnessy was appointed city manager of San Francisco. During his tenure, he built the Hetch Hetchy Reservoir, flooding a valley 170 miles east of San Francisco. The project included a sixty-eight-mile railroad, eighteen miles of tunnels, and a dam that was named after him. Bridges were involved as well, thus he was "Bridge-it" O'Shaughnessy.[+]

THE THEMES AND HAMMETT'S ERA

The Maltese Falcon was published in the same year as Ernest Hemingway's *A Farewell to Arms* and William Faulkner's *The Sound and the Fury,* novels noted for their modernist technique and their nihilistic message. The realism and naturalism movements that had begun to form late in the nineteenth century, focusing on accurate depictions of common people and the forces that cause humans to act as they do, had reached its maturity by the time Hammett began writing. World War I, which ended in 1919, had a profound effect on American writers. The brutality of the war traumatized Americans and caused them to speculate about life in a world where such horrible occurrences were possible. The hard-boiled novel, which presented emotionally isolated characters in search of values with only their instincts to guide them, is generally considered a response to the war. Hemingway's Jake Barnes in *The Sun Also Rises* (1926) and Frederic Henry in *A Farewell to Arms* (1929) are hard-boiled characters. So are the Continental Op and Sam Spade.

This hard-boiled stuff—it is a menace.

Dashiell Hammett, quoted in "Dashiell Hammett has Hard Words for Tough Stuff He Used to Write," *Los Angeles Times,* 7 June 1950.

The war also exposed Americans to European intellectual currents that were revolutionizing the creative arts. At the core of the various strains of modernism are the questions what do we know and how do we know it. When Pablo Picasso painted his flat-plane canvasses superimposing images of an object as observed from different perspectives he was examining the nature of perception. When the Surrealists expressed the chain of thoughts and sensations triggered by some sensual stimulation, they were examining how an individual's storehouse of memories and association affect what he or she perceives. Those central modernist questions about how one knows and what constitutes the truth are also the central questions of *The Maltese Falcon*. Faulkner approached the problem in *The Sound and the Fury* by presenting different perspectives on a story to let the reader sort out what to believe. Hammett approached the problem by showing the reader what Sam Spade knows and letting him sort out, as Spade does, the lies from the truth, the good from the bad.

The war caused people to examine what they believed, what values guided their lives. Families were torn apart when men joined the military. Many were sent abroad to witness or fall victim to combat. Others, including Hammett, stayed in the United States and experienced the terror of battle vicariously. It was a time that caused people to take stock of themselves and their institutions, to search their souls for the meaning of their lives. The significance of Sam Spade as a fictional character is that he is a loner. He looks to no one for guidance; he makes up his own rules; and he lives with the consequences of his behavior. In *The Maltese Falcon* there is only one requirement of Spade—that he pay tribute to the system of justice for the right to live in his city. As long as he does that, he can flaunt the law without penalty.

LITERARY TRADITION

The Maltese Falcon is a hard-boiled detective novel. Dashiell Hammett is credited as the originator of the form. Though there were others experimenting with the hard-boiled detective form at the same time as Hammett, he was among the first practitioners, and he is certainly the first hard-boiled detective novelist to write works of enduring value. The hard-boiled novel is a type of realism that concentrates on the seamy side of society. It features a main character, usually a private detective, almost always a loner, who fights against corruption. As the hard-boiled hero developed, he became a man who struggles to avoid corruption in a corrupt world, acting no meaner than necessary to do his job. Violence is a mainstay of the hard-boiled detective novel (though each of Hammett's novels is less violent than the one before it). The mood is consistently dark and pessimistic. The language, typically wisecracking street vernacular, was exaggerated by the hacks. Hammett sharply refined it. Because of Hammett's narrative technique, language defines character in his novels. Though there is no evidence of a direct link, Hammett is in the tradition of the vernacular writers who sprang from the realism and local-color movements. Like them, he wrote about common people, and he used their own language to describe them. When at the beginning of the novel Spade greets Effie Perine with "Yes, sweetheart?" and responds to the news that a customer is waiting for him with "Shoo her in, darling" (3), the reader has a quick sense of Spade's demeanor. When he tells Archer, who has just agreed to shadow Thursby for Brigid, "Well, don't dynamite her too much" (10), a crude sexual reference, he reveals his attitude toward Archer, Brigid, and women in general.

Hammett's primary literary influences were not simply crime writers though. He was an eclectic reader. Hammett biographer Diane Johnson points out: "He read pulps and Aristotle and Henry James. He also read the French—in particular Anatole France and Flaubert. He read the realistic Icelandic sagas of the thirteenth century with special interest, recognizing in their laconic and grim realism, their mannered but compelling narratives, their sophisticated appreciation of society and greed and honor, something that had to do with himself and with the way he could hope to write. It was to James, he would say later, that he owed his conceptions of literary style and his ideas of method, and to the sagas some ideas of tone."[5]

In a 12 December 1979 letter to Diane Johnson, Lillian Hellman said that Hammett's chief literary influences were Henry James and Fyodor Dostoyevsky, both masters of psychological fiction. Hammett's third-person novels, *The Maltese Falcon* and *The Glass Key*, both qualify in some respects as psychological novels; they explore what characters know, the quality of their knowledge, and how what they know affects their behavior. Hammett told humorist James Thurber that *The Maltese Falcon* was influenced by James's respected novel *The Wings of the Dove*

(1902).[6] James's novel is about a man, Merton Densher, who—encouraged by the woman he loves, Kate Croy—misrepresents himself as a lover of the wealthy dying Milly Theale to get an inheritance. When Milly Theale dies and leaves Densher a fortune, he is stricken with guilt and refuses to marry Kate unless she agrees with his decision to renounce the inheritance. She refuses to marry him unless he accepts it. Though the two novels seem to have little specific in common, they do share the theme of a man facing the corrupting influence of a greedy woman.

Diane Johnson points out further evidence of Hammett's high regard for James. In the introduction to *Creeps by Night* (1932), an anthology of mysteries by various writers, Hammett wrote:

> This business of making the reader feel that what cannot happen can and should not is a tremendously difficult one for the author. Addressing himself, as we have assumed he must, to the orderly minded reader, he cannot count on any native credulity or superstition to be taken advantage of.

> Atmosphere may be used to set the stage, but is seldom a great help thereafter and in fact more often an encumbrance than not.

> Brutality, often an excellent accompaniment and a means to an end, is never properly more than that in this field, and some of the finest effects have been secured with the daintiest touches. The most authentic single touch in 'The Turn of the Screw' [a famous story by James]—too well known as well as a bit too long for inclusion here—is not when the child sees the ghost across the lake, but when she turns her back to it, pretending interest in some rubbish at her feet, to keep her governess from knowing she has seen it.[7]

Johnson also points out that James Benet remembers being impressed with Hammett's close knowledge of James's work.[8]

In its emphasis on greed as a determining factor in the characters of Caspar Gutman, Brigid O'Shaughnessy, Joel Cairo, and Wilmer Cook, *The Maltese Falcon* has some similarity with the naturalists, particularly Frank Norris and Jack London, both of whom have associations with San Francisco and wrote in the generation before Hammett. Both explored the way in which base passions shape people's lives. In its coldly objective narrative technique, *The Maltese Falcon* is similar to the stories and early novels of Ernest Hemingway, a contemporary of Hammett's. Like Hammett, Hemingway developed a theory of literature that depended on implication; by narrowly and objectively reporting what happened, they suggested a rich range of emotions and a complex set of relationships. In his effective use of underworld slang, Hammett brings to mind the masterful vernacular fiction of Ring Lardner, who recorded the speech of uneducated people. In his thorough absorption of modernist attitudes toward perception, Hammett is in the company of William Faulkner, whose novels explore multiple perspectives and question the meaning of truth. In his concentration and near personification of a city, Hammett brings to mind John Dos Passos, whose depiction of New York is a study in the ways a city has personality that both reflects and affect the people who live there.

NOTES

1. *The Maltese Falcon* (New York: Vintage/Black Lizard, 1992), p. 177. Page references are to this commonly available edition. Quotations have been checked against the first edition. Subsequent references are noted parenthetically in the text.

2. Preface to Dashiell Hammett, *The Maltese Falcon* (San Francisco: North Point Press, 1984), p. viii.

3. Don Herron, *The Dashiell Hammett Tour* (San Francisco: City Lights Books, 1991).

4. See William Issel and Robert W. Cherny, *San Francisco, 1865–1932* (Berkeley: University of California Press, 1986), pp. 175–176.

5. Diane Johnson, *Dashiell Hammett: A Life* (New York: Random House, 1983), p. 36.

6. James Thurber, "The Wings of Henry James," in *Lanterns & Lances* (Alexandria, Va.: Time-Life, 1962), p. 77.

7. *Creeps by Night* (New York: Day, 1931), pp. 8–9.

8. Diane Johnson, *Dashiell Hammett: A Life* (New York: Random House, 1983), p. 308, note.

CRITICAL RESPONSE TO
THE MALTESE FALCON

RECEPTION

The Maltese Falcon was published four months after the stock-market crash of October 1929 that marked the beginning of the Great Depression. Many people lost their savings and their jobs. The American economy collapsed, and book sales suffered accordingly. Even in that depressed market, the book was a huge success, not just as a mystery novel, but as a work of literature that could be matched against any fiction being published. In *Black Mask* (September 1929) Joseph Shaw wrote, "We want to go on record as saying that this story is a marvelous piece of writing—the finest detective story it has ever been our privilege to read in book form, in any magazine of any kind, or in manuscript. Don't miss it."

On 23 February 1930 in the *New York Herald Tribune,* reviewer Will Cuppy wrote:

> This department announces a new and pretty huge enthusiasm, to wit: Dashiell Hammett. Moreover, it would not surprise us one whit if Mr. Hammett should turn out to be the Great American Mystery Writer. (The fact is, he may be that right now, and this department is merely hopping aboard the Hammett band-wagon ere it be too late—Herbert Asbury, Walter Brooks and Joseph Shaw have already discovered him.) The utterly convincing quality of Mr. Hammett's detective, Sam Spade, is the big news about "The Maltese Falcon"; Sam's 100 per cent authenticity is powerful enough to make one believe in the jeweled bird once presented by the Knights of Rhodes to the Emperor Charles V—a gadget which might turn up in almost any thriller. Add some most effective tricks of narrative and a satisfactory species of hard-boiled prose to his credit, too, not to mention a slick plot, boasting of three murders incidental to a search for the rara avis in San Francisco. The horsepower of Mr. Hammett's pen, especially in his brutal and very "different" ending, must be sampled

Dashiell Hammett in New York, circa 1931

to be believed—of a mystery author. In short, "The Maltese Falcon" is the best one outside the gay and polite classes, in Lord knows when. Read it and see.

Gilbert Seldes, reviewing the novel in the *New York Graphic,* wrote:

> The detectives of fiction have been knocked into a cocked hat—which is where most of them belong—by the appearance of Sam Spade in a book called The Maltese Falcon. It is the work of Dashiell Hammett; it is a novel and it is also a mystery story—the combination is so rare that probably not half a dozen good examples exist between The Moonstone and the present one.
>
> The central mystery is not an especially good one: three groups of people are after an object of enormous value. But everything else, characters, plot, and the general attitude of the author, are fresh and novel and brilliant. Spade himself is hard-boiled, immoral, with a free fist and a free tongue. After the high-minded detective heroes with their effeminate manners, their artistic leanings, and their elaborate deductions, he is as startling as a real man in a show-window of dummies. His actions and his language will shock old ladies.
>
> . . . the romance in the story is blown to bits by bitter realism.
>
> This book is far better written than most detective stories. . . . you read it with amazement and with wonder. Because this is the real thing and everything else has been phony. The publishers quote someone as saying that Mr. Hammett has done for the mystery story what Dumas did for the historical romance. I consider that an enthusiastic, but not unjustifiable, comparison.

Ted Shane, reviewing the novel in *Judge* magazine (1 March 1930), wrote:

> Should you stumble on a frantic hundred-and-fifty pounder at Madison and Forty-eighth Street hooking unheeding passersby; or if later in the day you should come on him pounding on bars, rudely accosting lady shoppers, insulting traffic cops and generally making himself painful around town, that would be us expressing ourself against him who hasn't read Dashiell Hammett. That twenty-minute hard-boiled boy has swept all the dilettante and drawing-room detecatiffs with the tiddledly-wink, card trick and cross-word puzzle mysteries out of Crime Hall and dragged in a free-for-all instead.

He writes with a lead-pipe and poisoned arrows as coups de grace. He stands alone as ace shocker. Hereafter even S. S. Van Dine must lower his monocle, cough up the encyclopedia and eat some humble pie.

We paeaned Hammett's "Red Harvest" till we went blue in the face and other publishers offered us bribes to lay off and give their tittivators a break. It was the pearl of underworld stories, and suggested the nice idea that the way to exterminate killers would be to let them slaughter themselves off. Then came "The Dain Curse," a love-cult mystery, overloaded with plot but 90 per cent pure bonanza. And now "The Maltese Falcon," a button-button-who's-got-the-falcon? of San Francisco. It is everything you want. The conventional ingredients of the typical guess-who are there but so handled as to bring on maximum pressure. The characters are hard, hatable and out of police headquarters family albums. Sam Spade, the private dick, is harder than Hammett himself. The writing is better than Hemingway; since it conceals not softness but hardness. It is the "Broadway" of mysteries and should have been chosen by a book club. Still unconvinced? Well, it's swell."

Donald Douglas, reviewing the novel in the *New Republic* (9 April 1930), wrote:

In real life, the important thing is to catch the murderer in the quickest round-up. In fiction, the important thing is not to catch the murderer for two hundred pages. And if in real life, our jaded presidents and unemployed wives find "escape" in detective fiction, then so do all readers of Norse Myths and the Scotch ballads and the exploits of romantic cowboys. The real, right detective story is and should be a myth wherein the demigod (disguised as a superman) pursues the demon-crook through the tangled maze of heart-shuddering adventure. For "real" murderers, you have the dullness of courtroom scenes and the dull evidence given by two-fisted dicks.

Until the coming of Mr. Dashiell Hammett in Red Harvest and now in The Maltese Falcon, the memorable detectives were gentlemen. The ever-delightful M. Lecoq and his copy, Mr. Sherlock Holmes, are fair gods against the gnomes. Their only worthy successor, Father Brown, is a priest. Scratch every other detective and you'll find a M. Lecoq. Now comes Mr. Hammett's tough guy in Red Harvest and his Sam Spade in The Maltese Falcon and you find the Pinkerton operative as a scoundrel without pity or remorse, taking his whiffs of drink and his casual amours between catching crooks, treating the police with a cynical contempt, always getting his crook by foul and fearless means, above the law like a satyr—and Mr. Hammett describing his deeds in a glistening and fascinating prose as "American" as Lardner's, and every bit as original in musical rhythm and humor.

There's nothing like these books in the whole range of detective fiction. The plots don't matter so much. The art does; and there is an absolute distinction of real art. It is (in its small way) like Wagner writing about the gnomes in Rheingold. The gnomes have an eloquence of speech and a fascinating mystery of disclosure. Don't get me wrong, bo. It's not the tawdry gumshoeing of the ten-cent magazine. It is the genuine presence of the myth. The events of The Maltese Falcon may have happened that way in "real" life. No one save Mr. Hammett could have woven them to such a silver-steely mesh. Elrick B. Davis in the *Cleveland Press* outdid them all:

HAMMETT BOOK SO GOOD IT STUMPS CRITIC
THE MALTESE FALCON IS BEST DETECTIVE STORY BY
LEADER IN THE FIELD

There are detective-story writers, and then there is Dashiell Hammett. I can think of no one in the world who is his match. . . . I find it hard to figure out a way to tell you how good a book The Maltese Falcon is. . . . the blood of everyone I know who has read it has pounded in plunging jets through every vein during all the reading. . . . And what an underworld story! We've had a flood of them lately, between boards and in the magazines and in the movies, but nothing to touch this. . . . it is made of reality. . . . The book is written with the snap and bite of a whiplash. . . . has a thousand virtues, of observation, of detail, of nuance, and of effect.

Walter Brooks, reviewer for *Outlook and Independent* (26 February 1930), called *The Maltese Falcon* "probably the best detective story we have ever read." William Curtis in *Town and Country* (15 February 1930) magazine wrote: "consider an amalgamation of Mr. Hemingway, Mr. [W. R.] Burnett . . . , Morley Callaghan and Ring Lardner . . . you would have a fair idea of the style and technique of Mr. Hammett."

In a scrapbook kept by Joseph Shaw there are letters from book reviewers. Scott Cunningham sent Hammett books to sign along with a letter that says, "I've just finished The Maltese Falcon, and Joseph Shaw erred in his estimate only by omitting a few other adjectives that should properly have been used along with 'finest'. The book is swell and it ought to sell a million copies." Herbert Asbury, reviewer for *The Book-man*, wrote, "I have actually read 'The Maltese Falcon' three times since Knopf sent me down a copy, and the more I read it the better I like it. I think it is much better than Red Harvest, and you may recall that I raved considerably about that. But the 'Falcon' is by all odds the best detective story I have read in years; indeed, I can't remember that I have ever read a better one. Sam Spade is perfect, and so is Brigid. In every respect the book is simply swell." Dorothy Parker, a writer and reviewer for *The New Yorker*, wrote:

> This is one of those letters that must start "I have never writ-ten to an author before."
>
> "I have never written to an author before.
>
> "I have just finished 'The Maltese Falcon.' Again, and ever more, I think you are great. Thank you for writing; Lord, what swell books."[1]

CRITICAL SURVEY

The Maltese Falcon has stayed steadily in print since its first publication, and scholars have generally concurred with the initial assessment. There have been some who have disagreed. Edmund Wilson wrote in *The New Yorker* on 14 October 1944 that "The Maltese Falcon today seems not much above those newspaper picture-strips in which you follow from day to day the ups and downs of a strong-jawed hero and a hardboiled but beautiful adventuress." He is nearly the lone voice of that position, however. Four years before Wilson's article, Robert Graves and Alan Hodge in England had declared that Hammett stood alone among Ameri-can detective novelists as a "first-rate writer," and by the end of the decade, Sinclair Lewis, André Gide, André Malraux, and Raymond Chan-dler had proclaimed his genius.

Formal critical assessment of *The Maltese Falcon* began in the 1940s with Howard Haycraft's pioneering study of the mystery genre, *Murder for Pleasure* (New York: Appleton-Century, 1941), and has contin-ued in a steady stream to the present. *The Maltese Falcon* is not a simple book, and as a result interpretations have varied. Generally, the criticism of the novel falls into two categories determined by the perspective of the critic, neither intrinsically more valuable than the other. The novel has attracted most attention from those critics who specialize in mystery fiction, and they, in turn, fall into two categories: teacher-critics and aficionados. The approach of teacher-critics is to place Hammett and the novel in the tradition of the genre, usually identifying him as a pioneer of a new type of mystery fiction—the hard-boiled novel. They tend to analyze Hammett's characters and literary techniques in comparison to those of other mystery writers. These critics, at their best, convey a clear sense of Hammett's achievement as a mystery writer. Their approach is often sharply focused on the genre and the literary achievements in the genre demonstrated by Hammett's novel.

The aficionados, who range from mystery novelists to plain fans, have made some of the most important contributions to an understanding of the book. Most of what is known about the setting of the book in San Francisco and the verisimilitude of the characters and the action comes from the research of these Hammett fans. Most often the genre critics and the Hammett aficionados publish in such periodicals as the now-defunct *Xenophile* and *Armchair Detective,* or the more academic *Clues.* These critics have typically been the pioneers in Hammett scholarship. William F. Nolan contributed the first checklists of primary and secondary bibliography to the *Armchair Detective,* and he developed that material into the first biographical study of Hammett, his *Dashiell Hammett: A Casebook* (Santa Barbara: McNally & Loftin, 1969). Novelist Joe Gores published his seminal article on the geography of the novel in *California Living* magazine, developed it for the Hammett issue of *City of San Francisco* (4 November 1975), and used that material as the basis for *Hammett* (New York: Putnam, 1975), his novel based on fact. Don Herron's *Dashiell Hammett Tour* (San Francisco: Dawn Heron Press, 1979; revised edition, San Francisco: City Lights Books, 1991) is a useful factual and visual guide to the setting for Hammett's fiction, especially *The Maltese Falcon. Clues,* the journal of the Popular Press at Bowling Green State University, is devoted to mystery fiction. It has published several interesting articles and important bibliographical studies of Hammett. Among the most useful bibliographical works is E. R. Hagemann's *A Comprehensive Index to Black Mask, 1920–1951* (Bowling Green, Ohio: Bowling Green State University Popular Press, 1982), which allows readers to identify all Hammett's publications in that important pulp magazine and to see as well who else was publishing at the same time.

A smaller number of so-called mainstream critics have offered interpretations of the novel. They are academic in approach, and their contribution is to apply the same analytical standards to *The Maltese Falcon* as to any other work, regardless of subject or form. Often that process involves identifying the novel with a genre, a mainstream literary tradition, an archetypal pattern, or a thematic pattern. Irving Malin in "Focus on 'The Maltese Falcon': The Metaphysical Falcon" (*Tough Guy Writers of the Thirties*, edited by David Madden, Carbondale: Southern Illinois University Press, 1968) compares Hammett to Hemingway, and Sam Spade to Odysseus, Jesus, and Samuel, the Hebrew leader named in the Bible. Jasmine Yong Hall in "Jameson, Genre, and Gumshoes: *The Maltese Falcon* as Inverted Romance" (*The Cunning Craft: Original Essays on Detective Fiction*, edited by Ronald G. Walker, Macomb: Western Illinois University Press, 1990) places the novel in a genre that traces back to the medieval romance. Christopher Metress in "Dashiell Hammett and the Challenge of New Individualism: Rereading *Red Harvest* and *The Maltese Falcon*" (*Essays in Literature*, Fall 1990) identifies Sam Spade with the spirit of individualism in the American novel.

A common approach to a literary work is to view it in the context of the author's life and times. Because Hammett's life has attracted so much study, there is an abundance of material to support this approach. There have been four biographies of Hammett. Richard Layman's *Shadow Man* (New York: Harcourt Brace Jovanovich, 1981) was the first. It is a carefully researched book that assiduously avoids speculation about Hammett's motives or the circumstances of his life. It was written without the cooperation of Lillian Hellman, who was alive at the time and controlled access to key documents related to Hammett's life. For the reader interested in *The Maltese Falcon*, Layman's book provides descriptions of hard-to-find stories by Hammett in which he developed characters and themes he used in his novel.

William F. Nolan's *Hammett: A Life at the Edge* (New York: Congdon & Weed, 1983) was aimed at a broader audience and attempts to draw a fuller portrait of Hammett. A fiction writer himself, Nolan brings to his biography an awareness of the pulp writer's challenges that is entertaining and useful. In his chapter on *The Maltese Falcon* Nolan concentrates on the detective: "Samuel Spade is, of course, like the Op, a direct extension of the author, a man caught up in an unstable universe of random violence, who survives by following a rigid self-imposed code of honor, who seeks to sift truth from lies, who trusts no one but himself" (91). Nolan goes on to say,

> *The Maltese Falcon,* when closely studied, is basically a series of brilliant dialogues, set in motion by offstage events. In this respect, it is totally unlike Hammett's first two books, in which violence was a major ingredient of the plots. It is as if Hammett had set himself the challenge of creating a violent novel without

the *use* of violence. Aside from a bit of scuffling and a punch or two, all of the physical action takes place beyond the reader's vision; the four killings are done offstage. We are shown the *effects* of murder rather than its execution, what its factual existence does to the men and women who share in it. Hammett gives us implied violence: guns are drawn and flourished, never fired; threats are made, tempers flare, accusations and cross-accusations abound—but Hammett keeps the tension taut as a stretched wire without ever resorting to violence. There is the constant, immediate feeling that, at any given moment, the scene will explode into bullets and blood, but Hammett resists the temptation, and suspense is therefore greatly intensified. Even at the climax, when one expects a shootout, we are given only conversation—crackling, menace-laden conversation, laced with double and triple meaning—designed to do the job we have come to expect from overt violence. When Gutman is finally killed by one of his own gang, we learn this as it is reported to Spade—just as we learned of the deaths of Archer and Thursby. . . .

Spade, a man of potential violence, uses only his personality, his shrewdness, to hold the game in check. (92–93)

The biography of Hammett authorized by Lillian Hellman, the executrix of his Estate, was Diane Johnson's *Hammett: A Life* (New York: Random House, 1983). Johnson had access to previously unpublished letters and was able to interview members of the Hammett family, providing very useful information related to the composition and publication of the novel.

In 1985 Julian Symons wrote a short, heavily illustrated biography of Hammett (San Diego & New York: Harcourt Brace Jovanovich) that provides a summation of what was known about him to that time. The biography contains little criticism, but Symons, a respected British mystery writer and critic, offers some opinions. Particularly interesting is his refusal to engage in speculation about the meaning of the Flitcraft parable. Summarizing various critics' interpretations, he concludes:

There are other theories, all based on Hammett's belief in the random nature of life. Without expressing positive disagreement with any of them, it should perhaps be added that with Hammett the most straightforward, least high-flown view of the Flitcraft story is likely to be the one he had in mind. It is possible that he was not contemplating a grand application of the story to all human existence but merely a personal reference to his own career to date. In that case the key sentence is "What disturbed him was the discovery that in sensibly ordering his affairs he had got out of step, and not into step, with life." Up to the time of his departure from San Francisco, Hammett had done his best to order his life sensibly, without much success. For several years afterward, however, he made no attempt to order it at all.

Whether this idea has any validity, those prone to fine-spun theories about Flitcraft in particular and Hammett's work in general should remember his response to Lillian Hellman on an occasion when he had killed a snapping turtle, first by rifle shot and then by an ax blow almost severing the head, only to find that the dead turtle had moved down the garden in the night. When Hammett started to cut away one leg from the shell, the other leg moved. Was the turtle alive or dead? Hellman rang the New York Zoological Society and was told that it was scientifically dead but that the society was not equipped to give a theological opinion.

"Then how does one define life?" Hellman asked Hammett.

"Lilly, I'm too old for that stuff," he replied.

He would always have been too old for some of the theories put forward about the meaning of Flitcraft. (71–72).

Joan Mellen wrote her *Hellman and Hammett* (New York: HarperCollins, 1996) after Lillian Hellman's death and thus was able to interview friends and acquaintances of her subjects who would not grant interviews during Hellman's life. But since the book begins with his meeting Hellman in 1930, there is relatively little information directly related to the novel. Her book is the most reliable account of the last half of Hammett's life.

There are two student guides to Hammett, each of which has a chapter on *The Maltese Falcon* and two short critical books on Hammett's fiction. The first critical study was Peter Wolfe's *Beams Falling: The Art of Dashiell Hammett* (Bowling Green, Ohio: Bowling Green University Popular Press, 1980). In his chapter on *The Maltese Falcon*, Wolfe argues that the book is "a subtle study of moral behavior and of degrees of emotional commitment and stress" (111–112). He says that "The feeling and the meaning of Hammett's most popular and enduring work inheres not in what the people do but why they do it. The main thrust of the Flitcraft story, for instance, comes in Spade's reason for telling it—to advise Brigid indirectly that, bedazzled though he may be for the moment, he will revert to the mentality of the private detective and arrest her for murdering Miles Archer, unless she talks him out of it" (125). He concludes, "Spade's desolation at the end tallies the cost of his professionalism, the novel's main subject; anyone who must keep watching for falling beams can't live at full stretch. Like Lawrence's *Women in Love* and Virginia Woolf's *To the Lighthouse,* both of which came out of the same decade as *Falcon,* Hammett's best book criticizes a vision while imparting and celebrating it. . . . The action of the novel describes matters less than the reactions—professional and moral—it provokes; Spade, whose job denies him the luxury of moral behavior, and his counterparts all reveal themselves most vividly in their responses to the drama bred by the elusive falcon. These revelations display control, substance, and consistency" (128).

Sinda Gregory's *Private Investigations: The Novels of Dashiell Hammett* (Carbondale & Edwardsville: Southern Illinois University Press, 1985) takes a formalist approach to Hammett's fiction. She says in her preface that she became "Caught up in the aesthetics of Hammett's vision" and "the skillful structure of his fiction" (xiii). She says, "*The Maltese Falcon* is a novel about mystery—it is, in fact, a declaration of the omnipotence of mystery and of the failure of human effort (on the part of both the reader and the detective) to ever dispel it. Throughout the novel nothing is as it seems, and that is the only truth on which we can rely" (88). Of Spade, she says that his "personal conduct and his code of professional ethics are shown to evolve from what is a fairly sophisticated philosophical position—a position identical to the Op's view that the universe is composed of a random series of unrelated, often destructive events" (97). She says that the Flitcraft parable is a statement of that belief. "Spade applies the implications of the Flitcraft story to his own situation: nothing is fixed, no values are absolute unless they are those which you yourself have arrived at in order to survive. A person can count only on oneself; the moment another person is allowed to affect or control you, you are once more at the mercy of forces beyond your control. And, of course, love is the most dangerous demand that can be made on a person, for it can force a man to 'play the sap' and abandon those defenses of job and code which are his only means of stabilizing a random, fluctuating world. The overriding fear is that love will not last, and when it goes, you have nothing between you and the devastating knowledge of falling beams" (98).

In 1983 William Marling published *Dashiell Hammett* in the Twayne United States Authors Series. In his view the Flitcraft story is central to the novel:

> The moral, which Brigid misses, lies at the level of Spade's ironic appreciation rather than in Flitcraft's insight into the nature of the universe. The universe may be material and organized by chance, one may die any second; but such an insight, as Flitcraft demonstrates, does not mean that randomness constitutes a way of life. Man is above all adaptive and habitual, traits not only rationally intelligible but rather predictable. Information keeps crystallizing in a chaotic universe. Spade, for example, has found Flitcraft. Herein lies the basic irony that pervades Spade's outlook: the world may not operate rationally, but rationality is the best net with which to go hunting. The chance event—the falling beam—drives men away from cover and adaptive responses for a short time.
>
> In telling Brigid this, Spade is explaining that his code is primary for him. It is the best adaptive response to the world in which he lives. . . . Spade has seen the potency of chance events—and love might be numbered among them—and he understands their relation to the patterns. Were Brigid at all perceptive about this story, she would see that each time she deceives him, Spade becomes more certain of her pattern. His "wild and unpredictable monkey-wrenches" repeatedly unseat her from romantic postures and reveal her fundamental avarice. But the uncomprehending Brigid only says "How perfectly fascinating" at the end of the Flitcraft story. . . .
>
> Hammett's most extraordinary fictional feat is the embodiment of this world view in the character of Sam Spade. Spade is a continuation of that interest, which Hammett expressed in *The Dain Curse*, in the deceptions that veil reality. Reality is Spade's psychological fulcrum, and yet he is more perfectly than the Op a knight of the detective code. But readers perceive him as flawed, cruel, and human, rather than as the holder of God-like powers. Hammett masks his character's power primarily by eliminating the first-person narrator, whose intimacy with the reader revealed his minor infidelities to the code and implied that he discussed his cases, a weakness alien to the entirely private personality of Spade. With a third-person point of view, the hero's person becomes more distant and independent. In addition, Hammett made Spade's code an innovation on the generic stan-

dard, a new version that allows him not only deception, but the pleasures of adultery and the rewards of betrayal. Such variations are the key mode of creativity in popular literature, allowing readers to enjoy generically or conventionally forbidden desires.

Yet Spade's code is only one of three moral climates. The reader is exposed equally to the worlds of the police and of the criminals, whose ethos Brigid shares. The exact distinctions between these worlds are blurred, and the reality/illusion question makes it clear that both Spade and the reader function, when they judge, on the basis of only some of the facts. More facts may be produced by "heaving a wild and unpredictable monkey-wrench into the works," as Spade says, but he never forgets that his facts, once linked, are still a construction of reality. (75–76)

In 1984 Dennis Dooley wrote his *Dashiell Hammett* for the Recognitions series of the Frederick Ungar Publishing Company. Dooley believes that Hammett's essence as a writer is his spiritual concern: "The present book follows this concern with spiritual issues, and what can only be described as the moral perspective, through Hammett's entire career—from his early days as a fallen-away Catholic of some ferocity to his later years as a communist manqué and patriot rejected by his own country" (xv). Unlike most critics, Dooley finds Spade to be an unsympathetic character.

His very name suggests both the gravedigger's implement and the playing card that symbolizes death. He is even compared to the devil himself—but with a paradoxical twist calculated to make us uneasy. . . .

He is the quintessential loner. Within weeks after he went into partnership with Archer, he admits later in the book, he was sorry. The man got on his nerves. And when Archer is killed tailing a man on behalf of their "customer" near the beginning of the book, Spade perfunctorily instructs his receptionist and Girl Friday Effie Perine to have their two names taken off the door and his own put on. It seems unlikely Spade will ever find a partner he wants to go into business with. He is too "high-handed," too given to being "wild and unpredictable," too distrustful finally to be tied comfortably to such an arrangement. He has never even been able to sustain a relationship with a woman, we are later told, beyond a few months. (100–101)

But the key element here is that the voice of Hammett's narrator is strictly neutral, no speaker at all, but an objective, totally, impartial voice that betrays not the slightest hint of affection or adulation concerning the detective hero. It is a voice that does not care whether Spade lives or dies, whether good triumphs in the end, or even whether the reader is impressed or exasperated by the main character's actions. And as such it is a logical extension of Hammett's earlier break with the popular conventions of his day.

By adopting the straightforward first-person narrative of the Op Hammett had consciously rejected the hagiographical tradition of detective-story narration stretching from Arthur Conan Doyle to S. S. Van Dine—in which the exploits of the detective hero are recounted in an awed, often abjectly admiring tone by a Watson figure. . . .

With *The Maltese Falcon,* he returned to the third person, while preserving the same clear-eyed objectivity he had brought into the genre six years earlier. The result was a morally ambiguous protagonist whose goodness is not presupposed from the start—and a story rich in complications of a very adult and realistic sort. (103–104)

All serious literary study begins first with the text and then with a bibliography. The primary bibliography of Dashiell Hammett's works is Richard Layman's *Dashiell Hammett: A Descriptive Bibliography* (Pittsburgh: University of Pittsburgh Press, 1979). Secondary bibliographies are included in William F. Nolan's *Dashiell Hammett: A Casebook* (1969), William Marling's *Dashiell Hammett* (1983), and in *The Critical Response to Dashiell Hammett,* edited by Christopher Metress (Westport, Conn.: Greenwood Press, 1994).

CRITICAL READINGS

Critical readings of a novel can be useful to a reader in formulating his or her own responses to the work. Students should keep in mind, though, that however forcefully a critic states an opinion, it has validity only insofar as it makes sense to an individual reader.

Typically critical articles contain at least three types of information. The first type is facts that may make the book more understandable. It is useful, for example, to know that *The Maltese Falcon* was set during Prohibition, and that when Dundy and Polhaus accept drinks from

Spade, they are, at least in spirit, violating the law, which prohibited the manufacture, sale, or transportation of alcoholic beverages, but not their consumption. One might use that fact to draw conclusions about the San Francisco detectives portrayed in the novel. The second type of information—verifiable observations about the plot and the characters—is equally fundamental to an informed reading of a novel. For example, the realization that Brigid whistles the song "En Cuba" upon getting out of bed in Spade's apartment on Friday morning and that Spade whistles the same song early Sunday morning as he is waiting with the crooks in his apartment for the sun to come up may provide the basis for a conclusion about their relationship. The third type of information—a critic's opinions about the meaning of the work—can be just as enlightening. The knowledge of literary techniques and traditions, the experience as a reader, and the perception that a good critic displays in explaining a work are important resources for a beginning reader to draw on. But that kind of information is not verifiable; it is opinion. However sensible, knowing, informed, and well presented such opinions are, the reader must judge by his or her own lights whether to accept them either in full or in part, or to ignore them altogether.

The articles that follow are representative of the critical responses to *The Maltese Falcon*. At their best they provide guidance in understanding the novel, but the responsibility for a final decision about what *The Maltese Falcon* means is up to the reader.

THE VIEW FROM THE IVORY TOWER

Detective stories do not often make their way into this department, but the Landscaper would be failing in his duty if he did not report that one of the recent books that gave him the greatest amount of pleasure was Dashiell Hammett's *The Thin Man* (Knopf, $2), Mr. Hammett being the distinguished author of *The Maltese Falcon*, among other books, and generally recognized as the top of the heap in his field. *The Maltese Falcon*, by the way, is now available in the Modern Library edition, a recognition it heartily deserves, since it is one of the finest thrillers ever to be put between covers.

Herschel Brickell, "The Literary Landscape," *North American Review* (March 1934): 238.

Elliot L. Gilbert, "Introduction: 'An Interest in Other Men's Lives,'" in *The Maltese Falcon* (Toronto, New York, London, Sydney & Auckland: Bantam, 1985), pp. xi–xvii.

Mystery story fans who concern themselves only casually with the history of the genre are likely to think of that history as falling into two distinct and consecutive periods: a so-called golden age, featuring eccentric, often aristocratic sleuths solving crimes set in country house libraries; followed by a rougher era of hard-boiled detectives prowling mean streets. But in fact there was a crucial decade early in the century when these two contrasting literary figures were developing simultaneously.

Consider, for example, the year 1920. That year Agatha Christie published her first detective novel, *The Mysterious Affair at Styles,* introducing one of the most famous of all golden age private investigators, Hercule Poirot. And in that same year H. L. Mencken and George Jean Nathan established *Black Mask,* the magazine that would pioneer the hard-boiled detective story and even give the new school of tough guy mystery fiction its name.

Parallels like these persisted throughout the decade. For instance, 1922 saw the first appearance in *Black Mask* of the hard-boiled fiction of one-time Pinkerton agent Dashiell Hammett, while the very next year produced Dorothy L. Sayers's debonair and aristocratic Lord Peter Wimsey. And 1929 offered an especially notable pair of detective debuts: Ellery Queen, the quintessence of the gentleman sleuth, in *The Roman Hat Mystery,* and Sam Spade, the best known of all tough guy private eyes, in *The Maltese Falcon,* a novel first published in five monthly installments in *Black Mask.*

Focusing on the simultaneous development of these two very disparate kinds of literary detectives allows us to consider a crucial characteristic that they have in common, one that links them in a kind of blood brotherhood despite all of their stylistic and sociological differences. Edgar Allan Poe first described that characteristic (in "The Murders in the Rue Morgue") as the detective's talent for "throwing himself into the spirit of his opponent, identifying himself therewith." Arthur Conan Doyle later made the same point when he emphasized Sherlock Holmes's ability to enter into other personalities through disguise. So did G. K. Chesterton with his description of Father Brown getting "inside the murderer, thinking his thoughts"; so, too, did Georges Simenon, designating empathy as the key to the success of his Inspector Maigret.

What Poe and the others were suggesting is that the essence of the detective, the thing that makes every true detective a detective in the first place, is an ability to see the world from a perspective other than his own. Most people—and that includes all the untalented policemen outwitted by great detectives in mystery stories—live in a world shaped by their own desires and expectations, a world they make in their own images, and hence they necessarily fail to grasp reality—fail to solve the mystery. In Poe's "Purloined Letter," for example, the prefect, M. G—, is unable to find the missing document because he looks for it only in places where he himself would have hidden it. Criminals are particularly guilty of imposing themselves and their views on the world, refusing to allow people and objects to have any independent existence. The great detective, on the other hand, can move beyond the deceptive screen of his own ego and thus see the world as it really is; his genius lies in being able to display, in Ross Macdonald's words, "an interest in other men's lives that often seems to transcend his interest in his own."

The Maltese Falcon offers a fine opportunity for testing this thesis about the great detective through examining the best known of all *Black Mask* sleuths, Sam Spade. And there is perhaps no better way to understand the working of his mind than to look at the story that the famous private eye tells Brigid O'Shaughnessy in Chapter Seven. It's the story of a man named Flitcraft who, after years of living a normal, comfortable life, is suddenly brought face-to-face with the dark and terrible reality of things outside that safe existence. On his way to lunch one day, he passes a construction site just as a heavy steel beam falls from ten floors up and lands right beside him in the street. "He was scared stiff, of course," Spade tells Brigid, "but he was more shocked than really frightened. He felt like somebody had taken the lid off life and let him look at the works."

It is the way in which Flitcraft responds to his shocking introduction to "the works" of life that Spade finds most appealing. Instead of rejecting the experience and withdrawing into an alternate world of his own making where he can once again enjoy the illusion of living safely, Flitcraft instantly accepts the painful reality he had discovered and adjusts his life to it. Significantly, the plot of *The Maltese Falcon* is an elaborate development of the Flitcraft anecdote. The book's strategy, strongly influenced by the post–World War I nihilism that Ernest Hemingway called *nada* and that indelibly marked all *Black Mask* fiction, is to take the lid off life and then record the ways in which a number of different people respond to "the works" that are revealed.

The response of the story's villains—Gutman, Cairo, Brigid—is to distort the world about them in one way or another to serve their own purposes, and Gutman's name and size sug-

Advertisement for *The Maltese Falcon*, from the scrapbook of Joseph Shaw

gests the method he, for one, has developed for doing this. Eating is the means by which we all convert organisms independent of us into more of ourselves. Everyone must do some of this converting to survive, but Gutman's vast bulk indicates that he is a pathological devourer of others, that his greatest need is to ingest the whole world and make it synonymous with himself. There's even something cannibalistic and incestuous (two more activities appropriate to a world peopled by versions of the self) about the way in which the fat man is willing to consume his own "son" Wilmer if that will help him attain his goal. "By Gad!" Gutman says to Spade, "if you lose a son it's possible to get another—and there's only one Maltese falcon."

As for the others, Joel Cairo is a homosexual—a symbol, for Hammett, of sterile self-love—whose hopeful view of Wilmer reflects his own desire rather than any reasonable expectation he may have for a return of affection. And Brigid O'Shaughnessy is an uninhibited liar, one who casually changes the version of reality she presents to others as the occasion demands, never telling the same story or giving herself the same name twice. Of course, all three of these characters commit or condone murder, the ultimate denial of another human being's independent existence.

The great symbol of success for these three is the fabulous Maltese falcon, and their search for it is a kind of parody of a medieval quest, like that of the Knights of the Round Table. King Arthur's knights roamed the world seeking the Holy Grail, symbol of the perfect purity and reality of God. The object of Gutman's search is the falcon, also associated with a group of knights, and represents for him the perfect purity and reality of gold. But, appropriately enough, the bird when found turns out to be worth nothing—*nada*. In a sense, it is fool's gold, a substance that is gold only to those who think it is, and thus a perfect reward for those who see the world as they wish it to be. For its entire value is the value Gutman and the others have given it by looking for it.

Sam Spade's response to the sight of the world with its lid off is different from that of Gutman and the others. Before Spade can demonstrate that difference, however, he must first arrange for his own survival. After all, if Flitcraft had actually been hit by the falling beam, he wouldn't have had the luxury of deciding how to deal with the experience. That survival involves a couple of steps, the first of which is absolutely basic. In a dangerous world full of pathological eaters like Gutman, Spade's first job is to keep from being devoured. In plain terms, this means that he has to be streetwise. He must know as much as he can about the world in which he operates, must belong entirely to it, even to the point of being nearly indistinguishable from the criminals he is hunting. When Thursby is found dead after Archer's murder, the police don't hesitate to make Spade a suspect. To them, he's as likely as anyone else to be guilty. Hammett makes this point about Spade's protective coloration on the very first page of the novel when he memorably refers to his protagonist as looking "rather pleasantly like a blond Satan."

But such coloration is not enough to assure the detective's survival in *The Maltese Falcon*. True, it will keep him from being devoured, and that is the most basic kind of survival. But if he is to survive spiritually and professionally too, he must find a way of existing in this Dantesque world without becoming a devourer himself. I've spoken of Gutman metaphorically as an obsessive eater, internalizing everything around him, changing reality to suit his own ends and therefore never able to find anything that is real. Spade escapes this fate by refusing to consume reality, by honoring, as do all great detectives, its independent existence. In this way, while he, like Dante, is required to be in the hell he's investigating, he is not *of* it, not defined by it. "Down these mean streets," Raymond Chandler has written about the hard-boiled detective, "a man must go who is not himself mean." Or as Spade puts it to Brigid O'Shaughnessy, "Don't be too sure I'm as crooked as I'm supposed to be."

It is in this famous last scene with Brigid that Spade clearly earns the right to be called a great detective. He does this, first of all, by solving the puzzle of Miles Archer's death. A few critics have attacked Hammett for failing to take this conventional murder mystery element seriously enough, but they miss the point. The killing of Archer is just a small part of a much more elaborate mystery, the whole baffling array of alternate "realities" that confront Spade all through the book, most of them created by the criminals, and out of which it is his business to pick the one that is true. The clearing up of Archer's murder is representative of that larger solution. It is punctuation, so to speak, coming at the end of the long, complex case.

Still, the solution to the Archer mystery shows Spade operating very much in the tradition of the great detective as it was first defined by Poe. Spade's technique is to enter imaginatively into the mind of his partner, to experience Archer's last minutes of life as if they had been his own. In this way, he is actually able to "see" the killer for himself. The most important clue to the mystery appears early in Chapter Two of the book, where police detective Tom Polhaus casually mentions some details of the crime to Spade. "His gun was tucked away on his hip," Polhaus says about Archer. "It hadn't been fired. His overcoat was buttoned." Spade, who for a moment almost becomes Archer, can see exactly what circumstances would explain these facts.

"Miles hadn't many brains," Spade tells Brigid when she suggests Archer had been murdered by Thursby,

> but he had too many years' experience as a detective to be caught like that by the man he was shadowing. Up a blind alley with his gun tucked away on his hip and his overcoat buttoned? . . . But he'd've gone up there with you, angel. . . . He was just dumb enough for that. He'd've looked you up and down and licked his lips and gone grinning from ear to ear.

Brigid is amazed at how accurately Spade has described the scene, almost as if he had been there himself. "How did you know he—" she stammers, "he licked his lips and looked—?" But in a sense Spade *had* been there, and his answer to Brigid concisely sums up the whole art of a great detective: "I knew Miles." Archer died because he didn't know Brigid, because he was too involved in his own familiar desires and plans to imagine the alienness of hers. Gutman is also destroyed by such narcissism. Though he has viciously betrayed Wilmer, he is too self-absorbed even to worry about the "kid's" revenge. Spade's comment when he hears about the fat man's death is the one a great detective would most naturally make. "He ought to have expected that."

The mystery of Archer's death, however, isn't Spade's greatest challenge in the story, and Hammett doesn't rely on the simple solving of a puzzle for the climax of his novel. The great moment, for both the detective and the book, comes only after Spade has told Brigid that he knows she is his partner's murderer. Brigid tries to tempt him not to turn her in, and Spade needs all the force of his special genius to resist her appeal to what she calls their love. Any other character in the novel would have been deceived by such an entreaty. But Spade knows Brigid just as he knew Miles Archer, and just as he knows himself—with the unsentimental acceptance of the truth that is his greatest strength.

For a moment he seems a bit confused and offers Brigid too many explanations for his decision. But in the end, all the different reasons come down to a single reason, the key idea of the story. "Listen," Spade says to Brigid when he has finished his list of explanations. "If that doesn't mean anything to you forget it and we'll make it this: I won't because all of me wants to—wants to say the hell with the consequences and do it." For Gutman, Cairo, Brigid, Archer, and those like them, wanting to do a thing is always a good enough reason for doing it. Such people are ruled entirely by appetite and by immediate self-interest. For them, there is no world but the one their desires make, no unchangeable reality, no consequences they can't devour except the last one, which devours them.

Spade is different. No matter how much all of him may want to, he will not deny reality. Like Flitcraft, and like all great detectives since Poe invented the genre, he looks steadily at whatever the world may offer him and starts from there. As a result, he isn't devoured and he doesn't devour; he survives. In Raymond Chandler's words, he is "the best man in his world and a good enough man for any world." Circumstances may sometimes force him to look and act like a devil, but he's a "blond" devil, and his is the only gold around that isn't fool's gold.

Robert I. Edenbaum, "The Poetics of the Private-Eye: The Novels of Dashiell Hammett," in *Tough Guy Writers of the Thirties*, edited by David Madden (Carbondale: Southern Illinois University Press, 1968), pp. 80–103.

> [The daemonic agent] will act as if possessed. . . . He will act part way between the human and divine spheres, touching on both, which suggests that he can be used for the model romantic hero, since romance allows its heroes both human interest and divine power. His essentially energetic character will delight the reader with an appearance of unadulterated power. Like a machiavellian prince, the allegorical hero can act free of the unusual moral restraints, even when he is acting morally, since he is moral only in the interests of his power over other men. This sort of action has a crude fascination for us all; it impels us to read the detective story, the western, the saga of space exploration and interplanetary travel.
>
> —Angus Fletcher, *Allegory*

Raymond Chandler, Dashiell Hammett's major successor in the tradition of the tough detective novel, Howard Haycraft, a historian of the form, and David T. Bazelon, a far from sympathetic critic, all agree that Hammett shaped the archetype and stereotype of the private-eye. Hammett's third novel, *The Maltese Falcon*, heads any list of tough guy novels of the thirties. The preeminence and popularity of that novel is not only due to its date of publication at the very start of the new decade, nor to the fact that eleven years later John Huston turned it into "the best private-eye melodrama ever made," according to James Agee (*Agee on Film*). And it is not only the vagaries of camp taste that have made Humphrey Bogart's Sam Spade a folk-hero a third of a century later. Sam Spade of *The Maltese Falcon* (1930), together with the nameless Continental Op of the earlier novels, *Red Harvest* and *The Dain Curse* (both 1929), and to a lesser extent Ned Beaumont of *The Glass Key* (1931) and Nick Charles of *The Thin Man* (1934) constitute a poetics of the tough guy hero of novel, film, and television script from 1929 to the present.

The characteristics of Hammett's "daemonic" tough guy, with significant variations in the last two novels, can be schematized as follows: he is free of sentiment, of the fear of death, of the temptations of money and sex. He is what Albert Camus calls "a man without memory," free of the burden of the past. He is capable of any action, without regard of conventional morality, and thus is apparently as amoral—or immoral—as his antagonists. His refusal to submit to the trammels which limit ordinary mortals results in a godlike immunity and independence, beyond the power of his enemies. He himself has under his control the pure power that is needed to reach goals, to answer questions and solve mysteries, to reconstruct the (possible) motivations of the guilty and innocent alike. Hammett's novels—particularly the first three, with which this essay will be primarily concerned—present a "critique" of the tough guy's freedom as well: the price he pays for his power is to be cut off behind his own self-imposed masks, in an isolation that no criminal, in a community of crime, has to face.

The Maltese Falcon is the most important of the novels in the development of the poetics of the private-eye because in it Hammett is less concerned with the intricacies of the detective story plot than with the combat between a villain (ess) who is a woman of sentiment, and who thrives on the sentiment of others, and a hero who has none and survives because he has none. As a result of that combat itself, the novel is concerned with the definition of the private-eye's "daemonic" virtue—with his invulnerability and his power—and with a critique of that definition.

The word "combat" has to be qualified immediately, for there can be unequal combat only when one antagonist holds all the cards and the other is always victim; when the one manipulates and the other is deceived; when the actions of the one are unpredictable and the responses of the other stock. These terms would seem to describe the villain and his victim of Gothic fiction from The Mysteries of Udolpho to The Lime Twig. But Hammett, in The Maltese Falcon, reverses the roles. Brigid O'Shaughnessy, the murderer of Sam Spade's partner Miles Archer, is the manipulated, the deceived, the unpredictable, finally, in a very real sense, the victim. Customarily in the detective story, the solution to the mystery—for example, the identity of the murderer—is known only to the murderer himself; terror makes everyone victim but the murderer, for only the murderer, the unpredictable element, can know what will happen next. In the first few pages of The Maltese Falcon Miles Archer is murdered, apparently by Floyd

Thursby. Thursby is killed; that is apparently a mystery (though it takes no great imagination to settle on the young hood Wilmer as the likely culprit). The ostensible mystery, then, is why Thursby killed Archer, and why he in turn was killed. In the last pages of the novel, however, the reader (and Brigid O'Shaughnessy) discovers that he (and she) has been duped all along, for Spade has known from the moment he saw Archer's body that Brigid is the murderer. Spade himself, then, is the one person who holds the central piece of information; he is the one person who knows everything, for Brigid does not know that he knows. And though Spade is no murderer, Brigid O'Shaughnessy is his victim.

Once the reader knows, finally, that Spade has known all along that Miles Archer, with his pistol tucked inaccessibly under his arm, would not have gone up a dark alley with anyone but a girl as beautiful as Brigid, and therefore must have gone with *her,* he can make sense out of an apparently irrelevant anecdote that Spade tells Brigid early in the novel. The story, about a case Spade once worked on, concerns a man named Charles Flitcraft who had disappeared without apparent motive. The likely possibilities—as nearly always in Gothic fiction, sex and money—are eliminated beyond doubt. The mystery is cleared up when Spade finds the missing man. Flitcraft's life before his disappearance had been "a clean orderly sane responsible affair," Flitcraft himself "a man who was most comfortable in step with his surroundings." The day of his disappearance, on his way down a street, a beam had fallen from a building under construction and missed killing him by an inch. At that moment Flitcraft "felt like somebody had taken the lid off life and let him look at the works." He left his old life on the spot, for "he knew then that men died at haphazard like that, and lived only while blind chance spared them." Flitcraft spends several years living under that Dreiserian philosophy, working at a variety of jobs, until he meets another woman identical to his first wife except in face, marries her, has children identical to those by his first wife, leads a life identical to the one he had led before his black epiphany. Spade had returned to the first Mrs. Flitcraft to tell her what he had learned. Mrs. Flitcraft had not understood; Spade had no trouble understanding. Brigid O'Shaughnessy, despite her fascination with Spade's story almost against her will (she is trying to find out what he intends to do in her case) understands no more than Mrs. Flitcraft did.

Flitcraft moves from a life—and a commensurate philosophy—in which beams do not fall, to one in which beams do, back to one in which they don't. There can be no doubt which of the two Spade subscribes to: "Flitcraft *knew* then that men died at haphazard" (my emphasis). That commonplace enough naturalistic conception of the randomness of the universe is Spade's vision throughout. The contrast is of Spade's life (that of the private-eye) in which beams are expected to fall, and do fall, and that of the suburban businessman, in which they do not—or, at least, do not until they do. Since they did stop in the years between, Flitcraft merely adjusted himself back to a world where they did not. In Spade's world, of course, they never stop falling. If Brigid were acute enough—or less trammelled by conventional sentiment—she would see in the long, apparently pointless story that her appeals to Spade's sense of honor, his nobility, his integrity, and finally, his love, will not and cannot work. That essentially is what Spade is telling her through his parable. Brigid—totally unscrupulous, a murderess—should understand rather better than Mrs. Flitcraft, the bourgeois housewife. But she doesn't. She falls back on a set of conventions that she has discarded in her own life, but which she naively assumes still hold for others'. At the end of the novel, Brigid is not merely acting her shock at Spade's refusal to shield her; that shock is as genuine as Effie Perine's at Spade for that same refusal—and as sentimental. Paradoxically, in *The Maltese Falcon* the good guy is a "blond satan" and the villain is as innocent as she pretends to be. For that matter Gutman, Cairo, even Wilmer, are appalled by Spade, and in their inability to cope with him are as innocent as Brigid.

This reading of the Flitcraft story accounts for Spade's overriding tone of mockery with Brigid whenever she appeals to his gallantry and loyalty based on her trust and confidence in him. His response to her talk of trust is, "You don't have to trust me . . . as long as you can persuade me to trust you." But, as we have seen, that is impossible from the very start, and Spade's saying so is a cruel joke on an unsuspecting murderer. To Brigid, Spade is "the wildest person I've ever known," "altogether unpredictable." Had she understood the Flitcraft story, she would have known that he is not unpredictable at all, but simply living by

Flitcraft's vision of meaninglessness and the hard knowingness that follows from that vision. Spade is in step with his surroundings as much as Flitcraft is in step with his. Except for a brief (but important) moment at the end when he is nonplussed by Effie, Spade is never surprised by anyone's actions as Brigid is continually surprised by his. Spade several times picks up mockingly on Brigid's words "wild and unpredictable." She asks at another point what he would do if she were to tell him nothing about the history of the falcon and the quest for it; he answers that he would have no trouble knowing "what to do next." Sam Spade (cf. Humphrey Bogart) never has to hesitate about what to do next. Brigid, of course, has no idea what he will do. When a thousand dollar bill disappears from the envelope holding Gutman's "payment" to Spade, the detective takes Brigid into the bathroom and forces her to undress so that he can make sure she does not have it hidden on her person. Brigid, incredulous, responds with the appropriate clichés: "You'll be killing something." "You shouldn't have done that to me, Sam . . ." But Spade will not be stopped by "maidenly modesty," for he knows that Gutman is testing him to see what he will do. The fat man finds out; Brigid still does not, and learns only when it is too late.

The rejection of the fear of death, perhaps the most obvious characteristic of the tough guy in general, is but another aspect of the rejection of sentiment. Spade fully expects those falling beams, and thus detective work is as much a metaphor for existence as war is in *The Red Badge of Courage* or *A Farewell to Arms*. In an exchange with the driver of a rented car on its way to one unknown destination in the unending series that is the fictional detective's life, the driver comments on Miles Archer's death and on the detective business.

"She's a tough racket. You can have it for mine."

"Well [Spade answers], hack-drivers don't live forever."

"Maybe that's right . . . but just the same, it'll always be a surprise to me if I don't."

The driver is a working-class Flitcraft; Spade, on the other hand, is heading towards another potential falling beam—though, in fact, the trip turns out to be a wild-goose chase planned by Gutman. And the final sentence of the dialogue—"Spade stared ahead at nothing . . ."—bears a double force.

Hammett's reversal of the trap of naturalism gives his heroes a kind of absolute power over their own destiny, a daemonic power, in Angus Fletcher's useful phrase. To stare into nothing and know it; to be as dispassionate about death as about using others—Wilmer, Cairo, or Brigid—as fall-guy: all this means that Spade can rob a Gutman of his ultimate weapon, the threat of death. When Gutman threatens Spade, the detective can argue that the fat man needs him alive; Gutman returns that there are other ways to get information; Spade, in his turn, insists that there is no terror without the threat of death, that he can play Gutman so that the fat man will not kill him, but that if need be he can *force* Gutman to kill him. Who but the tough guy can *make* the beam fall? In that lies the tough guy's power to set his own terms in life and death, a power that is the basis of his popularity in detective and other fiction.

To a generation of readers suckled on the violence of Mickey Spillane and Ian Fleming, it will hardly come as a shock to learn that detectives are as unscrupulous and amoral as "the enemy," as Spade calls them. In this book, though, Hammett seems to be consciously defining the nature of that unscrupulousness through Spade's relationship with Brigid, a relationship which itself becomes the major subject of *The Maltese Falcon* and itself exemplifies the terms of the detective's existence in the novel and in the fiction that ultimately derives from it. The dialogue between Sam Spade and Brigid does much of the work of developing the definition. For example, at one point Brigid says that she is afraid of two men: Joel Cairo and Spade himself. Spade answers, with his total awareness of what she means and what she is, "I can understand your being afraid of Cairo . . . He's out of your reach" (that is, because he is homosexual). And she: "And you aren't?" And he: "Not that way." Under the terms I am suggesting, this exchange must be read as follows: she says she is afraid of him; he says that that's not true because he's not out of her reach; he's right, she's not afraid of him; she should be because he *is* out of her reach. If she thinks him unscrupulous it is because she thinks he is after her and / or her money. She "seduces" him, thinking it will make a difference, but it doesn't. As soon as he climbs out of bed in the morning he steals her key to ransack her apartment, to find further evidence of her lies, though once again the reader doesn't know what he finds until the very end. The fact that Spade does not "cash many checks for

THE ADAKIAN STAFF ON HACKHEEL SPAM-MITT

Movies

Today: THE MALTESE FALCON; Something not-kosher about this bird. Ample proof that Hackheel Spam-mitt will get nowhere as a writer, and fast. Humphrey Gocart perambulates sto- ically thru the writer's wheeze-whim-sickly dialogue but the ivory-crapper aura of the plot funks up the fowl foully. D.H. should get his own bird.

Parody review from *The Adakian*, 27 May 1944, p. 2, the special DH at 50 Birthday Issue.

strangers," as his lawyer puts it, is the key to his survival, and it leaves him outside the pale of tenderness.

One further key to Hammett's demolition of sentiment is the all but passionless figure of Sam Spade and one further indication of the price immunity exacts is Effie Perine, the archetypal tough guy's archetypal secretary. Spade pays Effie the highest compliment of all in the classic line, "You're a damned good man, sister," but unlike many of her later peers Effie is not tough. In the course of the novel Spade baits Effie again and again by asking what her "woman's intuition" tells her about Brigid O'Shaughnessy; Effie is "for her"; "that girl is all right." The point is not simply that Effie is wrong. Even at the end, knowing that she has been wrong all along, that Brigid has murdered one of her bosses, she responds as a woman, with a woman's (from Hammett's point of view?) sentimental notions, with appalled distaste for *Spade*. The last word in the novel's is Effie's. She has learned of Brigid's arrest through the newspapers; Spade returns to his office.

> Spade raised his head, grinned, and said mockingly: "So much for your woman's intuition."
>
> Her voice was queer as the expression on her face. "You did that, Sam, to her?"
>
> He nodded. "Your Sam's a detective." He looked sharply at her. He put his arm around her waist, his hand on her hip. "She did kill Miles, angel," he said gently, "offhand, like that." He snapped the fingers of his other hand.
>
> She escaped from his arm, as if it had hurt her. "Don't, please, don't touch me," she said brokenly. "I know—I know you're right. You're right. But don't touch me now—not now."

Effie's response amounts to a definition of sentiment: the impulse that tells you to pretend that what you know to be true is not true, to wish that what you know has to be, did not have to be. In the vein of the romanticism of action that becomes doing what everything sensible tells you you cannot do. You're right, you're right, but couldn't you better have been wrong? As Hammett has made sufficiently clear in the course of the book, and particularly in the final confrontation with Brigid, exactly the point about Spade—and about the tough guy in general—is that he could not have.

The confrontation of Spade and Brigid rather than the doings of Gutman, Cairo, and Wilmer, who are disposed of perfunctorily offstage, is the climax of the novel. Spade makes Brigid confess to him what, as we have seen, he has know all along—that she is Miles Archer's murderer; then he tells her, to her horror, that he is going to "send her over." His theme throughout this sequence is, "I won't play the sap for you." Though he says, "You'll never understand me" (anymore than Mrs. Flitcraft understood her husband), he goes on, in an astonishing catalogue, to tote up the balance sheet on the alternatives available to him. He ticks off the items on one side: "when a man's partner is killed he's supposed to do something about it"; "when one of your organization gets killed it's bad business to let the killer get away with it"; a detective cannot let a criminal go any more than a dog can let a rabbit go; if he lets her go, he goes to the gallows with Gutman, Cairo, and Wilmer; she would have something on him and would eventually use it; he would have something on her and eventually she couldn't stand it; she might be playing him for a sucker; he could go on "but that's enough." On the other side of the ledger is merely "the fact that maybe you love me and maybe I love you."

The tabulation of pros and cons suggests that Spade is a bookkeeper calculating the odds for getting away with breaking the law. But that is inaccurate, for his final statement demolishes his own statistics and suggests that something else is at stake: "'If that [all he has been saying] doesn't mean anything to you forget it and we'll make it this: I won't because all of me wants to— wants to say to hell with the consequences and do it—and because—God damn you—you've counted on that with me the same as you counted on that with the others.'" The rejection of sentiment as motivating force, i.e., of sentimentality, is at the heart of the characterization of Sam Spade and of the tough guy in general. It is not that Spade is incapable of human emotions— love, for example—but that apparently those emotions require the denial of what Spade knows to be true about women and about life. The sentiment Spade rejects is embodied in all three women in *The Maltese Falcon*—Brigid, Iva Archer, and Effie: murderer, bitch, and nice girl, respectively. It is in this theme itself, paradoxically, that *The Maltese Falcon* has been weakened by the passage of time. As one reads the novel now, Spade himself still retains his force; he is still a believable, even an attractive (if frightening) character. Brigid, on the contrary, is not. (Just so, Hemingway's assertion of Jake Barnes' stoical mask in *The Sun Also Rises* still works, but the attack on Robert Cohn's romanticism seems to be beating a dead horse.) And yet it is the pitting of Brigid's sentimental platitudes against Spade's mocking wisecracks that may make this book the classic it is. This theme, too, signals a reversal in the naturalistic novel, for the tough guy in the tradition of Sam Spade can no longer be the victim of sentiment (cf., for example, Dreiser's Hurstwood or Clyde Griffith, or a Hemingway character defeated by the death of the woman he loves). On the contrary, he hedges himself so thoroughly against betrayal that he lives in total isolation and loneliness. Spade is last seen shivering (temporarily) in revulsion as Effie Perine sends the moral slug Iva in to him. The attractions of Brigid given up to the law, the possibilities of Effie lost, Spade is left with only Iva—or an unending string of Iva's successors.

The Hammett detective most pure, most daemonic, is the Continental Op of the first two novels, his purity indicated even in his namelessness. The Op, perhaps more than Spade, is free of sentiment, of the fear of death, of a past, of the temptations of sex and money. Like Spade he is capable of anything that his opponents are in the pursuit of his goals; in *Red Harvest* he goes further than Spade ever does in his responsibility for setting criminals against one another murderously. The Op in *Red Harvest* is much like Mark Twain's mysterious stranger that corrupts Hadleyburg: the stranger drops the bag of "gold" in the laps of the townsmen and watches them scramble; and so the Op in Personville (pronounced Poisonville). Both manipulate matters with absolute assurance and absolute impunity (cf. Spade as well). In *Red Harvest* twenty-five people are killed, not counting an additional unspecified number of slaughtered hoodlums, yet the only mishaps to befall the Op are to have a hand creased by a bullet and an arm stunned by the blow of a chair-leg. His powers come to seem almost supernatural, his knowledge of the forces that move men (sex and money) clairvoyance. His single-minded mission is to clean up the corruption no matter what the cost in other men's lives. The Op's own explanation of his motives—like those voiced to Gutman by Spade, a kind of personal grudge against those who have tried to get him—is not particularly convincing. It is tempting to say that the Op's apparently personal response to being picked on is the equivalent of Hemingway's characters when they are picked off, but Hemingway's characters do have identifiable human emotions, whether disgust, or relief from disgust, or love; Hammett's, because of the purely external mechanistic method, do not. The superhuman is so by virtue of being all but nonhuman.

Red Harvest offers a perfect role for the Hammett private-eye. Elihu Willsson, aristocratic banker-boss of Poisonville, gives the Continental Detective Agency in the person of the Op ten thousand dollars to clean up the town because Willsson thinks the local gangsters responsible for the murder of his son. After the Op discovers that the crime was one of passion (if passion bought and sold) unrelated to the bootlegging-gambling-political corruption of the town, Willsson tries to dismiss the Op, who refuses to be dismissed, "'Your fat chief of police tried to assassinate me last night. I don't like that. I'm just mean enough to want to ruin him for it. Now I'm going to have my fun. I've got ten thousand dollars of your money to play with. I'm going to use it opening Poisonville up from Adam's apple to ankles.'" Ten thousand dollars of your money to play with—there is the role of invulnerable power with the most possibilities open. The Op almost seems to forget he has the money; aside from his day-to-day expenses, all he uses of it is $200.10 that he reluctantly pays Dinah Brand for information. Hammett seems to want to establish the financial freedom of his character: with ten thousand dollars in hand how can the Op be suborned? Once that immunity is established it does not matter how (or whether) the money is spent.

The Op's immunity from temptation indicates something of the allegorical nature of the novels. Rather than being amoral, they establish moral oppositions of the simplest kind: if the proletarian novel is a version of pastoral in William Empson's witty formulation, the tough detective novel is a version of morality, with allegorical combat between the forces of good and evil, and the most obvious of object lessons. Don't be a sucker for sex (read "love"): better Spade with Iva than Spade with Brigid. Don't be a sucker for money: it leaves you wide open for the crooks *and* the cops. Myrtle Jennison (a minor character in *Red Harvest*) was once as beautiful as Dinah Brand: now she's bloated with Bright's

Disease (and Dinah herself dies of an ice-pick wound). Twenty-five men, slaughtered, were once alive (*Red Harvest*). And so on.

The morality of Hammett's detectives is basically defensive, as it must be in the Gothic world posited. As I indicated earlier, in the traditional Gothic novel (and as well in the naturalistic novel in this century) corruption and evil stem from two sources of power, two kinds of end—money and sex. Innocence (virginity in the older Gothic) is eternally threatened, usually for money; sex is used to gain money, and is in turn corrupted by money. Sexual and financial power are at most equatable, at least inextricable, for it is money which makes sex purchasable and sex which makes money attainable. The Op functions as a monkish ascetic who in order to survive must stay clear of money and sex, the only real temptations. Presumably he could walk off with Elihu Willsson's ten thousand, but of course he is no more tempted to abscond than he is to seduce Dinah Brand (he is just about the only male in the novel who doesn't). He unfixes a prize-fight, lets Dinah win a pile of money, but does not himself bet. When Dinah, puzzled, questions him, he claims he was not sure his plan would work; but there is no evidence that that is anything but a bluff. Dinah more understands the Op's immunity to cash than Brigid understands Spade's to love. For Dinah, trying to get money out of the Op in exchange for the information she has on the inner workings of Poisonville, "It's not so much the money. It's the principle of the thing." The Op, refusing, parodies her with her own words: "It's not the money . . . It's the principle of the thing." Everything about Dinah, particularly her body, can be bought; nothing about the Op can be, by money or sex or sentiment. In self-defense he must be untouchable; otherwise his invulnerability would be seriously compromised.

Like Spade, the Op in his immunity from temptation becomes god-like, perhaps inseparable from a devil, his concern not a divine plan but a satanic disorder. "Plans are all right sometimes . . . And sometimes just stirring things up is all right—if you're tough enough to survive, and keep your eyes open so you'll see what you want when it comes to the top." The Op's way of unravelling the mess in Poisonville is to "experiment," in his word, to see if he can pit one set of crooks against another, when he unfixes the prizefight, for example. The result, in that case and always, is more murder and further chaos impending. Dinah Brand's irony—"So that's the way you scientific detectives work"—is Hammett's as well. The Op's metaphor makes him the same kind of godlike manipulator the naturalist novelist himself becomes in *his* experiments with the forces that move human beings to destruction. The stranger in "The Man That Corrupted Hadleyburg" may drop the bag of money in the town, but it is Mark Twain who drops the stranger there; and Hammett the Op in Poisonville. The bitter enjoyment may be Hammett's and Mark Twain's as well as their characters'.

Ultimately the Op does discover that he is paying the price for his power—his fear that he is going "blood simple like the natives." "Play with murder enough and it gets you one of two ways. It makes you sick or you get to like it," he says as he tabulates the sixteen murders to that moment. The blood gets to the Op in both ways. He finds that he cannot keep his imagination from running along murderous lines on the most common of objects; he carries an ice-pick into Dinah's living room, and Dinah asks why.

> "To show you how my mind's running. A couple of days ago, if I thought about it at all, it was as a good tool to pry off chunks of ice." I ran a finger down its half-foot of round steel blade to the needle point. "Not a bad thing to pin a man to his clothes with. That's the way I'm betting, on the level. I can't even see a mechanical cigar lighter without thinking of filling one with nitroglycerine for somebody you don't like. There's a piece of copper wire lying in the gutter in front of your house—thin, soft, and just enough to go around a neck with two ends to hold on. I had one hell of a time to keep from picking it up and stuffing it in my pocket, just in case—"

> "You're crazy," [Dinah says].

> "I know it. That's what I've been telling you. I'm going blood-simple."

Out of his head on the gin and laudanum which he takes to relieve his own morbidity, the Op wakes the next morning to find his hand around the ice-pick, buried in Dinah's breast. It is not surprising that not only the authorities but one of the other operatives sent down from San Francisco and the Op himself think he may be Dinah's murderer. If the Op, like all men, is capable of all things, then he is capable of unmotivated murder. If the calculatedly nonhuman yields to human emotion and human weakness, defenses are down; loss of control and near-destruction follow. The point would seem to be, don't let your defenses down. No one, including the detective, is exempt from the possibility of crime. Thus, in *The Dain Curse* and *The Thin Man* the murderer turns out to be an old friend of the detective; in *The Maltese Falcon* it is the girl the detective loves (or may love); in *The Glass Key* a father (and U.S. senator) murders his own son; and in *Red Harvest* there is no one who might not be a killer—and most of them are, given those twenty-five some odd murders.

In *The Rebel* (Vintage Books) Albert Camus offers a brilliant analysis of the implications of the fear of emotion in the tough guy novel. The concomitants of the rejection of sentiment is the rejection of psychology itself and of everything that comprises the inner life in favor of the hedges themselves.

The American novel [the tough novel of the thirties and forties, Camus explains in a note] claims to find its unity in reducing man either to elementals or to his external reactions and to his behavior. It does not choose feelings or passions to give a detailed description of . . . It rejects analysis and the search for a fundamental psychological motive that could explain and recapitulate the behavior of a character . . . Its technique consists in describing men by their outside appearances, in their most casual actions, of reproducing, without comment, everything they say down to their repetitions, and finally by acting as if men were entirely defined by their daily automatisms. On this mechanical level men, in fact, seem exactly alike, which explains this peculiar universe in which all the characters appear interchangeable, even down to their physical peculiarities. This technique is called realistic only owing to a misapprehension . . . it is perfectly obvious that this fictitious world is not attempting a reproduction, pure and simple, of reality, but the most arbitrary form of stylization. It is born of a mutilation, and of a voluntary mutilation, performed on reality. The unity thus obtained is a degraded unity, a leveling off of human beings and of the world. It would seem that for these writers it is the inner life that deprives human actions of unity and that tears people away from one another. This is a partially legitimate suspicion . . . [but] the life of the body, reduced to its essentials, paradoxically produces an abstract and gratuitous universe, continuously denied, in its turn, by reality. This type of novel, purged of interior life, in which men seem to be observed behind a pane of glass, logically ends, with its emphasis on the pathological, by giving itself as its unique subject the supposedly average man. In this way it is possible to explain the extraordinary number of "innocents" who appear in this universe. The simpleton is the ideal subject for such an enterprise since he can only be defined—and completely defined—by his behavior. He is the symbol of the despairing world in which wretched automatons live in a machine-ridden universe, which American novelists have presented as a heart-rending but sterile protest (pp. 265–66).

Camus' analysis isolates both the success and the sadness of the tough novel. The success is that of the serious novel in general in that the correlation between the "voluntary mutilation" performed on reality by the author and that of the characters is complete; technique is subject matter in Hammett as much as in Joyce (though the analogy ends there). The excision of mind and emotion in tough dialogue, the understatement, the wise-guy joke-cracking cynicism—all the characteristics of Hammett's particular stylization—are matter as much as method. The sadness

First frame from a comic-strip advertisement featuring Sam Spade, circa 1946

lies in the thinness of the world that remains and in the terror that is the common denominator of all men, who must fear all other men and themselves, and whose primary occupation would seem to be the development and maintenance of a reflexive self-defense. Finally, the detective's motives are as hidden as the murderer's and as indeterminable. The inner world is so thoroughly left to shift for itself (if it exists at all) that there is some question as to whether Hammett's characters are more than Camus' "wretched automatons"—with credits to Hollywood for the terrorless charms of Bogart, Greenstreet, et al.

The Dain Curse is one of the more interesting of Hammett's novels, in part because it is concerned with the implications and consequences of the mechanistic method and the mechanical world, with the difficulty of discovering, not only the motives of the actors, but the actual events that took place. As a result *The Dain Curse* is by far the most complicated of the novels. It consists of three separate plots concerning the events surrounding the drug-addict Gabrielle Leggett, events which eventually include the deaths of her father, mother, step-mother, husband, doctor, and religious "counselor," among others. In the first sequence, an apparently trivial theft of a batch of inexpensive diamonds leads to several murders and to incredible disclosures about the history of Edgar Leggett and his two wives, the Dain sisters Alice and Lily, a history that includes, for example, Alice's training of the three-year-old Gabrielle to kill Lily. In the second sequence, her father and aunt / step-mother dead, Gabrielle, a virtual prisoner in the quack Temple of the Holy Grail, is involved in another round of deaths, and the Op does battle with a man who thinks he is God and with a spirit that has weight but no solidity. In the third, after still more murders and maimings— a total of nine, plus three before the time of the novel—the Op discovers that there was, as he had suspected, a single mind behind the many criminal hands at work in all three apparently unrelated sequences of events. The man the Op has known for several years as Owen Fitzstephan is actually a Dain, a master-mind whose prime motive is—love for Gabrielle.

After the second part, the Op gives the still-unsuspected Fitzstephan his reconstruction of the events at the Temple of the Holy Grail, then adds,

"I hope you're not trying to keep this nonsense straight in your mind. You know damned well all this didn't happen."

"Then what did happen?" [Fitzstephan asks]

"I don't know. I don't think anybody knows. I'm telling what I saw plus the part of what Aaronia Haldorn [the woman who runs the Temple, and, it is later disclosed, Fitzstephan's mistress and tool] told me which fits in with what I saw. To fit in with what I saw, most of it must have happened very nearly as I've told you. If you want to believe that it did, all right. I don't. I'd rather believe I saw things that weren't there."

And again the Op asks, "You actually believe what I've told you so far?" Fitzstephan says that he does, and the Op answers, "What a childish mind you've got," and starts to tell the story of Little Red Riding-Hood. In these novels there is no question of the complexity of, say, the relativity of guilt, for there is no ambiguity in human actions. As I have suggested, the allegory is fairly simple. The complexity is in the mystery of motive which results in the thorough-going ignorance that even the detective must admit to. What, finally, does move any human being—here, a criminal—to act? Put together a gaggle of the criminal and semi-criminal, the tempted and the merely self-interested, and it may be nearly as difficult to find out what happened as why. Similarly in *The Thin Man* Nora Charles is thoroughly dissatisfied with Nick's "theories" and "probablys" and "maybes" in his recon-struction of the events surrounding the death of Clyde Wynant. To the Op "details don't make much difference," details, that is, such as whether Joseph Haldorn really came to think himself God or merely thought he could fool everyone into thinking he was God. All that matters is that Joseph "saw no limit to his power." The same impossibility of determining truth recurs at the end of the novel: is Fitzstehphan a sane man pretending to be a lunatic or a lunatic pretending to be sane? It's not clear whether the Op himself thinks Fitzstephan sane. That again is a detail that doesn't make much difference, especially since people are capable of anything. Fitzstephan, like Haldorn, saw no limit to his power. The exact terms of the curse are irrelevant; he is lost in any case.

In *The Dain Curse* Hammett once again explores the detective's mask by means of a woman's probing, but the Op's motives are no more susceptible to analysis than the criminals'. Gabrielle wants to know why the Op goes to the trouble of convincing her that she is not degenerate or insane, cursed by the blood of the Dains in her veins. She asks the question the reader might ask: "Do I believe in you because you're sincere? Or because you've learned how—as a trick of your business—to make people believe in you?" The Op's response—"She might have been crazy, but she wasn't so stupid. I gave her the answer that seemed best at the time . . ."—doesn't answer the question for the reader any more than it does for the girl. Is it only a trick of his business or does he have a heart of gold beneath his tough exterior? Gabrielle is asking unanswerable questions, finally, because the removal of one mask only reveals another beneath. That may amount to saying that the toughness is not a mask at all, but the reality.

In their next encounter Gabrielle asks specifically why the Op went through the ugliness of supervising her withdrawal from drugs. He answers, with exaggerated tough guy surliness, "I'm twice your age, sister; an old man. I'm damned if I'll make a chump of myself by telling you why I did it, why it was neither revolting nor disgusting, why I'd do it again and be glad of the chance." By refusing to expose himself he is suggesting that he is exposing himself. Certainly his words suggest love for the girl, but he's hardly to be believed. He pretends to be hiding his sentiments under his tough manner, but it is more likely that he is pretending to pretend. Gabrielle has been the object of the "love" of a whole series of men: of the insane passion of Owen Fitzstephan and the only less insane of Joseph Haldorn, the High Priest and God of the Cult of the Holy Grail; of the petty lechery of her lawyer, Madison Andrews; and of the fumbling, well-meant love of Eric Collinson, who gets himself (and nearly Gabrielle) killed as a result. This view of love as destructive force, as we have seen, is an essential part of the occasion for the tough role. The Op, like Spade, has to think himself well out of it, though the reader does not have to agree.

In the last of this series of interviews in which Gabrielle, acting as the reader's friend, tries to comprehend the Op's tough role, the girl accuses the detective of pretending to be in love with her during their previous talk.

"I honestly believed in you all afternoon—and it *did* help me. I believed you until you came in just now, and then I saw—" She stopped.

"Saw what?"

"A monster. A nice one, an especially nice one to have around when you're in trouble, but a monster just the same, without any human foolishness like love in him, and—What's the matter? Have I said something I shouldn't?"

"I don't think you should have," I said. "I'm not sure I wouldn't trade places with Fitzstephan now—if that big-eyed woman with the voice [Aaronia Haldorn] was part of the bargain."

"Oh, dear!" she said.

It's tempting to take the Op at his word here, at least, and believe that he has been hurt by Gabrielle's unwittingly cruel words. But the pattern I have been developing makes it difficult to accept the Op's sensitivity about his toughness. It is more reasonable to assume that he is telling her, once again, what she wants to hear, suggesting that she is in some way unique in his life. If no sentiment whatever is involved in his actions, he is the monster she calls him. And, in fact, that is the case with the Op as with Sam Spade. Seen as figures in stylized romance, both men may be seen as daemons; as characters in realistic fiction they are monsters both.

The Glass Key is Hammett's least satisfactory novel, perhaps precisely because it is not allegorical Gothic romance, lacking as it does a godlike Spade or Op. It may be the case, as David T. Bazelon writing in *Commentary,* suggests, that Hammett was trying to write a book closer to a conventional novel, one in which characters are moved to action for human reasons such as loyalty and love. But Hammett's mechanistic method is unchanged and, as a result, it is still impossible to tell what is under Ned Beaumont's mask. Does Ned take the punishment he does out of loyalty to the political boss Paul Madvig, because Madvig picked him out of the gutter fifteen months earlier? Perhaps the reader's sense of propriety or decency fills in that answer, but there is no evidence that it is accurate. It can be argued, on the contrary, that Ned takes the vicious beatings, not out of loyalty but out of indifference to death (to falling beams, if you will). He "can stand anything [he's] got to stand," a gangster's sadism no more and no less than his (apparent) tuberculosis or a purely fortuitous traffic accident in a New York taxi. But "standing" punishment stoically (or suicidally) is not loyalty, not a basis for positive action; and without some clarification of motive, the sense of Ned's activities is merely muddy.

In a sequence that goes on for four brutal pages Ned tries repeatedly to escape his enemies despite being beaten after each attempt. But nothing stops him; as soon as he regains consciousness, he goes to work on the door again. It is tempting, once again, to take this behavior (which includes setting fire to the room) as motivated by loyalty, by Ned's overwhelming desire to warn Paul. But nothing of the sort is possible, for Hammett's descriptions of Ned's actions make it clear that most of his behavior—both his attempts to escape and to kill himself—are instinctual. He remembers nothing beyond his first beating, we are told. Action is determined mechanistically—or animalistically.

Ned's motives are essential to make sense of the climax of the novel when Ned allows Janet Henry, Paul's ostensible fiancée, to go off with him. His response to her "Take me with you" is hardly romantic: "Do you really want to go or are you just being hysterical? . . . It doesn't make any difference. I'll take you if you want to go." Yet there are indications earlier that Hammett wants to suggest the development of some kind of love between the two, growing out of their original mutual dislike, a love about which Paul Madvig has no doubt. The men have a falling out when Paul accuses Ned of lying to him because of Ned's own interest in Janet; at the end of the novel, Paul is confronted with the couple going off together. The questions remain whether Paul was right in the first place, whether Ned acted out of desire for the girl rather than loyalty to Paul, or for neither reason. But there is no basis for judgement, by Janet *or* the reader. Motives are once again indeterminable, but in this book it is necessary that they be determined. The result is not the richness of fruitful ambiguity but the fuzziness of inner contradiction.

The title of this novel, from a dream recounted to Ned Beaumont by Janet Henry, suggests once again the fear of unhedged emotion and thus of all human relationships despite the matching of Ned and Janet with which it ends. In the dream Janet and Ned are starving and come upon a locked house within which they can see food—and a tangle of snakes. To open the door there is a glass key; to get access to the food is to release the snakes. The fragile key breaks as the door opens, and the snakes attack: apparently to get at the heart's need is to open a Pandora's box. Given the tawdriness of the "love" relations in *The Glass Key*—Taylor Henry's unscrupulous use of Opal Madvig's love, Janet Henry's of Paul's—there is not much chance that Ned and Janet will escape the snakes ("I'll take you if you want to go"). Once again in these novels it would seem that the only safety is in not letting down your guard in the first place: do without the food and you escape the snakes.

It is perhaps significant that Ned Beaumont is not actually a detective, though he functions as one in trying to clear up the mystery of the murder of Taylor Henry. However, there is a professional detective in the novel, Jack Rumsen, who is interesting for his unHammett-like behavior; it is not Sam Spade or the Op who would say to a man trying to solve a crime, "Fred and I are building up a nice little private-detective business here . . . A couple of years more and we'll be sitting pretty. I like you, Beaumont, but not enough to monkey with the man who runs the city.'" That modification of the private-eye character in the direction of the cynicism and timidity of self-interest prepares the way for Hammett's last novel, *The Thin Man,* published three years later. Nick Charles is the least daemonic of Hammett's heroes, but then he's only an ex-detective. However indifferent he may have been to death in the past, now he wants to be left out of danger, to be able to enjoy his wife, her wealth, and his whiskey. Nick Charles and his boozing is what happens to the Op/Spade when he gives up his role as ascetic demi-god to become husband, man of leisure, investor in futures on the stock market.

The Thin Man is perhaps less concerned with murder and the private-eye than with the people around the murder—with a wide range of social types spiritually sibling to the Alfred G. Packer of the long entry Gilbert Wynant reads in *Celebrated Criminal Cases of America.* The man-eaters Mimi, Dorothy, and Gilbert Wynant; Christian Jorgensen, Herbert Macauley, the

Quinns, the Edges; as well as under-world characters like Shep Morelli and Julia Wolfe are little less cannibalistic than Packer. Nick Charles has no interest in their problems; it is his wife who drags him into the search for the missing Wynant against his will. The martini-for-breakfast cracking wise of William Powell and Myrna Loy more than anything else accounts for the popularity of *The Thin Man*. Despite Nick Charles' tough manner, Hammett's tough guy had been retired for good before this book appeared.

In Hemingway's story "In Another Country" the Italian major whose wife has just died fortuitously of a cold says, "[A man] must not marry. He cannot marry . . . If he is to lose every-thing, he should not place himself in a position to lose that. He should not place himself in a position to lose. He should find things he cannot lose." Knowing that, and despite that knowledge, Hemingway's characters of course always put themselves in a position to lose. They continually fall in love, knowing just how vulnerable that makes them, and they continually lose. Their hard exterior is merely a mask for the fine sensibility on a perpetual quest for good emotion. Hammett, in his best novels, literalizes the Hemingway mask and produces "monsters" who take the major's advice. The Hemingway mask is lifted every time the character is alone; he admits his own misery to himself—and to the reader—and exposes his inner life. The Hammett mask is never lifted; the Hammett character never lets you inside. Instead of unimpaired control and machinelike effi-ciency: the tough guy refuses "to place himself in a position to lose." For all (or most) intents and purposes the inner world does not exist: the mask is the self. It is that "voluntary mutila-tion" of life that is the subject matter of these novels as much as Hemingway's stoical mask is of his. Hammett uses the relation-ships of Sam Spade with Brigid O'Shaughnessy, of the Continen-tal Op with Dinah Brand and then with Gabrielle Leggett as proving grounds to indicate just how invulnerable his tough

DRUNK IN ANCHORAGE

Main Street in Anchorage was a procession of bars and liquor stores. Sam didn't bother much with the liquor stores. Off the wagon, he was as effusive as he was withdrawn when sober. He wanted company for his drinking, anybody's company. And with his natural Toid Avenue and Toity-Toid Street tough-guy accent, he could talk to anybody. And did.

Smashed, crocked, jugged, loud, boisterous, talking nonsense, then eloquence, then just four letter words. The gamut, including weep-ing.

E. E. Spitzer, "With Corporal Hammett on Adak," *Nation* (5 January 1974): 9.

guys are. In each case the woman tries to find out what the man is; in each case the toughness is tested—and found not wanting. In the fantasy of detective novel readers and movie-goers who are themselves victims of a machine-ridden universe, loneliness is not too high a price to pay for invulnerability.

Joe Gores, "Dashiell Hammett," in *AZ Murder Goes Classic: Papers of the Conference,* edited by Barbara Peters and Susan Malling (Scottsdale, Ariz.: Poisoned Pen Press, 1997), pp. 63–82.

In 1925, a short, dumpy, fortyish man told a self-styled Russian countess who was trying seduce him:

> You think I'm a man and you're a woman. That's wrong. I'm a manhunter and you're something that has been running in front of me. There's nothing human about it.

In 1956, a tall, solid, fortyish man said to himself, after interviewing a teen-age hooker who was mainlining heroin:

> The problem was to love people, try to serve them, without wanting anything from them. I was a long way from solving that one.

Both are fictional private investigators. The first, never named, is known only as The Continental Op. He is Dashiell Hammett's essential detective. The second is Lew Archer, Ross Macdonald's durable detective hero.

That Hammett is Macdonald's literary grandfather—by way of Raymond Chandler's Philip Marlowe—there can be no doubt Macdonald said that, "As a novelist of realistic intrigue, Hammett was unsurpassed in his own or any time." He even named Lew Archer after Miles Archer, whose murder in the opening stanzas of *The Maltese Falcon* sends his partner Sam Spade out into the San Francisco streets in the quest for the jewel-encrusted black bird.

So why is this picture out of focus? Where did Hammett's singular detective hero come from, and what happened to him in the three decades between those two quotes?

Samuel Dashiell Hammett (Dashiell was his mother's maiden name) was born in St. Mary's County, Maryland, in 1894. His father (a Democrat) ran for political office from the wrong party (Republican) and was virtually run out of the county, so Hammett grew up in Philadelphia and Baltimore. He left school at the age of 14; during the next few years he held several kinds of jobs—messenger boy, newsboy, office clerk, timekeeper, yard-man, machine operator, and finally stevedore.

Probably at about 18, he became an operative for the Pinkerton Detective Agency. Based on my own experiences as a private detective, I have a hunch he perhaps started out as office boy rather than field man, but there are no records from those years, and in any event he soon became an operative.

WW I interrupted his sleuthing and injured his health. He was an ambulance driver (not in the war zone), and in a one-vehicle accident rolled an ambulance full of sick and injured soldiers. No one was damaged further, but Hammett was so shaken by the incident that he never drove a motor vehicle again.

He also contracted TB in the service, and was in and out of veterans' hospitals for several years until he grew tired of it, discharged himself, moved to San Francisco in 1920, married Josephine Dolan—a nurse whom he'd met in a VA hospital in Seattle—and returned to sleuthing for Pinkerton's.

He and Jose had two daughters, but his tuberculosis eventually made it necessary for him to live apart from his family. They never really got together again as man and wife, although Hammett bought Josie a house, supported her all his life, and provided for the education of his daughters. They never divorced, contrary to the impression left by Lillian Hellman in her autobiographical writings, and Hammett never stopped spending several weeks each year with his family.

He finally quit detective work and started writing ad copy for Al Samuel's Jewelry store on Market Street. A co-worker there, Peggy O'Toole, served as his major inspiration for Brigid O'Shaughnessy in *The Maltese Falcon*. In 1975, while researching my novel *Hammett*, I tracked down Peggy O'Toole; she would only talk to me on the porch of their Sonoma home, because her husband was still suspicious about her and Hammett from those long-ago days in the 1920s. She didn't know she had served as a major literary inspiration—and had never read *The Maltese Falcon!*

During these early years he was trying to write—fiction, poetry, fact pieces, criticism—and had his first crime story published in 1922; in 1923 his first Continental Op story was published in *Black Mask*. During this brief eight-year creative burst in San Francisco (1923–1930), he turned out four novels (*Red Harvest, The Dain Curse, The Maltese Falcon,* and *The Glass Key*), and an even sixty short stories and novelettes.

His fiction made him the unquestioned master of detective-story fiction and made a lasting impression on American letters. But the 1934 publication by Knopf of his fifth novel, *The Thin Man,* virtually marked the end of his creative career: during his last 27 years he wrote a few book reviews, a few radio scripts and motion picture rewrites, and for a few months the continuity of the Alex Raymond–drawn comic strip, *Secret Agent X-9.*

During WW II, Hammett again served in the army, this time in the Aleutian Islands where he edited a post newspaper that has since become famous in its own right. After the war, he was hounded by HUAC—House Unamerican Activities Committee—commie-hunters in Congress, and jailed for contempt by refusing to state whether he was a member of the Communist Party and because he said he "didn't know" the names of any card-carrying Communists. This jail-time gave him emphysema, which completed the destruction of his health begun during his Army service in WW I.

During subsequent testimony before the Senate came the famous exchange between Hammett and "Tail-Gunner" Joe McCarthy, the red-baiting Senator who almost destroyed the American system of government. McCarthy asked, "If you were me, Mr. Hammett, would you allow your books to be on the shelves of American libraries?" To which Hammett replied, "If I were you, Senator, I wouldn't allow there to be any American libraries."

He died in 1961 in the home of his long-time consort, Lillian Hellman.

Many theories have been advanced for Hammett's long creative silence. Some say his chronic alcoholism destroyed his ability to work; others that his ill-health did the same thing.

More pragmatic observers like San Francisco private detective David Fechheimer, one of the country's great Hammett experts—he even has X-rays of Hammett's teeth—disagree. Fechheimer feels that Hammett was earning huge amounts of money ($60,000–$75,000 a year) from rights, royalties, and residuals during the 1930s and 1940s when federal income taxes were idiosyncratic at best and a very good income was $2,000 year. So why should he write?

Writers know very well why he should write even though he didn't need the money: for a writer, it is impossible not at least to try. The best argument against the "why write?" theory is that during many of those years he was trying desperately to complete a non-mystery novel called *Tulip* of which a sizeable fragment exists. I know Bill Nolan disagrees with me on this, but I find the fragment, about a writer trying to write anything but compelling.

My own theory about the long silence is what I call the "*Mr. Roberts* Syndrome." *Mr. Roberts* was a Pulitzer-Prize winning play and subsequent high-grossing movie by Thomas Heggen about Heggen's adventures on a non-combat naval vessel during World War II. The trouble for the very-successful Heggen was that the only thing he had to write about was his wartime experiences. He hadn't had any other experiences, but the imperative to write was still there. So he drowned himself, if I remember correctly, in his bathtub.

I think a variant of this is what happened to Hammett's career as a novelist. When he left San Francisco in 1930 for the big bucks and bigtime of Hollywood and then New York, he was riding the crest: he had created a new kind of American fiction. In Hollywood he met Hellman and her circle of friends who all considered detective fiction low-class and definitely not "literature"—in quotes, of course.

The irony is that Hammett was already being recognized as a major American novelist, but because he was a Pinkerton op moving in a smart set with radically different concerns, he came to have contempt for what he had been writing about and for himself. The *Tulip* fragment bears poignant testimony to the fact that he couldn't write about anything that wasn't rooted in his Pinkerton experiences.

His solution was to write nothing at all. Instead of drowning himself, he drowned his talent.

The urge to write remained, of course, so he poured his creativity into Lillian Hellman's plays. There are many critics who claim they can isolate huge hunks of Hellman's work which actually were written by Hammett; there is no doubt that his finger-prints are all over her plays.

I find it significant in the extreme that while Hellman wrote extensively after Hammett's death—memoirs, screenplays, adaptations, and translations of European dramatists—she never wrote another original play of her own after his death in 1961. So far as I know, not even a single scene of her own.

Could the disapproval of the literati really carry such weight with someone struggling to be a writer? Well, in 1955, when I wanted to do my Master's Thesis at Stanford on the stories of Hammett, Chandler, and Macdonald, I was informed by the University that since these stories were not literature, obviously graduate papers could not be written about them. I took comfort from the fact that back about 300 years, the Bodleian Library of Oxford University refused shelf room to the manuscripts of William Shakespeare's plays on the same grounds.

The term most often applied to the hard-boiled detective novel, even today, is "realistic." The writer is primarily a creator, not a commentator. He is less concerned with realism in a literary sense than with reality in a literal sense. Realism is a word that critics and reviewers love—John Mason Brown rhetorically asks, "If realism isn't real, then isn't it trash?"

Mike Avallone has always called critics "one-legged runners" and there are many of us who would say he is not in every instance wrong. Anyway, let's look at the critics' "realism" for a moment. Realism of character is very far from Lillian Hellman's sort of hothouse creations—I think Hammett's help to her was more in the way of construction of scene and movement of story than in *whom* she chose to write about.

Realism in its best sense equals truth; and ironically it was perhaps that element in Hammett's work that Hellman's friends—and many critics—scorned. But it is that truth which makes his work so seminal and successful. Fiction's truth takes what is there and refines it until the very essence of truth—more true than fact itself—is there on the page.

Of course in some ways, realism is subjective—as any judge learns from listening to eyewitnesses of the same event. On the other hand, real people look, dress, and act in certain ways; when they talk, they talk in certain ways. It is the writer's job, whatever his subjective feelings, to take these true elements of real people and heighten and shape them without losing the underlying reality.

Never easy to do. It is a commonly held maxim that artistic realism is the miner's canary of a civilization: extreme realism in sculpture and drama marked the beginning of the decline for both the Greek and Roman empires. Could it be that a coarsened realism that anticipates artistic decline is emotional? That the writers begin to believe that the emotion surrounding the reality is the reality itself?

Anyway, such extreme realism (as is often seen in today's novels, film, and television) gives a certain hard reality to Hemingway's off-hand comment about New York when he was hand-delivering a manuscript to Knopf. In his hotel room he found that the row of books on the shelf were only fake backs of books, and said, "I think we are an outfit on the way out."

Let's stick with Hemingway for a moment. He once wrote of Mark Twain:

All modern American literature comes from one book by Mark Twain called *Huckleberry Finn* . . . it's the best book we've had. All American writing comes from that. There was nothing before. There has been nothing as good since.

My wife Dori would give *Moby Dick* the honor of the Great American Novel; I'd split the honor between the two. I think the Great American Novel has to appear every fifty years or so anyway, because society keeps changing.

There is a whole school of literary thought, by the way, that believes Ernest Hemingway was a major literary influence on Hammett. However, the late Lee Wright, mystery editor for many years at Random House, always held that Hemingway learned his clipped, precise style from Hammett. Indeed, in *Death in the Afternoon*, Hemingway remarks that his wife is reading *The Dain Curse* ("Hammett's bloodiest yet") aloud to him. Of course in one of the Op short stories a woman the Op interviews is reading *The Sun Also Rises*. Tit for tat.

But I still agree with Lee Wright. Hammett, flat broke in San Francisco, would have had no access to Hemingway's earlier stuff published only in Europe. Furthermore, he had been appearing in *Black Mask* for two years before Hemingway's first collection of short stories, *In Our Time,* was published by Scribner's in 1925.

It is the writer's job as *writer* to chronicle life as he sees it, as Twain chronicled life on the Mississippi, as Melville chronicled life on a New Beford whaler, rather than directly comment on it. His subjective appraisal of that reality he is interpreting will seep through—as Twain's and Melville's did—because the writer is always concerned with the *real*—as opposed to the *realistic*. English novelist John Braine says, in a discussion of Charles Dickens' work:

An intense concern for the real—that's what the novel is all about. It starts with a passionate and devouring interest in things as they are.

So are Hammett's detective stories "real"? Is any hard-boiled detective novel "real"? When I started writing, Hammett, Chandler, and Macdonald were the gods of the hard-boiled field. If you wanted to write in this genre, you had to read these men; and if you read them, you found in their works—despite the necessities of genre—all the hallmarks of fine literature: economy of expression, creation of character with a few bold strokes, realistic depiction of milieu, and sentiment without sentimentality. Raymond Chandler wrote of Hammett:

Hammett was spare, hard-boiled, but he did over and over what only the best writers can ever do at all. He wrote scenes that seemed never to have been written before.

The private eye tale, as created in the 1920s and developed in the 1930s, faced a special challenge because of the English countryside murder mysteries so epitomised by the wonderful novels of Dame Agatha. The American private eye tale had to put fictional murder back where it realistically belongs, in a dark alley at three in the morning. It had to do this while being coarse, gutty, tough, and gritty—or it wouldn't sell to its primary market, the pulps. Again, it is Raymond Chandler, writing of himself and his fellow writers at *Black Mask,* who puts it best:

We were trying to get murder away from the upper classes, the week-end house party and the vicar's rose garden, and back to the people who are really good at it.

Detective novels present the writer with very specialized problems. First, the mystery or detective novel demands a *plot.* And I don't mean the loosely-knit tapestry a mainstream novelist can get away with—500 pages of navel-gazing doesn't cut it. The mystery demands a tightly-knit series of causes and effects. There is a stern logic involved here that, if ignored, will destroy the effectiveness of the novel.

Second, while demanding this tightly-knit series of causes and effects, the mystery also demands a compression of many of the essential dimensions of the story. Something—in the hard-boiled tale a lot of somethings—has to be happening all the time. Often at the *same* time.

Raymond Chandler put it this way: "The detective story deliberately outrages probability by telescoping time and space."

And how's this for a killer: the James Brady novel *Six Days of the Condor* becomes *Three Days of the Condor* as a Robert Redford film. Ruthless telescoping of time and space. And hey, wait a minute! The Faye Dunaway character was a *photographer!* With a telephoto lens! Oh, reductions within reductions!

So what does a writer do if he wishes to be at once mysterious and realistic? How to give a "flat response," as they sometimes like to say in the music field, while at the same time being evocative and compelling? Why is *The Maltese Falcon* so much more real—and to my mind readable—than *The Unpleasantness at the Bellona Club?* What did Hammett do that Dorothy L. Sayers did not?

Very simply, in Hammett's work the people are real even when his plot is full of twists and turns, even if the time and space in which these events take place is outrageously telescoped. Hammett's characters and the backgrounds against which they move are meticulously true to life.

The reader feels that these things *could* happen to these people, maybe even are *likely* to happen to them. The author cheats not in what happens, but in making it happen in a few days, rather than months or years, and in making it happen here and now in a single case rather than on a dozen different investigations in a dozen different places.

This balancing act, this uneasy alliance between plot and incessant action on the one hand, and character, setting, and atmosphere on the other, is the true art and accomplishment of the hard-boiled detective story. Understanding this is the key to understanding the literary form Hammett created. As Fred Dannay (under the Ellery Queen pseudonym he shared with his cousin, Manny Lee) writes:

> We would not label Hammett a "realist" and merely let it go at that. . . . We would call him a "romantic realist". . . . The secret is in Hammett's method.

Hammett tells his modern fables in *terms* of realism. . . . His *stories* are the stuff of dreams; his *characters* are the flesh-and-blood of reality. . . .

Okay. We've got it. Romantic realist. But wait a minute. There were other private eye writers before and after Hammett just as realistic in character and setting, just as masterful of time and story, just as fanciful in plot and purpose. What made Hammett somehow stand out? What made his, apart from Hemingway's and Chandler's very different prose styles, the most emulated style of story-telling in American letters? How did he turn the crude stuff bequeathed him by Carroll John Daly into lasting literature?

Howard Haycraft, writing about Hammett, almost gets it— but doesn't understand the point he himself is making. He says:

Because of their startling originality, the Hammett novels virtually defy exegesis even today. . . . As straightaway detective stories they can hold their own with the best. They are also character studies of close to top rank in their own right, and are penetrating if shocking novels of manners as well. . . .

Then, merely in passing, Haycraft also notes that Hammett was for eight years a field operative with the Pinkerton Detective Agency. He adds off-handedly:

It was this last experience . . . which principally gave him the backgrounds and many of the characters for his stories. . . .

What Haycraft fails to realize, or at least fails to state, is that Hammett was writing about a different set of manners: those of the hunter and the hunted. The mores he was examining were those of the criminals he knew—and hunted. *Hunted.* No other writer before Hammett had been a manhunter. His detective experience gave Hammett a *mind-set* that no other writer of his day, and damned few of ours, has had.

His novels stand or fall by the quality of their detectives *as detectives*. This is what sets Sam Spade and The Op apart from other detective heroes. Hammett was to stress this in his introduction to the Modern Library edition of *The Maltese Falcon*:

Spade . . . is what most private detectives I worked with would like to have been and what quite a few of them in their cockier moments thought they approached. A hard, shifty fellow, able to take care of himself in any situation, able to get the best of anybody . . . whether criminal, innocent bystander or client.

David Fechheimer, my nominee for today's most creative, off-beat, and successful real-life private detective, remarks, in the

Preface to the gorgeous North Point Press edition of *The Maltese Falcon,* that:

> The San Francisco I live and work in as a detective is still Spade's city. . . .
> Just as Joyce created Dublin, Hammett created San Francisco. The City is not
> just a setting for the novel; it is a character, flowing through the dialogue like
> fog. . . . Looking again at *The Maltese Falcon,* a story about a detective written by
> a former detective, from my perspective as a detective, I see the authenticity of
> Spade's character and the plausibility of the details.

This stubborn hewing to the reality of the private detective, based on his own Pinkerton experiences, is what sets Hammett's central character apart from all who went before and all who were to come after. No matter how exotic and fanciful his plots, he never abandoned that reality. Not because he was worried about Literature with a capital *L.* He was worried about the rent.

He was not a writer learning about private detection in order to create a detective hero; he was a detective learning about writing in order to make a living. This meant that as he wrote, he retained the detective's subconscious attitudes toward life. It is this subconscious state of mind, I believe, that separated his work from that of Chandler or Macdonald and their followers. The stories he told were about *real* private eyes, because real private eyes were what he knew about most intimately, and the reading public recognized it instantly.

But not necessarily the critics. According to Leo Gurko, the fictional private eye is:

> A variant of the tough guy . . . (a) sensual and utterly amoral man who, like the
> males in Hemingway, lives by the quickness of his reflexes rather than by the
> keenness of his intelligence. . . . He makes love to three or four sexually mag-
> netic women, consumes four or five quarts of hard liquor, smokes cartons of cig-
> arettes, is knocked on the head, shot, bruised in fist fights from seven to ten
> times—while groping through a dense fog as far as breaking the case. . . .

Well, all right, okay so far. We certainly all have met this chap Gurko describes. But then he goes on:

> This unstained biological egotism, in its literary context, is best seen in . . .
> Dashiell Hammett's *The Maltese Falcon.* Its central figure, Sam Spade, is a charac-
> teristic specimen.

Sutherland Scott expands upon the theme with the same carelessness of observation and analysis:

> Sam Spade . . . is father to all the tough private investigators. . . . he loves and
> leaves his women with catholic abandon; he must be held responsible for the
> bottle in the desk drawer. . . . *The Maltese Falcon* introduces the inevitable fat,
> sinister man. . . . There is also the usual collection of seductive blondes and
> brunettes. . . .

Let's measure the foregoing criticisms against the novel ourselves and see where it takes us. Gurko's stupid, punchdrunk, alcoholic, chain-smoking letcher bears no resemblance to Sam Spade at all. Or to *The Maltese Falcon,* a subtle novel of intrigue and innuendo, things half-understood, half-seen through San Francisco's pervasive fog.

True, Spade takes guns away from Joel Cairo and the murderous youth, Wilmer Cook—but he gives them back again. He is punched in the face by a cop once, is drugged by Casper Gutman and kicked in the head by Wilmer. He shoots nobody, he does not even carry a gun. Four men are murdered in *The Maltese Falcon,* none of them on-camera, none of them by Spade. He is smarter than anyone else in the novel, and he outwits everybody—cops and bad guys alike.

Spade's office is small, but it is not shabby. It is a suite of rooms and is not, when the book opens, a one-man office. The appearance of Spade's office bottle of booze is of such startling brevity that it deserves quotation in full here:

Spade . . . took a bottle of Manhattan cocktail and paper drinking cups from a desk-drawer. He filled the cup two-thirds full, drank, returned the bottle to the drawer, tossed the cup into the wastebasket. . . .

Spade is not celibate, but he is hardly a satyr. He has had an affair in the past with Iva Archer, his partner's wife, but that is finished as far as Spade is concerned. We catch a glimpse of Brigid O'Shaughnessy asleep in Spade's bed, but nothing more than that. Many assume that Spade has been sleeping with his secretary, Effie Perrine, but there is no evidence of this at all. The only other attractive woman in the book is Rhea Gutman, daughter of Spade's fat antagonist. Spade does no more than impatiently walk her around a hotel room to get knock-out drops out of her system so he can question her.

Are the antagonists in detective stories as crude and rude as the critics would have them? Is Casper Gutman so sinister? By any objective appraisal, he is a bumbler. So much so, in fact, that Spade at one point scowls at him and bursts out irritably:

Jesus God! Is this the first thing you guys ever stole? You're a fine lot of lollipops! What are you going to do next—get down and pray?

Those Gutman hires betray him; Spade outwits him; when he finally possesses the black bird he has spent seventeen years of his life pursuing, it is a worthless lead substitute; and in the

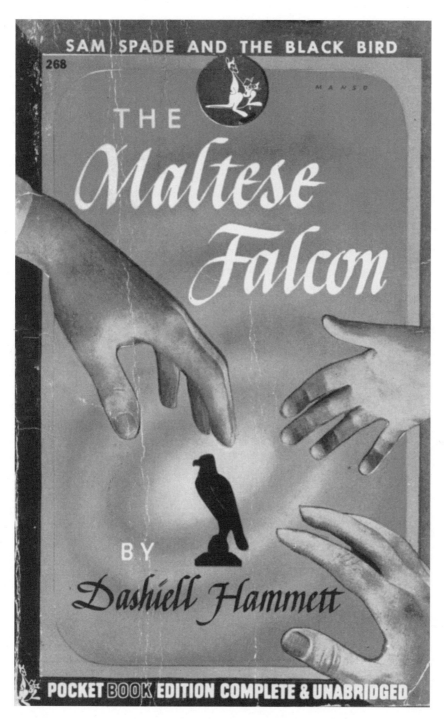

Front cover for the first paperback edition of *The Maltese Falcon*

end, worst bumble of all, he is shot dead by Wilmer. Is Gutman a master criminal, or is he Everyman—Gutman, after all, literally means Good Man—with his impossibly, hopelessly romantic quest? If so, isn't his portrayal a throw-away bit of virtuosity that scorns the capital *L* in favor of a compelling story and an unforgettable character?

As for the charge of unstained biological egotism, Spade solves the crimes by using his intellect and his knowledge of human nature, not his fists or his guns, and turns both of the murderers over to the police. And they are the actual murderers. No one is framed. Justice is done—deliberately—by Samuel Spade, Esq.

When Hammett published the first Continental Op story in the October 1, 1923, *Black Mask*—a rural tale called *Arson Plus*—he did not, as is so often thought, create the American tough private eye in fiction. That distinction, if such it can be called, must go to Carroll John Daly, who fathered Race Williams and Terry Mack. But it is instructive to glance at Daly's work for a moment. Here we meet Race Williams in *Knights of the Open Palm:*

> "Race Williams, Private Investigator," that's what the gilt letters spell across the door on my office. As for my business; I'm what you might call a middle-man—just a halfway house between the dicks and the crooks. It don't mean nothing, but the police have been looking me over so much lately that I really need a place to receive them.

Daly was never one to abandon a good thing. When we meet his other private eye, Terry Mack, we might notice a certain similarity of phrasing and content:

> So for my line, I have a little office which says "Terry Mack, Private Investigator," on the door; which means whatever you wish to think it. I'm in the center of a triangle; between the crook and the police and the victim. The police have had an eye on me for some time, but only an eye, never a hand; they don't get my lay at all.

Both pieces were written in 1923, and Terry Mack and Race Williams are, perhaps, distant uncles to Sam Spade and the Continental Op. But anyone who has read Hammett's work—or even seen John Huston's superb adaptation of *The Maltese Falcon*—can see how unique and far from these precedents Hammett's hero was.

In analysing this hero, it is well to remember that Sam Spade appeared in only one novel and three indifferent short stories from the closing years of Hammett's creative surge. The Continental Op, on the other hand, appeared in two novels and 29 short stories. The Op is the fictional distillation of the genuine article. He is, above all, a superb detective. He is a better detective than Spade, because he does not get emotionally involved. Ellery Queen points out:

The Continental Op might easily be Sam Spade's older brother. He's just as hard, just as hardbitten, just as hard-boiled. A less spectacular workman at times (but only at times), he is equally efficient as a manhunter.

More efficient, in fact. The Op stories are a condensed course in the techniques of detection. He is more physical than Spade, and his San Francisco is filled with more underworld types than Spade's. Of course Spade has a one-man office, while The Op is a fieldman in the Continental Detective Agency's San Francisco office. No affairs with Iva Archers for the Op; he barely exists outside his work.

In this he is distressingly like a real agency detective. When I was a young field agent with the L. A. Walker Company, I might, in a single month, be sent to work in Eureka, Vallejo, San Francisco, Oakland, San Jose, Fresno, Bakersfield, and Palm Springs. If working out of DKA's head office in San Francisco, I would average 5,000 miles a month in my car without ever leaving the city. Everything except work, including eating, sleeping, and socializing, was on a catch-as-catch-can basis.

It is the Op who makes Hammett's art so seminal to the literary tradition that he founded. And it is to the Op, tough, pragmatic, not imaginative but with a detective's highly-developed intuition concerning his cases, that we must turn if we are to understand the very real detective that Hammett himself must have become during his Pinkerton years.

What are the characteristics of the Hammett detective? First he's a man both mentally and physically competent in his job. Spade is more cerebral than the Op: he tends to think or talk himself out of sticky situations. The Op tends to find a more physical solution to his problems. Here he is at work in *The Whosis Kid:*

I twisted around, kicking the Frenchman's face. Loosened one arm. Caught one of his. His other hand gouged at my face. . . . Clawing fingers tore at my mouth. I put my teeth in them and kept them there. One of my knees was on his face. I put my weight on it. My teeth were still in his hand. Both of my hands were free to get his other hand. Not nice, this work, but effective.

As I have said, Sam Spade doesn't even carry a gun. He tends more to take them away from other people. The Op, doing his work on the pulp pages of *Black Mask,* also tries to avoid gunplay; but if he has to use his gun, he makes sure he has whatever edge he can get so his gun will be effective. In a totally black apartment with a man who wants him dead, the Op crawls silently into the bedroom. Why? Only one door. The other man has to come through that door to get him. So. . .

I . . . felt for my watch, propped it on the sill, in the angle between door and frame. I wriggled back from it until I was six or eight feet away, looking diagonally across the doorway at the watch's luminous dial. The phosphorescent numbers could not be seen from the other side of the door. . . . On my belly, my gun cocked, its butt steady on the floor, I waited for the faint light to be blotted out.

Unlike the stereotyped private eye of fiction, Hammett's detective lone-wolfs it only when he has to. Spade uses Effie Perine for legwork whenever possible; consults a lawyer on legal angles; pumps Tom Polhaus of the local police for information; and shamelessly talks hotel dicks into rousting people he doesn't like and searching hotel rooms for him.

The Op is even less inclined to work alone. He brings in other operatives, he brings in the police, he uses any routine which promises to grind out the answers he needs. Above all else, the Hammett detective—especially the Op—is dogged.

In *The Scorched Face* there is more real investigative procedure in one page than will be found in most complete private eye novels. The Op sets out to make a list that he hopes will establish a pattern of linked suicides among the upper stratus of wealthy San Francisco women. Let him describe the process:

We spent all the afternoon and most of the night getting the list . . . it looked like a hunk of the telephone book. . . . We could check off most of the names against what the police department had already learned of them. . . . The remainder we split into two classes . . . the second list was longer than I had expected, or hoped. There were six suicides in it, three murders, and 21 disappearances. . . . For four days I ground this list. I hunted, found, questioned, and investigated friends and relatives. Three times I drew yesses. . . .

I had the names and addresses of 62 friends of the Banbrock girls. I set about getting the same sort of catalogue on the three women. . . . Fortunately, there were two or three operatives in the office with nothing else to do just then.

We got something.

Can you imagine Mike Hammer doing that? Or even Philip Marlowe? But it is what real detectives do all the time. I spent my first week at L. A. Walker Company running down forty-two people at 122 different addresses in San Francisco. The last address was in Colma. In the cemetery. The absconder had died six months before he was assigned to me.

Dave Kikkert, my boss and later my partner at DKA, had known the man was dead when he assigned me the case. It takes a certain mentality and blind determination to pursue a maze of conflicting leads with the relish and certainty of a beagle after a rabbit when in reality nothing is certain. That would be a drawback in most professions, but Dave knew it is a plus to a detective. And Hammett, instead of growing softer and more fanciful as he matured as a writer, dug deeper into the reality of detection.

Although Hammett's detectives are on the side of the law, like contemporary detectives they are not scrupulously law-abiding. They have been hired to do a certain thing, discover a certain fact or object. There are municipal, county, state, federal agencies, and legislative bodies constantly churning out laws and regulations—many directly contradictory to the others. So if a detective must bend the law, well—so be it. Any detective who observed them all would get very little done.

At DKA our motto—unspoken by the field men except among ourselves—was "a felony a week whether we need it or not." Hammett's detectives, in an age when weaker law-enforcement agencies were all jealous of their own turf, have a much wider latitude of action than do private eyes of today. They break the law constantly, sometimes with deadly results. Almost everything the Op does to bring Poisonville to the boil in *Red Harvest* is illegal. He lies, cheats, suborns, even kills. It is not unreasonable to assume his actions are based on those of real operatives.

In *$106,000 Blood Money*, the Op learns that another operative has sold out to the baddies and that only one of the baddies who knows about the sell-out is still alive. He arranges that both operative and baddie are shot down and killed.

In *Zigzags of Treachery* he sends a blackmailer out to face the police with a gun the Op knows has a broken firing pin.

These stories all combine Hammett's superb imagination with the countless cases he worked as a Pinkerton Op; it is impossible to tell where fact ends and creative invention

THE *TLS* ASSESSMENT

Mr Hammett has not published a novel for more than 16 years, and it is to be hoped that he will soon complete the major work on which he is rumoured to be engaged; for at his worst he has provided us always with entertainment, while at his best he is an artist intent on presenting his intensely personal vision, in terms of action rather than psychology, of the violent, cruel and treacherous world we live in to-day.

"A Man Called Hammett," *Times Literary Supplement* (London), 17 November 1950, p. 728.

begins, and it matters little. What emerges rings with truth.

Hammett's detective goes by his gut feelings. Spade tells the fat man of Wilmer Cook:

Keep that gunsel away from me. . . . I'll kill him. I don't like him. He makes me nervous. I'll kill him the first time he gets in my way. I won't give him an even break. I won't give him a chance. I'll kill him.

In the end, of course, it is Wilmer who does the killing. Of the fat man. So Spade was right about him. Hammett's detective does not believe in chivalry, does not give the other fellow (or woman) an even break. Spade turns the killer of Miles Archer over to the police no matter what it costs him personally. The Op does the same thing with Princess Zhukovski in *The Gutting of Couffignal*.

The Op is ruthless—or merely realistic?—in *Fly Paper* when he must stop a huge criminal named Babe McCloor. The Babe is not at all intimidated by the Op's gun.

"I can still get to you with slugs in me."

"Not where I'll put them. . . . If you think smashed kneecaps are a lot of fun, give it a whirl."

"Hell with that," he said, and charged.

I shot his right knee.

He lurched toward me.

I shot his left knee.

He tumbled down.

"You would have it," I complained.

He twisted around, and with his arms pushed himself into a sitting position facing me.

"I didn't think you had sense enough to do it," he said through his teeth.

This passage may no longer represent a private detective's life, but even today it has a symbolic truth. And it was real for the tough-guy street culture of Hammett's day. As an *amateur* student of paleoanthropology, I must make a case for the accuracy of Hammett's perception of the nature of man.

Spade and the Op not only put the job first, they like the job. I've read and enjoyed many contemporary detective writers who make their detective heroes somber men or women who dislike themselves and their work, but these are not Hammett's detectives, nor are they real detectives. Both of them derive much of their enjoyment from their job, and take a lot of pride in it. As the Op says in one of the stories:

I'm a detective because I happen to like the work. . . . And liking work makes you want to do it as well as you can. Otherwise there'd be no sense to it. . . . In the past 18 years I've been getting my fun out of chasing crooks and solving riddles. . . . and I can't imagine a pleasanter future than 20-some years more of it.

It seems to me that human nature hasn't changed too much in the genus Homo's 2.7 million year history. We are here today because a great many of us enjoyed the hunt and were very good at it; and a great many of us still enjoy the hunt. I have read and enjoyed many mysteries in which the detectives are strongly motivated by empathy and a desire to better society, but I think Spade and the Op know all too well that the fellow to whom you give the even break will often be the one who gets you.

One of our field agents was run off by a Lutheran minister with a loaded double-barreled shotgun, and the next day the same man of God tried to run me down with his car.

I think that in our deepest nature we all know the game, because we are all descended from survivors. But we don't want to think about this dark side of ourselves, and if we're lucky we won't have to. The detective, on the other hand, lives it every day, and he knows he is not always going to be popular with those around him.

When a character in *The Dain Curse* looks at the Op "as if I were something there ought to be a law against," and says sarcastically, "I hope you're satisfied with the way your work got done," the Op replies, "It got done."

The manhunter—real-life, or Hammett's—is, frankly, not concerned with truth in the abstract, only with enough truth to do the job he has been hired to do. Nora Charles complains of this at the end of *The Thin Man,* when Nick says to her:

"Now, are you satisfied with what we've got on him?"

"Yes, in a way. There seems to be enough of it, but it's not very neat."

"It's neat enough to send him to the chair," I said, "And that's all that counts."

Again, it is Hammett himself who most neatly sums up his detective when he writes of the Op:

I see him . . . a little man going forward day after day through mud and blood and death and deceit—as callous and brutal and cynical as necessary—toward a dim goal, with nothing to push or pull him to it except he's been hired to reach it.

When you're a manhunter, that goal is seeking out other human beings and taking from them something they treasure—their illusions, their gold, their freedom, perhaps only their chattels, perhaps their greatest treasure, life itself—and doing it dispassionately. It's all part of the job. In *The Maltese Falcon* is a passage I have often seen quoted, but which none of the commentators has really understood. Spade is talking with Brigid in the famous closing moments of the book:

Don't be too sure I'm as crooked as I'm supposed to be. That kind of reputation might be good business—bringing in high-priced jobs and making it easier to deal with the enemy.

The Enemy. Right there is the core of Hammett's detective hero. The man he is tracking is *The Enemy.* The detective's pride, indeed his own estimation of his worth as a man, derives in part from his assessment of himself as a manhunter. Hunting *The Enemy.* Hammett's detective has the pitiless knowledge that when he faces *The Enemy*, it is going to come down to *him* or *me.*

Only one of them will walk away from it a whole person.

This is the detective Hammett has bequeathed us. A proud, independent, crafty, intelligent, tough, hard-minded protagonist who closely mirrors the ideal real-life investigator. Whether he is a scoundrel or a hero depends upon who hires him and the context within which history places his work.

For myself, I am grateful that Hammett, the detective who yearned to write, took the lumpy, unformed clay he was handed, and molded it into a new ideal, found in it the hard, clear fossil of our essential nature, without embellishment. It is not that the writers who follow him can't embellish and improve on his model; we can, and we must. But I'm glad that Samuel Dashiell Hammett went straight to the complicated heart of our most ancient nature to mold a new reality for American letters.

John Paterson, "A Cosmic View of the Private Eye," *Saturday Review* (22 August 1953): 7–8, 31–33.

Sam Spade, the hardboiled hero of Dashiell Hammett's "The Maltese Falcon," in a rare moment of weakness permitted his readers an oblique insight into his motivation as a human being. He told the story of Flitcraft. "Flitcraft," he said "had been a good citizen and a good husband and father, not by any outer compulsion, but simply because he was a man who was most comfortable in step with his surroundings." One day passing an office building under construction he was narrowly missed by a beam that fell ten stories. In the moment he realized that he had based his life on false assumptions. He had assumed that life "was a clean orderly sane responsible affair"; he now discovered that "he, the good citizen-husband-father, could be wiped out between office and restaurant by the accident of a falling beam." That afternoon he found it necessary suddenly and mysteriously to abandon his family, his business, and his community.

He had, of course, his reasons. He had seen life with the lid taken off and he had acted accordingly. He had dissociated himself from the clean orderly life he had known and begun his readjustment to a world in which beams fell.

This fable explains, I think, the revolt of the hardboiled wing led by Hammett in the Twenties and Raymond Chandler in the Thirties against the practitioners of the historic detective story. For the society postulated by the older school, which flourished in the Twenties and which has continued to flourish in spite of the schism, resembles in its essentials the staid, comfortable, secure society of the pre-1914 period, the period before the beams begin to fall. In the age of the Boom, the Great Depression, flappers, gangsterism, and the Fascist Solution it recalls the sober gentility and crude optimism of an earlier and more complacent generation; it asserts the triumph of a social order and decorum that have all but passed away. It is the virtue of the insurgent wing, on the other hand, that it attempts more closely to approximate the central experience of the age, the experience of a war epoch, of an age of transition in which men are less confident of their values and their motives, less pleased with the society they have constructed.

Thus two worlds, two notions of society, are represented in the detective fiction of our day: the one embodied in the pompous and transcendent sleuth, the other in the grim and badly battered private dick. To understand them is to understand something of the social and cultural climate of our period.

The first thing to be said about the transcendent detective is that he functions in a closed, controlled, and static universe. It is a world in which things do not happen, they have already happened; it is a world that does not admit the adventitious; it is a world from which all but the most counterfeit human emotions have been banished. Its people need not *become,* they need only *be;* its hero need not *do,* he needs only *interpret.* It is therefore in miniature a kind of timeless and unchanging universe such as long geometricians and men with a weakness for order might dream of. Reducible to mathematical law and formula and therefore predictable, it is eminently suited for the operations of the serene and confident intelligence. Closed, untouched by the shouting in the streets, it yields easily to the mastery of the single and transcendent mind. It holds no final secrets. It is marked, therefore, by an unswerving optimism, for it contains nothing that cannot be remedied and explained. It is that very rarest of worlds, a world that is not so complicated that it cannot be solved.

Nothing could disturb for long the fierce immutability of such a world, the operation of its stringent laws, the clarity of its light. Not the ludicrous appearance of its blood-bespattered dummy or the shrieks of its paper-thin heroine. It is the complicated day-dream of the twentieth-century citizen. For it resembles the kind of world he would like to believe he lived in— where beams do not have the habit of falling.

The world of the private detective, however, is something else altogether. For dangerously open and dynamic as it is, charged with fear and change, it is the world we recognize everywhere around us. It is the place where things happen and people act, and where the things that happen and the people that act are not predictable. It is the place of violent and irrational human behavior, a region where law and formula do not apply. It is the place where people could not possibly say, "A mathematical deduction from facts can never be false." They would be more likely to say, "If I knew everything I'd never want to turn the lights off at night." It is not, therefore, susceptible to the workings of the radiant and all-powerful mind, and he who would master it must bring with him qualities other than those of the intellect. Certainly it is a world within whose unhappy boundaries infallibility and total success are so implausible as to be ridiculous. Hence, if the universe of the transcendent detective has the elements of a day-dream, the universe of the private eye has all the naked intensity of a nightmare. It is preeminently the place where beams fall.

Splendid as he is, the transcendent sleuth has about him little of the unique other than his superb intelligence and an endearing eccentricity or two, like a passion for orchids or for the violin (a touch of whimsy that suggests that even a god may stoop to human pleasures). Perfectly at home in the vicarage, the country house, and the walnut-paneled study, he is virtually indistinguishable in his values and his sympathies from the middle-class men and women he has agreed to relieve, whose enchantingly small and ordered world he has elected to safeguard. For he generally derives from the professional classes, the doctors, the lawyers, the university professors, or from the ranks of the leisured upper classes who find in crime and its detection a satisfactory and a socially useful hobby. And in everything he reveals this derivation. If he does express, on occasion, a contempt for the bumbling ineffectuality of the police authorities and for his obtuse and boyishly admiring foil, who stands for a rather vacant humanity, it is on the whole a friendly contempt, and there is, in fact, in his relations with the staid little inspector and other members of a hapless humankind something of the spirit of *noblesse oblige*. But certainly he is, and never doubts that he is, on the side of the angels. And although it is certain to require articulation—the transcendent sleuth acts upon the assumption that society is basically sound, its laws admirable and crime a wicked aberration.

The transcendent sleuth then has been, for all his arrogant power, a member of the professional classes; he has had a stake in the community and has been understood to sympathize with its ideals. But the private detective, in the parlance of his world the shamus, has no real community. He is the symbol of the isolated individual who, in the sense that he has been estranged from the community rather than banished from it, is an exile. He speaks for men who have lost faith in the values of their society.

His professional and social status is in the highest degree anomalous. In his capacity of private detective he is the member of a craft not wholly accepted, a craft barely tolerated by the authorities; and we are allowed to suspect that he has had some friendly and profitable association with the underworld. His methods tend frequently to be unorthodox and are not, in fact, substantially different from those of his less-idealistic antagonists. He has neither the certitude nor the sanctity of the great omniscient; he occupies the dim uneasy region that lies between right and wrong, between the legitimately constituted social order and the rapacious criminal underworld. He trusts neither the one nor the other and is himself not trusted by either party. Hence he cannot ally himself to any recognized class, authority, or institution within the social framework; for guilt and innocence are not immediately, if ever, identifiable, and he must be guided by the grimmest skepticism.

He is moving in a bewildering world of disintegrated values where evil cannot be isolated and destroyed as it could be in the fairy-tale world of the transcendent sleuth. Here in the tangled web of crime and corruption, and playboy and police chief, businessman and thug, killer and political boss are joined in one general confraternity. No one is above suspicion. "We do not live," writes Chandler describing this gargoylish age, "in a fragrant world—gangsters can rule cities, perhaps even nations; a screen star can be the fingerman of a mob; the mayor of your town may have condoned murder as an instrument of money-making . . ."

Hence, for the private eye crime and guilt are coextensive with society itself, and in his person he expresses a fierce exasperation with and loathing for it. In this connection his frequent and bitter clashes with the official police force, with which the transcendent sleuth had always enjoyed friendly relations, take on a particular significance; for its faults are now no longer those of mere ineffectuality but also those of the very vice and corruption that characterize the "enemy" itself. If the transcendent sleuth, then, has acted upon the assumption that society justifies itself, the private detective acts upon the assumption that society is decadent and evil. And as he stands for the alienated of our time, his is the virtual declaration that the ends of the individual and the ends of society are no longer one.

Thus we remember him with pity and affection as a figure of intense and sometimes terrible loneliness, as the member of a soiled and disillusioned knighthood whose ordeal it is to assert himself on behalf of right—without even the luxury of knowing he is right. He is, in fact, and most of all in Dashiell Hammett's operative, the portrait of a primitive and animal dignity in the face of the particular viciousness and suffering of our age. For he ventures into the perverted and amoral universe of the twentieth century, into a place where gunmen will not sleep at night without covering the floor around their beds with crumpled newspaper, into a place where men can say, "I wanted it and I found it. I want it and I'm going to have it." And he triumphs in this world not because he is infallible, not because he is omniscient, but because he has pride, integrity, and courage. He is, in the final analysis, the apotheosis of the everyman of good will who, uncertain of his own values and certainly alienated by the values of his time, seeks desperately and mournfully to live without shame, to live without compromise to his integrity. He is everyman's romantic conception of himself: the glorification of toughness, irreverence, and a sense of decency too confused and almost half-ashamed to show itself.

For it is the character of this man that in the world this side of fiction he is generally ineffectual. He is subject to strange fears and anxieties, is seldom free of bitter memories of the cowardices and humiliations in the office, at him, and in the streets; and he is prone to make compromises and concessions by day that destroy his pride by night. In his identification, however, with the proud and immensely durable figure of the private detective he has his compensation: he is now the common man become suddenly, magically aggressive, become purified by righteous and legitimate anger—and become, at last, devastatingly effective. He is lonely, but he is proud; he is fallible, but he endures; he has suffered, but he has not surrendered his ideals; and if the cost to himself has been great, he has triumphed. Perhaps in the end he has gained nothing, changed nothing. There is always at the end of the hardboiled novel a moment of depression when the mission is completed, the enterprise ended, as if this little victory had cost too much in terms of human suffering. But there is always, too, the notion that human dignity and human integrity have somehow been vindicated, and that this has been worthwhile.

The first to appear in their field, Dashiell Hammett's Continental Op and his successor, Sam Spade, have not yet been surpassed—not even by Chandler's Philip Marlowe—in the hardboiled tradition of detective fiction. Hammett's hero is, first of all, most intensely the denizen of the dark borderland between good and evil. His disillusion and despair are more complete, his values more ambivalent, his loneliness and isolation more incurable than those of the young knights who will follow him. Certainly, he has none of the spiritual and intellectual fastidiousness of the pompous sleuth from whom he represents a departure, against whose world he stands as a reproach.

Small, hard-bitten, kind, and middle-aged, moved by some vague inner compulsion, he determines as the Continental Op in "Red Harvest" to rid a small Far-Western town of the organized criminal forces that have attached themselves to it. Entirely dependent upon his own resources, resources of integrity, intelligence, and courage, he seeks by sowing dissension among them to wreak their extermination. He is appalled, however, when he comes to take a grim and secret pleasure in this necessary carnage. "I've got a hard skin," he admits disconsolately, "all over what's left of my soul, and after twenty years of messing around with crime I can look at any sort of murder without seeing anything in it but my bread and butter, the day's work. But this getting a rear out of planning deaths is not natural to me. It's what this place has done to me." His dilemma is thus a familiar one. With the breakdown of legally constituted law and order, he, the lonely man of conscience, has assumed in his own small compact person the role of public judge and executioner. And having assumed this dangerous power and the terrible kind of freedom that accompanies it, he has also assumed all the loneliness and doubt of the individual who in a period of distress has only the authority of his own being to refer to.

Max Thursday, the hero of the Wade Miller stories, operates under a similar constraint. In "Guilty Bystander" he has been responsible for the death of six men and, though blameless from the point of view of law, suffers at the close under the fear that he has become spiritually brutalized. The sequel, "Fatal Step," describes among other things his desperate attempt to convince himself that he has escaped the infection—as it turns out, an abortive attempt, for he is forced, despite his willing otherwise, to kill, and the book closes down on his depression. "He held his face in hands, but between his fingers he could see the asphalt garishly painted by the howling fire. It was the color of blood."

In both the Continental Op and Max Thursday, then, the hunter himself is not sure, the hunter himself has been of the hunted. He thus carries in him the conscience of individuals not wholly convinced of the righteousness of their society, and the conscience of all men who, if they are not on the side of the devil, are not altogether sure, in the circumstances of a moral and social confusion, they are on the side of angels.

This is even more true of Hammett's Sam Spade, of the nature of whose allegiance we can never be absolutely sure. He reacts to the murder of his partner, for example, with a contented grin. "I think we've got a future," he tells his secretary, "I always had an idea that if Miles would go off and die somewhere we'd stand a better chance of thriving. Will you take care of sending flowers for me?" But we are never permitted to think too badly of him. For his fallen partner has proved to be none too savory a character, and the loyalty and admiration of his secretary, who is as artless and wholesome as any girl has a right to be, is never forfeited. Even the implications of Joel Cairo's words are not altogether to be trusted. This greedy and malicious homosexual had said at their first meeting, "I made somewhat extensive inquiries about you before taking any action and was assured that you were far too reasonable to allow other considerations to interfere with profitable business relations." But Spade will later say, "Don't be too sure I'm as crooked as I'm supposed to be. That kind of reputation might be good business—bringing in high-priced jobs and making it easier to deal with the enemy."

Even in context, however, we cannot be certain he means what he says. The best, and the least, that can be said is that we sympathize with him. For, appearances notwithstanding, we sense that he has acted upon some obscure impulse towards justice and decency which he could not name even if he would. He prefers, for example, to surrender to the police the murderess whom he happens to love rather than accept the love of a woman who happens to be a murderess. And, more significantly, when he gives his reasons—and he gives them, it must be said, only under duress of the moment—he names in a spirit of bitter mockery no less than eight. This more than anything else reveals his central character, marks him a child of the twentieth century, for it is clear that when a man has so many reasons to advance he is not really sure of any of them. He is not sure what his motives are.

The Continental Op – Sam Spade saga has no continuation. After the publication of "The Maltese Falcon" Hammett abdicated the literary scene, perhaps because he had exhausted the possibilities of his subject matter. Certainly the symbolism of his private eye has not since received more thorough exploitation, more vivid statement: alone he has invaded the predatory world of compulsive greed and dispassionate murder and has won what alone remains of victory—the personal victory. What exactly he has gained, even in this sense, is not immediately apparent. Certainly it is neither the certitude of victory nor the rapture of victory. Returned to his desk in the final scene of his career in fiction, he is in fact a bleak, lonely, and unhappy figure, without home, without love, without community, conscious perhaps that his victory is far from final and that it may have cost him far too much.

Dashiell Hammett is, I think, with so many of his literary contemporaries, protesting the horrors of a savagely competitive society, the horrors of an urban-industrial civilization. For when we scrape the tough exterior of his hero we find not heart of stone and nerves of steel but the tortured sensibility of the Nineteen Twenties, its romantic isolation and its pessimism, its inability to find grounds for action. With Chandler's Philip Marlowe, however, we pass into another world, the world of the Depression. He retains, of course, many of the attitudes of his predecessor, his toughness, his irony, his loneliness. But he has none of Spade's conviction of persisting failure, his sense of futility and defeat, none of his perhaps tragic implications. There is about him little of the spirit of a man who wins and does not win, who wins and cannot win. For he represents the moral and social ardor of the Depression years, the impulse towards reform; and he is frequently prone to feelings of boyish optimism.

In the first place, tough and brave though he may be, Marlowe is a much more respectable figure than Spade. He went to college and "can still," he asserts belligerently, "speak English if there's any demand for it." And if he is "a little bit of a cynic," as his client notes, he is no more so than is proper in one who aspires to knight errantry. For he does betray all the characteristics of the first-class crusader.

This is apparent in the deadly seriousness with which he takes his craft. "The first time we met," he says angrily, "I told you I was a detective. Get it through your lovely head. I work at it, lady, I don't play at it." Clearly the words of a man who knows what he means and what exactly he must do in the world, the words of a man who can, that is, afford social consciousness. We get another glimpse of this aspect of the private detective when we discover Marlowe is in a jail cell pondering ruefully the two worlds, the nice, sane, comfortable world he has rejected and the ugly world to which he has committed himself. "I knew a girl," he meditates, "who lived on Twenty-fifth Street. It was a nice street. She was a nice girl. She liked Bay City. She wouldn't think about the Mexican and Negro slums stretched out on the dismal flats south of the solid interurban tracks. Nor of the waterfront dives . . . the sweaty little dance-halls . . . the marihuana joints, the narrow fox faces watching over the tops of newspapers. . . ."

But Marlowe is not only the social crusader; he is also the moralist, almost the prude. Sam Spade could never have said, on discovering a nymphomaniac disposed in his bed, what Marlowe said. "It's so hard," he said, "for women—even nice women—to realize that their bodies are not irresistible." For Spade, in his grim odyssey through the underworld, was always too ambivalent a character to express an opinion one way or the other. He acted, but he acted inscrutably, almost without point of view. Marlowe, however, finds it difficult to conceal his contempt for the diseased world in which he must move.

Nevertheless he is, like the boy next door, a rather pleasant character and articulated the longing, universal in our day, for an honorable if not a pleasant world. Chandler describes his thus:

He is a poor man or he would not be a detective. He is a common man or he would not go among common people; he has a sense of character or he would not know his job. He will take no man's money dishonestly and no man's insolence without a due and dispassionate revenge; he is a lonely man and his pride is that you will treat him as a proud man or be very sorry you ever saw him.

After this, he must indeed have seemed a wonderfully attractive symbol to the men who lost their pride in the bread lines and employment offices of that decade.

Unfortunately, the private detectives who succeed Sam Spade and Philip Marlowe represent a progressive deterioration of the type. We have noted the essentially romantic temperament of Hammett's Sam Spade. But where in him it has been implicit, in the lesser creations it is crudely explicit. The result is rather revolting sentimentality: the hardboiled novel turns soft at the center. There are signs even in Philip Marlowe of this contagion. "Knights have no meaning in this game," he muses, bitterly in love with himself. "It wasn't a game for knights."

Humphrey Bogart as Sam Spade, Peter Lorre as Joel Cairo, Mary Astor as Brigid O'Shaughnessy, and Sidney Greenstreet as Caspar Gutman in the scene from the 1941 movie of *The Maltese Falcon* in which Spade delivers the statuette

But if we admit that Marlowe is not always quite as fatuous as he appears here, we cannot, I fear, extend the same charity to his colleagues in fiction: for in the more recent of the hardboiled writers, among them Geoffrey Homes and George Harmon Coxe, the private dick virtually wears his heart on his sleeve. The pressure of the war may have had something to do with it, for not only does he indulge himself in feelings of romantic self-pity but, more intolerable, comes to terms with the community and accepts unblushingly the just rewards of virtue and tractability. He may appear in the beginning as the haggard outcast, grown a little weary and emaciated in the service of obscure ideals, but the reader is usually ravished to discover that he has, in the end, found this way back to the warmth of the community—generally in the arms of the sweet and wholesome American girl. Witness, for example, the voluptuous anguish of rugged Humphrey Campbell in the toils of a love-emotion: "A breathlessness, an inside singing that he was much too old for; too old and too tough and too beat up around the edges." As it turns out, however, this was not really so. And the modest passion of the strong man is rapturously consummated in the final pages of Home's "Six Silver Handles." This pattern is repeated in Coxe's "Woman at Bay." The hero, who has achieved romantic 4-F status in the Spanish Civil War and is now a member of the OSS, not only recovers a vital manuscript establishing the disloyalty of a big chemical concern, but is reunited in the arms of his ex-wife who has been wrongly, it seems, suspected of Vichyite connections.

The private eye as we find him today represents, then, a betrayal of everything Sam Spade and, to a lesser extent, Philip Marlowe, stood for. He is the rehabilitated private dick, the private dick gone soft. He may, it is true, point the way to a period of greater stability and confidence, a period in which the intractability of a Sam Spade, who is *par excellence* the creature of crisis, could have no justification. But I doubt it.

I am an inveterate Sam Spade man myself.

Peter J. Rabinowitz, "'How Did You Know He Licked His Lips?': Second Person Knowledge and First Person Power in *The Maltese Falcon*," in *Understanding Narrative*, edited by Rabinowitz and James Phelan (Columbus: Ohio State University Press, 1994), pp. 157–177.

"What do You Want Us to Think the Facts Are?" Epistemology and Detective Fiction

Classification is an occupational hazard for any theorist of detective stories—in part because there are so many convenient but competing axes for sorting them out. You can, for instance, differentiate novels according to the location of the guilt they uncover—say, between Hercule Poirot stories (where detective and criminal are kept rigorously separate) and Oedipal stories (where, as in William Faulkner's *Intruder in the Dust* or Raymond Chandler's *The Big Sleep*, a key discovery is a discovery of the detective's own guilt). Alternatively, you can organize them according to their treatment of time—between backward-facing stories (for instance, Sir Arthur Conan Doyle's *A Study in Scarlet*) where the key events precede the detective's intervention, and

THE PRESS ATTACK

Hammett likes to joke that he takes no exercise more vigorous than rolling his own cigarettes. For decades he has led an owl-like existence, mostly at night, oiling his internal combustion machine as much with alcohol as with food.

It seems odd for a former TB case, 57 and frail, to stick his chin out in front of a six-months Federal prison sentence by refusing to disclose how the Civil Rights Congress dug a hole in the ground for a quartet of convicted Communist arch-conspirators.

But it is not surprising to his friends. Outside of his specialized form of literary genius (now withered by long disuse), they say Hammett's chief qualities, as revealed by his career, have been cynicism, an impulse toward martyrdom and an amazing physical endurance.

Oliver Pilat, "The Strange Case of Dashiell Hammett," *New York Post,* 23 July 1951, pp. 2, 24.

stories where the primary events are those provoked by the investigation itself—say, Sara Paretsky's *Bitter Medicine*. It is also popular to distinguish stories stylistically, as between classical British and hard-boiled American.

In this essay I want to work along another axis, looking at detective stories in terms of the way they conceptualize the nature of truth. Mikhail Bakhtin argues that "when the novel becomes the dominant genre, epistemology becomes the dominant discipline" (15), and from this perspective the detective story would seem one of the most novelistic of subgenres. Granted, this is complex terrain that engages a number of intersecting questions, both epistemological and metaphysical. Nonetheless, I think we can draw a crucial, if rough, dividing line between two sorts of texts. The first relies on what we might call the Fort Knox noting of truth, a phrase with a double resonance for connoisseurs of early detective fiction, since one of the first attempts to chart out the "rules" for classical detective novels was Ronald Knox's "A Detective Story Decalogue." Fort Knox novels, often embodying positions associated with empiricism, realism, and especially positivism (as Knox puts it, "all supernatural or preternatural agencies are ruled out as a matter of course" [194]), rest on the twin assumptions that the truth exists and that it can be found through rational procedures. That is, their plots are constructed on the belief that the truth value of a particular claim can be determined according to some external and transcendent standard independent of the perspective or context of the individual making the claim, a standard that is available to the skilled detective. Most traditional detectives, from Oedipus and Sherlock Holmes through Mike Hammer and Travis McGee, take the Fort Knox position, assuming, as Michael Holquist puts it, that "the mind, given enough time, can understand everything" (141). Indeed, Ellery Queen built the notion of an independent standard and a single solution into the very format of some of his best novels, offering an explicit challenge to the reader at the point where all the necessary information to reach the one right answer had been provided.

Even many of the traditional novels that appear to trifle with these conventions end up firmly wedded to them. Queen's *Ten Days' Wonder*, for example, reads in part as a subversion of the Fort Knox position, suggesting that more than one solution might fit the available facts. Still, in the end, the novel does not equivocate about what really happened: we may be tricked by false stories, but there is ultimately a difference between true and false accounts, and they can be distinguished in practice, if not always in time to prevent misfortune. Similarly, Anthony Berkeley's *The Poisoned Chocolates Case,* which multiplies the number of possible explanations, ultimately determines one to be the true story.

In contrast, such postmodern detectives as Jacques Revel (in Michel Butor's *L'Emploi du temps* [*Passing Time*]) or Witold (in Witold Gombrowicz's *Cosmos*) resist the siren call of positivism. Philosophically, they're allied with what might be called the barter school of truth, a school often associated with what Katheryn Doran has aptly called the "seductive conflation of epistemological skepticism and metaphysical relativism."[1] Unlike Fort Knox adherents, champions of this position believe that perspective inevitably influences any account (or attempted account) of reality. As a result, what will "count as" truth is always a context-dependent construction.[2]

As I have suggested, there are numerous variations within this broad grouping. In *Les Gommes* (*The Erasers*), for instance, Alain Robbe-Grillet surprisingly combines metaphysical realism with his epistemological skepticism, suggesting that there is a true narrative of the events, although it is inaccessible to any of the characters in the world of the novel. *Cosmos* appears to be more thoroughly postmodern, suggesting that no transcendental narrative exists at all, although the novel's (probably coincidental) intertextual references to the life and music of Alban Berg confuse the issue.[3] Still, despite their differences, the novelists in this second camp reject the belief that we can determine the truth of particular claims; at most, we make truth discursively and rhetorically by telling stories and negotiating among them, bartering truth claims in exchanges that are either taken up or not according to the needs of a particular social context (including its power relations).[4] For these counter-cultural detectives, the search is not for some empirically verifiable "truth" but rather for some coherent story "about" the world, preferably one with enough persuasive power to gain acceptance from whoever needs to be convinced.

For the most part, these novels do not pursue their philosophical quarry all the way to the most radical skepticism (although Paul Auster, in his *New York Trilogy*, comes close). In particular, most do not deny the existence of brute material facts, and do not throw doubt on the possibility of direct observation of the present. But, much like Alain Resnais and Robbe-Grillet's *L'Année dernière à Marienbad* (*Last Year at Marienbad*), they suggest that the past (even the immediate past) exists only in the form of present material objects. "History" (and any detective story necessarily involves its characters in some attempt at historical reconstruction) is consequently a matter of inventing stories about those present objects. Any story that can account for those material objects has equal validity; whether or not it is accepted thus depends not on its fidelity to what is the case, but rather on its barter value for the particular context in which it is presented.

"The Soft Grey Sheen of Lead": Clipping the Wings of the Maltese Falcon

Traditionally, Dashiell Hammett's *The Maltese Falcon* has been read as a straight hard-boiled detective story, with little interest in erudite philosophical issues. This is not to say, of course, that the novel has not been widely read as a serious social critique. Liahna K. Babener, for instance, is typical in claiming that the novel's "target . . . is the duplicity of the Horatio Alger myth" (78). But on the whole, there's been little interest in considering *The Maltese Falcon* as a philosophical novel fundamentally "concerned with stories and storytelling" (Schulman 400).[5]

There is good reason, of course, for the customary readings. The novel first appeared in the context of the early *Black Mask* school, and many of its surface features—its clipped, tough "masculine" dialogue; its complex, fast-moving plot; its cynical antisentimentalism—appear to invite the reader to apply the same reading strategies demanded by other tough novels of the period, rather than, say, the strategies demanded by such then avant-garde contemporaries as Woolf or Pirandello, much less the strategies later demanded by Robbe-Grillet and Auster. Yet different features emerge as significant for readers of different historical periods. And as we grow accustomed to thinking and rereading in postmodern terms, the stability of Hammett's novel increasingly begins to dissolve, as Percy Walton and Kathryn Gail Brock's parodic readings have in their different ways demonstrated.[6] From the arrival of Brigid O'Shaughnessy in Sam Spade's office, it's a novel in which the plot consists not of events but of continual acts of narrativizing and renarrativising about events that may or may not have taken place. Even Lieutenant Dundy, the character most committed to meaning what he says (21), finds that he has to invent stories ("Nobody saw it, but that's the way it figures" [22]) and deal with the inventions of others: "What do you want us to think the truth is?" he asks Brigid O'Shaughnessy with a scowl of aggravation (75). The characters are not centered subjects, but assume a dizzying series of self-conscious roles that cast doubt on traditional notions of identity: Brigid O'Shaughnessy's carefully choreographed transformations in particular, from the timid Miss Wonderly clasping her handbag to the teary, love-wracked beseecher of the final confrontation, confirm that this is a world in which the equation between who you are and what your story is, is more than a dead metaphor (22). The stability of gender, too, is undermined, not only by the dynamics of the Gutman-Wilmer-Cairo trio or the fight between Cairo and Brigid O'Shaughnessy over the boy in Constantinople (68), but even more by Spade's boyish but femininely seductive secretary Effie Perine. Novelistic clichés—the reliability of women's intuition, the joviality of the fat man—are turned inside out. Messages—even a condolence note to a love upon her liberation from a husband she detested—are severed from their senders. Clues—for instance, the hole in the newspaper that Spade finds in Cairo's hotel room—are often marked by absence rather than presence, just as Archer's murder in the San Francisco fog is celebrated by the erasure of his name from the door of the detective agency's office.

To the extent that there is a story, it is a story of a search without a beginning. Spade's first words to Brigid O'Shaughnessy may be "Suppose you tell me about it, from the beginning" (5), but since he doesn't expect "it" to be believable, he hardly expects that it will have a real origin. More important, the search is a search without an ending, except the promise of endless deferral. It's consistent, then, that in common with much postmodernist thought, the novelistic acid eats away at the distinction between fiction and history. Indeed—and it came as a shock when I called up the OCLC catalog on my computer to check this out—the historical texts that Casper Gutman uses to buttress his story about the falcon turn out to be "actual" historical works, and the stories that he tells fit the facts that we know. Thus, although Ernie Bradford's version of the story puts into question the Knights' power and their undiluted enthusiasm for Malta (which apparently required them, in addition, to garrison Tripoli: "It is indicative of the desperate straits to which the Order had been reduced that they agreed to the Emperor's offer"), his account confirms the basic story of the "annual nominal rent of one falcon" (123).[7] The assessment of Effie Perine's fictional historian-cousin Ted ("the names and dates are all right, and at least none of your authorities or their works are out-and-out fakes" [139]) thus collapses the distinction between the authorial and narrative audiences.[8]

Money—the anchor of capitalism—is deconstructed as well. Gutman may claim that the cash he hands to Spade is "actual money, genuine coin of the realm" that somehow transcends the merely discursive: "With a dollar of this, you can buy more than with ten dollars of talk" (174). But the novel represents a world of counterfeiters, too (119), and even Gutman's apparently legitimate thousand-dollar bills can not only disappear, but even change the very nature of their being; at the end, the one remaining bill has been transformed from a payment into an "exhibit" (215–16).

Then, too, although the novel has sometimes been treated as a Hemingwayesque endorsement of a masculine code of honor and loyalty, the novel's intertextual links with Prosper Mérimée's 1829 short story "Mateo Falcone" serve to undercut the code, too, as well as traditional bourgeois notions of the family. Mérimée's brutal little anecdote concerns a father who executes his own son out of devotion to a higher code of conduct—for the child, bribed with the promise of a silver watch, has turned a fugitive over to the government authorities, becoming "the first of his line to have committed a betrayal" (Mérimée, 65). Hammett twice inverts this scenario: when Gutman, who "feel[s] towards Wilmer just exactly as if he were [his] own son" (178), nonetheless agrees to turn him over to the police in exchange for the falcon, and again when Spade turns over Brigid O'Shaughnessy.

Most striking, of course, is the falcon/phallus itself (what Sam Spade calls a "dingus"): for the transcendental signifier that ostensibly gives meaning and value to the world of the novel displays the "soft grey sheen of lead" (202), as it turns out to be just another counterfeit of a unique original that may or may not exist. No surprise, then, that in this novel, pistols—for instance, the "tools bulging [Wilmer's] clothes" (95)—keep multiplying and changing hands, a thematic ploy that reaches comically Ionesco-like proportions when the guns are all (or nearly all) shut up in the closet during the long negotiation scene. No surprise, either, that the other variant of the phallus—the crucial fall guy—miraculously disappears from a crowded room.

The Maltese Falcon, like most other postmodern detective stories, refrains from challenging the existence of an observable material present, although like them it rhetoricizes history. History becomes a matter of telling stories about present objects, and any story that can account for the material traces of the past—any story, as Spade puts it, that "seems to click with most of the known facts"—will "hold," as long as you have the power to persuade your listeners to go along with it (115). Nor does the novel confront the abyss by endorsing either despair or aesthetic free play. Rather, in common with such other macho preexistentialists as Hemingway, Hammett seems to be trying to propose a way of controlling one's environment (and preserving "self," in body if not in soul) in a world where truth is relative and where violence (whether in the form of gunshots or of beams falling from construction sites) erupts without warning. Spade's "way of learning is to heave a wild and unpredictable monkey wrench into the machinery" (86), and his refusal to "settle" into a "groove" (64) is, to a large extent, what ensures his survival and success, not to mention his status as a hero.

"Wait Till I'm Through and Then You Can Talk": Power and Narrative Technique

I do not want to overstate the extent of *The Maltese Falcon's* post-modernism. As I pointed out, there are also numerous conventional signals that invite us to read the novel as a traditional hard-boiled text: this is a world of real violence and real corpses, without any of the ghostly ambiguities of perception that haunt Auster's trilogy, and without any of the nagging ambiguities of plot that make the world of Butor's *L'Emploi du temps* (where we never even find out whether or not there was a crime) such an unsettling experience. Still, the presence of these deconstructive counter-forces fundamentally disturbs the equilibrium of the text; and the reader who picks up on the novel's questioning spirit is apt to be taken aback when the novel's postmodern unraveling itself falls apart in the paradoxically tight-knit ending.

The clarity of the conclusion is no doubt partly a result of the pressures of genre: Hammett was apparently not yet ready to give us a detective story without an ending. But there's also a deeper sexual-political cause. If any poststructural interpretive doctrine has acquired general currency, it is the belief that texts assert what they're at most pains to deny. And if the clear epistemological and metaphysical structures of traditional realist detective fiction aim to deflect our attention from metaphysical and political aporias, what is being furtively asserted by this text when it so steadfastly refuses to assert anything at all? What I'd like to suggest here is that, through its very rhetorical structure, the novel deconstructs its own postmodern refusal to take a stand—its own rejection of what Casper Gutman calls "plain speaking and clear understanding" (105)—covertly reasserting precisely those traditional values it so ostentatiously undermines, and falling back on an unexamined myth of absence. And the novel does so because it reaches a rhetorical impasse, where, in order to follow through on its own barter-school program, Hammett and Spade would be required to accept women as independent subjects.

The novel turns into a self-affirming artifact most clearly through its treatment of embedded narratives, stories within stories. In order to explain how this happens, I'd like to introduce two distinctions: one between two kinds of transmission as a story moves from one level to the next, the other among three types of narration. To begin with transmission: when light waves travel from one medium to another, one of two things can happen. If they hit perpendicular to the surface of the new medium, they continue on in the same direction, in a straight line; but if they hit obliquely, they are refracted, and move off at a different angle. Similarly, when a story moves from one medium to another, one of two things can happen. In straight line transmission, intervening levels of narration do not in any significant way deflect the story being told. In Voltaire's *Candide,* the Old Woman's tale has the same claim to authenticity as the narration that frames it. More elaborately, in Mary Shelley's *Frankenstein,* Safie's letters are presented with four levels of embedding. We know them only from Walton's letters, which include Victor Frankenstein's narrative, which in turn includes the monster's story, which in turn includes the letters—or at least copies that he made of them, copies we're told of, but never shown (108). Nonetheless, as readers, it is as if we have direct access to the letters; the intervening levels don't interfere in any way with our rhetorical connection to the originals.

In refractive transmission, by contrast, each intervening level bends the story, so that our attention as readers is necessarily divided between what is narrated and the twists introduced by the act of narration itself. Indeed, such embedded stories are thus both refracted and refractory, in the sense that they resist easy interpretation. Thus, for instance, in Mikhail Lermontov's *Hero of Our Time,* we learn about the characters as much from how they narrate as from what is said about them, and the differences between the accounts given by Pechorin and those given by Maxim Maximich are crucial to our sense of the novel.

Now either type of transmission—straight line or refractive—is in principle consistent with a Fort Knox notion of truth: for while the Fort Knox doctrine hinges on the assumption that the truth is *potentially* available, it does not follow that a particular individual will be capable of (or interested in) actually finding it. Much of Poirot's detection, therefore, consists of sorting out conflicting refracted narratives, some consciously false, some simply mistaken, in order to discover the transcendent truth at their origin. But while the Fort Knox notion does not necessarily entail straight line transmission, straight line transmission *does* entail Knoxism. Straight line transmission inevitably involves both the possibility and the actuality of identity between two versions of a story—not merely a possible partial overlap (as in *As I Lay Dying,* where Cash and Darl may partially confirm each other's narrative of Jewel's past), but an absolute match between the telling and the told, *as well as* a way of determining that that match has occurred. Because of this, we can't have straight line transmission in a world where the very act of perception changes (in some versions, even creates) what is perceived. The barter notion of truth therefore necessarily requires refractive transmission.

My second distinction is among first, second, and third person narration. Although this distinction is commonplace in narrative theory (enough so that as long ago as 1961, Wayne Booth called it "overworked" [150]), its value has been obscured by the grammatical terminology, which encourages us to concentrate on the surface manifestations of the text. But surface does not always match significant structure: Faulkner's *Intruder in the Dust* uses third person grammar, but the narrative has all the characteristics of a retrospective first person novel. I would like to propose, then, that we reconsider the terminology, and think of narrative person not as a grammatical category—nor even what Genette calls a "narrative posture" (*Narrative Discourse* 244)— but rather as a rhetorical situation embracing not only the teller but the audience as well.[9]

To be schematic for a moment: let us assume that narrator A says to audience B that referent C did something. (I'm using the term "referent" here because the terms "subject" and "object" introduce too many ambiguities of meaning.) In the simplest type of what I'm calling third person narrative, the three positions (A, B, and C) are clearly distinct, and the third of them is, moreover, absent from the scene of reception. "A photograph of Mama Chona and her grandson Miguel Angel—Miguel Chico or Mickie to his family—hovers above his head on the study wall beside the glass doors that open out into the garden. When Miguel Chico sits at his desk, he glances up at it occasionally without noticing it, looking through it rather than at it." So begins Arturo Islas's *The Rain God* (3), and we know that Miguel Chico is neither telling nor being told the story. In first and second person narration, however, some of these positions are collapsed. In the simplest type of first person narration, it is the narrator and referent who are collapsed: "Last year, on the evening of March 22, I had a very strange adventure" (Dostoevsky 1). And in second person narration, most often found in spoken discourse (or its novelistic representation), it's the distinction between audience and referent that's collapsed: "You are about to begin reading Italo Calvino's new novel, *If on a winter's night a traveler.* Relax. Concentrate. Dispel every other thought" (Calvino 3).[10]

For the most part, these rhetorical categories overlap with traditional grammatical categories. Thus most first person narratives in my sense are composed in the grammatical first person. But as I've suggested, *Intruder in the Dust* is rhetorically a first person narrative, since narrator and referent are identical, despite the grammatical construction that describes Chick in third person throughout. Likewise, we learn at the end of Albert Camus's *La Peste* (*The Plague*) that we've been reading a first person narrative in which the narrator refers to himself in the third person.

Despite such famous exceptions as Butor's *La Modification* and Calvino's *If on a winter's night a traveler,* second person is rarely used as the top—that is, the most inclusive—level of narration (I'm calling on this rather informal terminology in large part because the more familiar terms Genette uses in *Narrative Discourse*—extradiegetic, diegetic, metadiegetic—are so cumbersome).[11] Indeed, even some of the rare text that are second person in grammar are not second person in rhetoric. For instance, Rex Stout's *How Like a God* (1929) is written, except for the brief interchapters, in a grammatical second person. But, as the third person interchapters make clear, it's really a variant of first person narration—an internal monologue that we might call narcissistic narration—in which the narrator is speaking to himself about himself.[12]

This relative scarcity of complete second person texts, coupled with the popularity of Genette's homodiegetic/heterodiegetic distinction (which seems to remove second person narration as a serious option [but see *Narrative Discourse Revisited* 133–34]), has resulted in a widespread tendency to brush second person narration aside. But while second person narration is rare on the top level of narrative organization, it's found widely in smaller narrative units. In particular, as Robyn Warhol has shown, it's found in direct address to the reader, especially in eighteenth- and nineteenth-century fiction; and it is frequent in embedded narration—where it is a dramatized *narratee* rather than the narrative or authorial audience of the text as a whole that's being narrativized. It certainly occurs at a crucial juncture in *The Maltese Falcon*.

What is useful about this reconception of person is that by stressing the relationship not only between narrator and story but also between narrator and audience, we get a handle not only on epistemological issues (the questions about what the narrator knows stressed by so many traditional studies of point of view) but on issues of power as well. In particular, this analysis underscores that second person narration, especially second person refractive transmission, opens up the possibility of feedback—feedback not in its current trendy meaning, as when a Dean tells faculty or students to provide some "feedback" on the latest course evaluation form, but in its more precise acoustic/electronic meaning, the screech that occurs when an infinite loop is created between a microphone and a speaker that is simultaneously serving as both the input and the output of the microphone. That's because in second person narration, the referent of the story, being also the audience, is *present* at the site of reception, and thus always has the potential to insist on retelling his or her story in his or her own way, a further act of narration that can itself become embedded in the story that the original narrator is telling, and so on *ad infinitum*. In contrast, a third person narration, even when refracted, has an absent referent, and hence closes down the possibility for feedback. When Spade tells Brigid O'Shaughnessy the Flitcraft story, for instance, his transmission is clearly refractive. The curve between Flitcraft's own story and Spade's story about that story shows up in Spade's ironic stance toward the story he tells, in the judgmental element introduced through the act of telling: "I don't think he even knew he had settled back naturally into the same groove he had jumped out of in Tacoma. But that's the part of it I always liked" (64). But the feedback potential in that ironic distance never drowns out the present rhetorical situation, for Flitcraft—if he exists—isn't present, and hence has no opportunity to provide commentary on the tale.

It is more difficult, however, to reduce feedback in second person refracted narrative. There are two primary ways of silencing a referent-audience: conversion and coercion. Conversion has several variations. One can, for instance, seduce the audience into accepting the narrator's version of the story by offering pleasure. That kind of seduction forms the central intrigue in *Marienbad*, as X tries to persuade A that his stories about what happened to them last year are worth believing. In a very different way, we see the same kind of technique when Spade tries to create a story that will work with the District Attorney: "He's more interested in how his record will look on paper than anything else. . . . To be sure of convicting one man he'll let half a dozen equally guilty accomplices go free. . . . That's the choice we'll give him and he'll gobble it up" (180).[13] Alternatively, one can mediate between conflicting stories until some mutually acceptable version is found: that's what happens, for instance, in the conversation between Violet Stoke and Charles Watkins in Doris Lessing's *Briefing for a Descent into Hell*, or between Spade and Gutman when they negotiate a trade of the fall guy for the falcon.

But whether in the form of seduction or mediation, conversion-generated silencing places the audience in a subject position—a position to make choices. One can avoid that necessity through the second alternative, sheer force—what Spade resorts to when casting Wilmer as the fall guy. When dealing with men, these two alternatives seem adequate—even when dealing with gay men, although Spade (and Philip Marlowe, too) seems to prefer violence as an alternative to offering subjecthood. Violence is especially characteristic of his dealings with Wilmer. He alternately beats up and negotiates with Cairo, but he never extends the option of serious negotiation to Wilmer, who seems to get more deeply under his skin—perhaps because his "hard masculine neatness" (93) casts more doubt on the meaning of Spade's own masculinity than does the effeminacy of Cairo, with his smell of *chypre*. Spade beats up Wilmer before he tells him, "This will put you in solid with your boss" (121), and Spade's brief second person narrative before Wilmer is chosen as the fall guy ("Two to one they're selling you out, son") is similarly accompanied by silence rather than feedback ("The boy did not say anything" [184]).

Something quite different, though, happens in his final scene with Brigid O'Shaughnessy. There's certainly no literal violence at this climax of the plot (perhaps some residue of chivalry makes him squeamish about knocking her out—although it's significant that he's willing to force her to strip in his quest for the palmed thousand-dollar bill). But neither is Spade willing to give her the freedom

HAMMETT QUESTIONED BY MCCARTHY

THE CHAIRMAN: . . . Mr. Hammett, if you were spending, as we are, over a hundred million dollars a year on an information program allegedly for the purpose of fighting communism, and if you were in charge of that program to fight communism, would you purchase the works of some 75 Communist authors and distribute their works throughout the world, placing our official stamp of approval upon those works?

Or would you rather not answer that question?

MR. HAMMETT: Well, I think—of course, I don't know—if I were fighting communism, I don't think I would do it by giving people any books at all.

THE CHAIRMAN: From an author, that sounds unusual.

Hammett's testimony before the Permanent Subcommittee Investigation of the Senate Committee on Government Operations, chaired by Senator Joseph McCarthy, 26 March 1953.

to negotiate her future. This refusal is all the more strikingly noticeable because of its jarring contiguity with the lengthy give-and-take with Gutman. One cannot, of course, be absolutely sure of Spade's (or Hammett's) reasons for this: Spade may feel (although the prior events in this novel would hardly support this belief) that she is more duplicitous than Gutman. It may be, as I've suggested earlier, that Hammett feels an aesthetic need to close off the infinite possibilities of his text.

Still, it's hard to ignore Spade's uncharacteristically obsessive insistence that he "won't play the sap" for her (212–15). He's told her earlier, half in jest, that "You don't have to trust me, anyhow, as long as you can persuade me to trust you" (65), and there is good reason to believe that, because of her sexual allure—because it's "easy enough to be nuts about" her (214)—her powers of persuasion are more than Spade wants to handle. Certainly her sexual power has been deadly for Thursby, Captain Jacobi, and especially for Miles Archer. Spade, of course, considers himself less "dumb" (208) than Archer ("You've got brains, yes you have" he tells his leering partner sarcastically when he starts to make his move on Brigid O'Shaughnessy [10]), and less of a "sucker for women" than Thursby (207). But there's evidence that Gutman's claim "We mere men should have known better than to suppose ourselves capable of coping with her" (192) applies to Spade more than he would sometimes like to believe. After all, Gutman requires drugs to shut Spade up, but Brigid O'Shaughnessy manages to shut him up by simply putting "her open mouth hard against his mouth" (89).

In the final scene, Spade is intensely aware of his power as he reviews his past with Brigid O'Shaughnessy: "You came into my bed to stop me asking questions" (212). And he's well aware of the way that the continued presence of her body, always an embarrassment in an act of narration, makes the outcome of a life-threatening seduction or negotiation doubly doubtful ("Last night you came here with them and waited outside for me and came in with me. You were in my arms when the trap was sprung" [212]), especially since she is fully aware of both the danger of the situation and the source of her power ("God damn you—you've counted on that" [215]). There is much to be said about the reasons for and implications of Hammett's and Spade's attitudes toward women—it's significant, for instance, that both Brigid O'Shaughnessy and Effie Perine are consistently objectified by the author's (although not the characters') insistence on calling them by full name, first and last.[14] But for my purposes here the effects, not the causes, are of primary concern. For finding himself unwilling to have Spade either batter Brigid O'Shaughnessy or let her negotiate, Hammett silences her with a rhetorical, rather than a physical, coercion, a sleight of pen that reinscribes what Percy Walton has called the "dominant colonizing norm," a "singularizing effort . . . that . . . ignores difference when it accepts its own desires as more important than the desires of the space it seeks to dominate" ("Paretsky's V.I." 203–204).

Specifically, in their famous final confrontation, second person narration is *treated as* a third person narration. That is, although Brigid O'Shaughnessy is literally both audience and referent of the discourse, Spade's account of her story is made definitive, as she is rhetorically objectified as absent and hence silent (her few remaining snippets of dialogue do nothing to challenge the narration). What makes this rhetorical sleight-of-hand possible? She says nothing because she has nothing to say: no feedback loop is started up because—and both Brigid O'Shaughnessy and Spade *know* this—no dissonance is registered between her perception and his. "How did you know he—he licked his lips and looked—?" she asks (209), and in asking this question, she affirms the consonance of their stories, and consequently affirms the straight line of his transmission. On the surface, perhaps, the potential for dialogue continues: "Wait till I'm through and then you can talk," he tells her (214). But because she has already accepted the congruence of the stories, she can do nothing but confirm the correctness of his version of her story; she tries one last barter—with body, rather than text (215)—but it's a futile gesture and the doorbell rings just as she puts her arms around him.

It's worth distinguishing between Hammett's and Spade's performances here. It's Spade who tells the story, but it's the implied author who creates Brigid O'Shaughnessy's assent. That assent serves to end the story and contain the woman without violence, and its sheer dramatic power makes it easy for the reader to accept without question. But under the surface, the ending comes at tremendous epistemological cost. For in order to guarantee that assent, Hammett has to resort, at this key moment, to a straight-line embedded narrative. And in this apparently purely formal choice, Hammett smuggles in precisely the Fort Knox conception of truth that his novel has been at such pains to resist. It grounds Spade's story as true, but it deconstructs the patient deconstruction of foundationalism that forms the very basis of the novel's epistemological project.

No wonder, then, that Effie Perine seems so depressed at the end—refusing to let Spade touch her—when she has to go along with this epistemological turnaround. As I've suggested, this "lanky sunburned girl" with a "boyish face" (3) has had gender-crossing license throughout the novel—as Spade says, "You're a damned good man, sister" (160). (No doubt her name, with its echoes of "peregrine," gives her some falcon/phallic privileges.) But when she says, "I know—I know you're right" (217), she realizes that there's no longer any opening for the kind of dialogue that has enlivened their relationship up until now. For most of the novel, Spade has given her the choice of siding with Brigid O'Shaughnessy, even against him ("You're sore because she did something on her own book," she argues; "Why shouldn't she?" [153])—and Effie Perine has belied the clichés about women's rivalry by remaining steadfast in her loyalty to Brigid O'Shaughnessy; even though they're both sexually attracted to the same man. But the ending of the novel proves that female bonding has been a mistake—that there is, in fact, a right and wrong to the situation, and that Effie Perine has simply been wrong.

Spade's situation is no more upbeat than Effie Perine's. Throughout the novel, he has prided himself on his flexibility and unpredictability. But although he enters his office with cheerful lines on his face and clear eyes, the superficially bland final sentences strike a very different note. Effie Perine enters Spade's inner office to announce that Iva Archer, the indefatigable mistress Spade has been trying to elude for the entire novel ("I wish to Christ I'd never seen her" [27]), has arrived once again at the office. "'Yes,' he said, and shivered, 'Well, send her in'" (217). The echo of his decision to turn Brigid O'Shaughnessy in to the police ("I'm going to send you over" [211]) underscores the connection between Spade's rhetorical victory over Brigid O'Shaughnessy and his philosophical defeat. For in the wake of the Knoxian solution has come a chilling kind of return to things as they were—and while sentimental readers may want to see that final shiver as a sign of despairing romantic loss, it's more likely that it comes from a resigned recognition that he has forfeited his philosophical decenteredness and that, like Flitcraft, he has found himself trapped once again in the same groove that he has been trying to jump out of for the entire novel.

NOTES

1. Personal communication.

2. This distinction, of course, has close connections to Steven Mailloux's distinction between foundationalist accounts of interpretation and rhetorical hermeneutics in *Rhetorical Power*. There is, as well, a link to the two ways of conceptualizing truth often classed as correspondence theories (where statements are deemed "true" according to their correspondence to some determinable external state of affairs) and coherence theories (where statements are deemed "true" according to internal standards that include such things as consistency, inclusiveness, and logical relations). The distinction, of course, has been important for literary theorists as well, especially for the New Critics. See, for instance, Brooks and Warren (27). I am warned by my philosopher friends, though, that I do not want to wander through the thickets of this distinction. Special thanks to Elizabeth Ring and Katheryn Doran for their invaluable assistance on these issues.

3. For a fuller discussion, see my *Before Reading*, 178–83.

4. In defining the subgenre in this way, I am taking a substantially different route from that of Holquist, in his discussion of "metaphysical" detective stories. He sees postmodern detectives' recognition of chaos ("they dramatize the void" [155]), but does not discuss the novels in terms of the way they *create* a truth.

5. For the most part Schulman, too, views the novel from a social rather than an epistemological perspective, since those stories are motivated by "a market society world that systematically demands improvisation, acting, and the manipulation of appearances, people, and feelings." Still, he is one of the critics who recognizes the philosophical issues as well. See in particular 408–9.

6. My thinking in this direction was begun through conversations with Kathryn Gail Brock nearly a decade ago, and the influence of her "parodic" reading on the following paper is enormous. Walton's arguments, in "You're in My Burg," similarly stress parodic elements in the text; and although she is less interested in determining an authorial reading than I am, the overlap between our essays is considerable.

7. See, for instance, Carutti: "Gli abasciatori di Malta vennero a rendere omaggio al nuovo Re e offerire il falcone, annuo tributo che Carlo V avea imposto all'ordine dei Cavalieri gerosolimitani in ricognizione della movenaza dell'isola dalla corona di Sicilia" [The ambassadors of Malta came to render homage to the new king and to offer the falcon, the annual tribute which Charles V had imposed upon the order of the Knights of Jerusalem in recognition of his granting of the island from the crown of Sicily] (391). Thanks to Maureen Miller for help with historical research.

8. For fuller discussion of the difference between authorial audience, narrative audience, and narratee, see *Before Reading,* chapter 3.

9. See also Genette's discussion of the problematic nature of grammatical categories, *Narrative Discourse Revisited* 104 ff. See also Bal 121 ff. In refusing to discuss grammatical difference, though, Bal skims over other differences that, as we shall see, really matter.

10. Of course, there are any number of possible variants. For instance, we might want to distinguish between "normal" third person and what I call third person private, where the narrator and audience are identical, as when someone writes a note to him- or herself, or a secret diary entry about someone else. And when we introduce the distinctions between implied author and narrator, or between authorial audience and narrative audience, the possible permutations increase radically.

    For valuable discussions of second person narration in particular, see also Kacandes, Morrissette, McHale, Richardson, and Boheim. McHale's "calculus" of "possible communicative situations" (96) provides one useful way of sorting out texts; Richardson's distinction among three different types of second person narration—which he conceptualizes in a way quite different from mine—is likewise illuminating. Bonheim's approach is, in places, similar to my own in its attention to which narrative positions have been collapsed; and his numerous distinctions, too, are often valuable in charting out this hazy area. But especially toward the end of the essay, he puts more stress than I do on grammatical surface. He also minimizes the importance of brief second person interpolations, as well as cases where "the use of second person is . . . more a matter of rhetoric than of point of view" (71). Although he is here using the term rhetoric in a narrower sense than I am, his essay avoids treating rhetoric in the broader sense too, and hence the issues of power that are central to my argument.

11. For an excellent discussion of Calvino's techniques here, see Phelan, chapter 5. Camus's *La Chute* seems to begin as second person narrative, but it's not really sustained, as much of the novel reverts to first person.

12. See also McHale's discussion of this sort of narration as "self-addressed interior dialogue" (101–4).

13. On the surface, this seems a third person narrative, and at least with respect to its past tense aspects, it is. But there's a double story here, and the main story is intended to narrate to the DA what his role will be: it is

hence a future tense second person narrative—or, since the story is never actually told, a hypothetical future tense second person narrative. A Greek term would be useful to describe this kind of narrative situation.

14. Hammett uses a similar technique to create distance in *The Glass Key*, although there it is not tied to gender. For further discussion of Hammett and women, see, for instance, Marling.

BIBLIOGRAPHY

Babener, Liahna K. "California Babylon: The World of American Detective Fiction." *Clues* 1.2 (1980): 77–89.

Bakhtin, M. M. *The Dialogic Imagination: Four Essays.* Trans. by Caryl Emerson and Michael Holquist. Ed. by Michael Holquist. Austin: University of Texas Press, 1981.

Ball, Mieke. *Narratology: Introduction to the Theory of Narrative.* Trans. by Christine van Boheemen. Toronto: University of Toronto Press, 1985.

Bonheim, Helmut. "Narration in the Second Person." *Recherches anglaises et américaines* 16 (1983): 69–80.

Booth, Wayne C. *The Rhetoric of Fiction.* Chicago: University of Chicago Press, 1961.

Bradford, Ernie. *The Shield and the Sword: The Knights of St. John.* London: Hodder and Stoughton, 1972.

Brock, Kathryn Gail. "Reason is Convention: Parody in The Maltese Falcon." Unpublished manuscript.

Brooks, Cleanth and Robert Penn Warren. *Understanding Fiction.* 2nd ed. New York: Appleton-Century-Crofts, 1959.

Calvino, Italo. *If on a winter's night a traveler.* Trans. by William Waver. New York: Harcourt, Brace, Jovanovich, 1981.

Carutti, Domenico. *Storia di Vittoria Amedeo Il: Il primo Re Di Casa Savoja.* 3rd ed. Torino: Carlo Clausen, 1897.

Dostoevsky, Fyodor. *The Insulted and the Injured.* Vol. 6 of *The Novels of Fyodor Dostoevsky.* Trans. by Constance Garnett. New York: Macmillan Company, n.d.

Genette, Gérard. *Narrative Discourse: An Essay in Method.* Trans. by Jane E. Lewin. Ithaca: Cornell University Press, 1980.

Genette. *Narrative Discourse Revisited.* Trans. by Jane E. Lewin. Ithaca: Cornell University Press, 1988.

Hammett, Dashiell. *The Maltese Falcon.* 1930. New York: Random House/Vintage, 1989.

Holquist, Michael. "Whodunit and other questions: Metaphysical Detective Stories in Post-War Fiction." *New Literary History* 3.1 (Autumn 1971): 135–56.

Islas, Arturo. *The Rain God.* 1984. New York: Avon Books, 1991.

Kacandes, Irene. "Are You in the Text? The 'Literary Performative' in Postmodern Fiction." *Text and Performance* 13 (1993): 139–53.

Knox, Ronald A. "A Detective Story Decalogue." 1929. Rpt. in *Art of the Mystery Story: A Collection of Critical Essays*. Ed. by Howard Haycraft. New York: Carroll and Graf, 1983. 194–96.

Mailloux, Steven. *Rhetorical Power*. Ithaca: Cornell University Press, 1989.

Marling, William. "The Hammett Succubus." *Clues* 3.2 (1982): 66–75.

McHale, Brian. "'You Used to Know What These Words Mean': Misreading *Gravity's Rainbow*." *Language and Style* 18.1 (Winter 1985): 93–118.

Mérimée, Prosper. "Mateo Falcone." 1829. In *Carmen and Other Stories*. Trans. by Nicholas Jotcham. Oxford: Oxford University Press, 1989. 54–66.

Morrissette, Bruce. *Novel and Film: Essays in Two Genres*. Chicago: University of Chicago Press, 1985.

Phelan, James. *Reading People, Reading Plots: Character, Progression, and the Interpretation of Narrative*. Chicago: University of Chicago Press, 1989.

Rabinowitz, Peter J. *Before Reading: Narrative Conventions and the Politics of Interpretation*. Ithaca: Cornell University Press, 1987.

Richardson, Brian. "The Poetics and Politics of Second Person Narrative." *Genre* 24.3 (1991): 309–30.

Schulman, Robert. "Dashiell Hammett's Social Vision." *Centennial Review* 29.4 (Fall 1985): 400–419.

Shelley, Mary. *Frankenstein*. 1831. New York: Bantam Books, 1981.

Stout, Rex. *How Like a God*. New York: Vanguard Press, 1929.

Walton, Priscilla. "'You're in my Burg': Sam Spade's San Francisco." Paper presented at the meetings of the Popular Culture Association, New Orleans, April 1993.

Walton. "Paretsky's V.I. as P.I.: Revising the Script and Recasting the Dick." *Literature/Interpretation/Theory* 4 (1993): 203–13.

Warhol, Robyn R. *Gendered Interventions: Narrative Discourse in the Victorian Novel*. New Brunswick: Rutgers University Press, 1989.

NOTE

1. Scrapbook in the Philip Durham Collection, Special Collections, UCLA.

ADAPTATIONS OF *THE MALTESE FALCON*

Because the dramatic scenes in *The Maltese Falcon* are so vivid, the novel was regarded as an ideal original for screen adaptation. There were three attempts, two of them laudable, but Hammett had no hand in any of the movies made from his book. The first movie from the novel was *The Maltese Falcon* produced by Warner Bros. in 1931. Ricardo Cortez played Spade as a ladies' man; Bebe Daniels was Ruth Wonderly; Dudley Digges played Gutman; Una Merkel was Effie Perine. The screenplay was by Maude Fulton, Lucien Hubbard, and Brown Holmes. Adhering closely to the plot of the novel, the movie was a success at the time of its release, and subsequent critics have praised it. When this version of *The Maltese Falcon* was shown on television, it was retitled *Dangerous Female*.

Five years later, Brown Holmes adapted another version of the novel for Warner Bros. *Satan Met a Lady* took considerable freedom with the plot, presumably to differentiate it from the earlier movie. Starring Warren William as the detective Ted Shayne, Bette Davis as his client Valerie Purvis, and Alison Skipworth as the mysterious Madame Barabbas, this version of Hammett's story was less successful than the first. Shane meets Purvis on a train and agrees to help her find Madame Barabbas. When he locates her, Madame Barabbas hires him to find Valerie Purvis, who has a jewel-encrusted ram's horn. A working title for this version, by which it is sometimes known, was *The Man in the Black Hat*.

The third try proved a charm for Warner Bros. The 1941 John Huston version of the novel is considered a movie classic. When the American Film Institute compiled its list of the 100 greatest movies of the past 100 years in 1999, the 1941 version of *The Maltese Falcon* was ranked number 23. *The Maltese Falcon* was the first movie directed by Huston. He had worked as a screenwriter for Warner Bros., and the success of his screenplay for *High Sierra*

Page from the 1946 comic book based on *The Maltese Falcon*

Warren William and Bette Davis in a scene from *Satan Met a Lady*, the 1936 movie based on *The Maltese Falcon*

(1941), which starred Humphrey Bogart, convinced the studio heads to allow him a chance to direct. Huston also wrote the screenplay for the movie, though the script is so close to the novel that little writing was required. The cast was brilliantly chosen. Humphrey Bogart hardly matches the description of Spade in the novel, but his performance was so compelling that he became Sam Spade for many readers who saw the movie. He was a well-known actor before *The Maltese Falcon;* after it he was a star. Mary Astor is Brigid O'Shaughnessy. Peter Lorre plays Joel Cairo sensitively and accurately. Sidney Greenstreet, making his film debut at age sixty-one, after a career as a stage actor, is brilliant as Gutman. He was nominated for an Academy Award as best supporting actor.

There are some departures from the plot of the novel. The murder of Archer, which is reported in the novel, is depicted in the movie. What Hammett called the to-bed and homosexual scenes are either omitted or toned down to meet the morality-code standards

HAMMETT ON SCREENWRITING

"You need to simplify a story as much as possible when you're going to make a picture of it," he said. "If you don't you'll have too many lines and so lose your full effect. No, I didn't work on the thing at all. I was doing originals most of the time. I believe it's better to have somebody else than the author do adaptations, because the story isn't so rigid in the mind of the man who hasn't written it."

Marguerite Tazelaar, "Film Personalities: A Private Detective Does His Stuff in Hollywood," *New York Herald Tribune,* 12 November 1933, V: 3. Hammett is quoted after sale of movie rights to *The Glass Key* (Paramount, 1935).

imposed on movies at the time. The scene in which Brigid spends the night with Spade is indicated with a kiss, and he does not leave her the next morning to search her apartment; rather, she shows up in his office, as in the book, reporting the break-in. Rhea Gutman as a character is omitted. In the movie, when the $1,000 bill is found missing, Spade only stares at Brigid before accusing Gutman of palming it. The movie leaves Gutman alive at the end and adds a famous, some think corny,[1] last line. When Spade hands the falcon over to Polhaus, the detective says "It's heavy. What is it?" and Spade replies: "The, er, stuff that dreams are made of."—a reference to William Shakespeare's *The Tempest*, Act IV, in which Prospero says, "We are such stuff / As dreams are made on, and our little life / Is rounded with a sleep."

There are curious, seemingly officious, changes in the script for the sake of what Huston considered historical accuracy. For example, the caliber of the gun Brigid uses to shoot Archer is changed from a "Webley-Fosbery automatic revolver. . . . Thirty-eight, eight shot"[2] to a ".44 or .45" possibly, as one critic suggests, because Huston felt the gun Hammett described was "too rare and valuable to have belonged to Thursby."[3] A more likely reason for the change may have been to make the gun conform to the police description of the gun used to kill Thursby. And at the end when Spade tells Brigid, "Well, if you get a good break you'll be out of San Quentin in twenty years and you can come back to me then" (210), Huston changes the name of the prison to Tahatchapi, a women's prison. For the most part, however, the changes in dialogue are made to meet the practical concerns of adaptation, especially the need to keep the movie to an acceptable running time. Huston was so successful that he effectively blocked further attempts to adapt the novel for the screen.

Almost immediately after its publication, Sam Spade and *The Maltese Falcon* entered the popular culture. Wildroot Haircream used comic-strip depictions of Sam Spade's adventures as advertisements in daily newspapers. *The Adventures of Sam Spade* was broadcast as a radio serial on CBS radio in 1946–1949 and on NBC in 1949–1951. *Academy Award Theatre* broadcast a radio version of the novel in July 1946, and Screen Guild did it in May 1950. There was even a comic book based on *The Maltese Falcon*. While Hammett took a fee as script consultant for *The Adventures of Sam Spade,* he had no hand in the program nor in any of the other knockoffs of his novel. In 1932 he wrote three Sam Spade short stories: "A Man Called Spade" (*American Magazine,* July 1932); "Too Many Have Lived" (*American Magazine,* October 1932); and "They Can Only Hang You Once" (*Collier's,* 19 November 1932). Then he was done with Sam Spade.

NOTES

1. See James Naremore, "John Huston and *The Maltese Falcon,*" *Literary Film Quarterly,* 1 (1973): 249.

2. *The Maltese Falcon* (New York: Vintage / Black Lizard, 1992), p. 14. Page references are to this commonly available edition. Quotations have been checked against the first edition. Subsequent references are noted parenthetically in the text.

3. See Peter P. Gillis, "An Anomaly in *The Maltese Falcon,*" *ANQ,* 8 (Summer 1995): 29–30. Gillis says the gun in the movie is a .45. It is identified twice as a .44 or .45.

RESOURCES FOR THE STUDY OF
THE MALTESE FALCON

STUDY QUESTIONS

1. Explain what Sam Spade means at the end of the novel when he tells Brigid O'Shaughnessy "I won't play the sap for you."

2. Choose a statement by one of the critics cited above and develop an argument disagreeing with it.

3. Explain the significance of the narrative voice in *The Maltese Falcon*. How would the novel have been different if Sam Spade were the narrator?

4. Does Brigid O'Shaughnessy love Sam Spade by the end of the novel?

5. Does Sam Spade love Brigid O'Shaughnessy by the end of the novel?

6. Using the floor plan of Spade's apartment, plot the movements of the characters in Chapters XVIII–XX.

7. What is the significance of the timing of Spade's recitation of the Flitcraft story?

8. Stage a scene from *The Maltese Falcon*.

9. After reading the novel, watch the movie John Huston made from it. Compare the two in terms of character development and thematic emphasis. Is the movie a faithful representation of the book?

10. Why does Hammett include the brief scene at the beginning of Chapter XVI in which the theater owner hires Spade to find out whether his employees are stealing from him?

11. Discuss the Maltese falcon as a symbol. What does it symbolize?

12. Does the falcon have a different meaning for different characters? For the reader?

13. Discuss the concept of the tribute in the novel.

14. Chapter III of the novel is titled "Three Women." There are scenes involving the three women in Spade's life: Brigid O'Shaughnessy, Effie

Perine, and Iva Archer. Describe the attitudes of the three toward Spade and his attitudes toward them. To whom is he closest?

15. On a map of San Francisco, trace the action of the novel.

16. Discuss the clothing of the characters in the novel. What do clothes contribute to our understanding of the main characters in the novel?

17. Identify elements of the plot that position the novel in time and place.

18. Why does Spade tell Brigid the Flitcraft parable?

19. What does the Flitcraft parable mean?

20. Research the real Maltese falcon and comment on the accuracy of Gutman's history of the fictional statuette.

21. Discuss the relationship between Iva and Miles Archer.

22. How does Sam Spade demonstrate his professional expertise as a private detective? Find five examples of his trade craft.

23. What is Spade's relationship with Effie Perine? Support your opinion with evidence from the novel.

24. Who introduced the fake falcon? Support your opinion.

25. Is Rhea Gutman really Caspar Gutman's daughter? Why or why not?

26. Explain Rhea Gutman's disappearance after Spade leaves her drugged at the Hotel Alexandria.

27. What are the qualities that give the novel "the absolute distinction of Real Art"?

GLOSSARY OF LITERARY TERMS

Black Mask School: the group of writers who published in *Black Mask* magazine and pioneered hard-boiled detective fiction. The Black Mask School can be divided into overlapping chronological groups. The first predates Joseph Shaw's editorship, which lasted from November 1926 to November 1936. Dashiell Hammett, Carroll John Daly, Paul Suter, and Erle Stanley Gardner are included in this group. The second group is the writers shaped by Shaw. Hammett is also included in this group, as are Raoul Whitfield, Paul Cain, James M. Cain, Horace McCoy, Cornell Woolrich, and Raymond Chandler.

Denouement: a final scene or chapter that explains mysteries and straightens out misunderstandings between characters and the author and reader. The word means "unknotting" in French.

Diction: the author's choice of words. Hammett used a simple diction that reflected the speech of the real models for his characters. He used street slang.

Double entendre: a word or figure of speech used so that it can be understood in two ways, one of which is usually sexual or slighting. The words mean "double understanding" in French.

Embedded plot: a plot entirely contained within the main plot, often called a subplot. Embedded plots may be dream sequences, as in Hammett's *Red Harvest,* or anecdotes, as in *The Maltese Falcon.* Embedded plots should be examined for their relation to the theme of the main plot.

Femme fatale: a beautiful, dangerous woman who leads men into difficult or doomed situations. The phrase means "fatal woman" in French.

Genre: a category of literary work. The term, which comes from the French for "type," is used loosely to designate works that have some common characteristic. Some consider genre to designate subject matter. These users would call romance fiction and mystery fiction genres. Other traditional critics use the term to designate broad types of fiction: novel, poem, short story. Some critics call hard-boiled fiction a genre, but traditionalists would say that it is a content subcategory of the mystery-novel subgenre.

Genre Fiction: a subcategory of fiction defined by subject matter. Mystery fiction, science fiction, romance fiction are examples of genre fiction.

Hard-Boiled Fiction: unsentimental fiction, usually narrated in the first person by a determined and yet resigned person, usually a man and often a detective, who struggles with the bleakness of modern life. Hard-boiled fiction is typically set in a big city, where there are no clear-cut moral guidelines. The protagonist must determine his own values based on a personal sense of right and wrong. The hard-boiled hero struggles against the dark forces of the world he encounters. The name comes from

177

slang usage late in the nineteenth century that derives from the phrase "tough as a hard-boiled egg."

Marxism: the economic and social theories of Karl Marx and Friedrich Engels, developed from their doctrines of the mid-nineteenth century, especially their *Communist Manifesto* (1848) and Marx's *Das Kapital* (1867). Marxist literary critics examine the material or economic circumstances of the production of literature, the economic story it narrates, and the ways in which it shows class struggle. Marxist critics struggle to find some political message or some indication of class conflict in Hammett's fiction.

Narrative: in its simplest sense, the telling of the story. Narrative theory uses the term to point to such formal aspects as who tells the story, how much the teller knows, the order in which the events are told, and the ratio of scene versus summary. In this sense, narrative means the formal apparatus of storytelling.

New Historicism: a school of criticism that believes literature always reflects economic, social, and political circumstances and that readers are basically consumers of cultural objects. New Historicists attempt to "put the history back" into texts that had been considered timeless and ahistorical. The history favored is that of the common man, rather than the great one.

Noir: from the French for "black"; bleak, pessimistic fiction about corruption, lust, greed, and betrayal of the type that became popular after World War I. Hard-boiled fiction often provided the original stories for noir movies, called film noir. Notable examples are John Huston's *The Maltese Falcon* (1941), Billy Wilder's *Double Indemnity* (1944), and, more recently, Roman Polanski's *Chinatown* (1974).

Objective style: a strictly maintained third-person point of view, in which the author describes only what a bystander would see and expresses no interpretation of the characters or the action. Hammett's *The Maltese Falcon* is a well-known example, but *The Glass Key* actually carries out the technique more faithfully.

Omniscience: a point of view used by the author in which he or she knows all and sees all. The author can look into characters' minds and tell readers some or all of the characters' thoughts as well as the unseen qualities of places and objects. There are degrees of omniscience: in "character-bound omniscience," the author looks only into the mind of a specific character, usually the protagonist. "Limited omniscience" usually means that the author restricts omniscience to a few characters. Omniscience must be combined credibly with point of view. Omniscience must be carefully controlled and sharply limited in detective and mystery novels to create suspense and to avoid disclosing the revealed plot.

Plot: literary theorists, beginning with Aristotle, have argued and refined the concept of plot. For most students it is enough to differentiate plot from story. A story is what happens; a plot is how an author constructs the telling of a story to make it into literature. Plot involves causality, characters and their motivations, a structure that may not be chronological, and narration.

Point of view: the position from which the author narrates the plot. If the narrative is presented from the point of view of a single person, that character is referred to as the "point of view character." The Continental Op is the point of view character in *Red Harvest* and *The Dain Curse*, as detectives almost always are in hard-boiled fiction. "Point of view" may refer to the character who tells the story, or in a third-person narrative it may refer to the perspective the narrator adopts in telling the story.

Popular Culture: the term adopted by scholars who focused attention on the cultural interests of the average person. In literature, popular-culture scholars studied best-sellers and works of genre fiction rather than classic works. They attempted a leveling of cultural standards, arguing that the tastes of the general reader have as much standing as those of cultural traditionalists.

Scene: a sequence of actions set during a short period of time in a particular place. The scene includes dialogue, action, and descriptive details. Beginning with *The Maltese Falcon,* Hammett arranged his novels in sharply focused, vividly depicted scenes in which characters' speech and actions and their responses to the speech and actions of others reveal the plot. The opposite is "summary" plotting, in which the author summarizes events that occur over an extended period of time.

Simile: a figure of speech in which two unlike things are compared, using the connective "like" or "as"—"my love is like a rose." The direct comparison— "my love is a rose"—is a metaphor, but both terms are commonly grouped under the label of metaphor.

Style: the way the author uses the elements of writing to express his or her idea and individuality. Word choice, sentence type and length, punctuation, and ratio of scene to summary are some of the elements of a style. In classical rhetoric, the best style was thought to be that best matched to the purpose of the writing. The modern use of the word also includes the author's distinctive verbal patterns.

Tone: the general impression of a work on the audience. Elements of tone may include the perceived attitude of the author toward the audience or the mood the author elicits. The tone of *Red Harvest* is serious and pessimistic; the tone of *The Thin Man* is humorous and mocking.

Vernacular: the native speech or language of a place as spoken or written by inhabitants; everyday language used by ordinary people. Hammett uses diction and speech rhythms to express vernacular speech. His detectives and crooks use street slang, which is an element of vernacular speech.

GLOSSARY OF PEOPLE, PLACES, AND TERMS IN *THE MALTESE FALCON*

5*: **General Delivery.** Mail sent to a recipient care of a post office for pickup in person. General Delivery mail was often for itinerant people who either had no permanent address or did not wish to reveal an address.

6: **St. Mark.** A fictitious hotel probably modeled on the St. Francis at Union Square and the Mark Hopkins. Both are on Powell Street, the St. Francis at the foot of Nob Hill, the Mark Hopkins at the top.[1]

10: **Dynamite.** *The Random House Dictionary of American Slang* uses this passage from *The Maltese Falcon* as an example of the usage meaning "to speak aggressively and insistently in an attempt to sell, persuade, impress, or seduce." However, Spade's comment seems to have a more vulgar connotation, suggesting sexual intercourse.

11: *Celebrated Criminal Cases of America.* Volume of true crime stories by Thomas S. Duke, Captain of Police, San Francisco. The volume was published with the approval of the Police Commissioners of San Francisco by James H. Barry in 1910. The volume was a favorite of Hammett's. He refers to it in *The Dain Curse* and *The Thin Man* as well.

14: **Machine.** Automobile.

32: **Coronet.** Apartment building probably modeled on the posh Cathedral Apartments at 1201 California Street.

40: **Remedial.** Remedial Loan, a real pawn shop.

42: *Chypre.* A heavy sandalwood scent often used in soaps. Chypre is also an Elizabethan usage for mischievous sprite.

45: **Levantine.** A person from the Eastern Mediterranean region. A levant is also one who welshes on a bet.

51: **Hotel Belvedere.** Modeled on the Hotel Bellevue, one block from the Geary Street Theatre.

52: **Herbert's Grill.** Actual restaurant in 1928 at 151 Powell Street, since closed.

53: **Geary Theatre.** A real theater, where actor George Arliss played Jewish moneylender Shylock in William Shakespeare's *The Merchant of Venice* in December 1928.

53: **Marquard's.** A real restaurant that billed itself in 1928 as "A Restaurant for Epicures."

78: **Bulls.** Police.

92: *En Cuba.* Song by Eduardo Sanchez de Fuentes. Originally published in English as "Tu (you) Habanera" by Jerome H. Remick in 1906; the song was republished in 1928 as "En Cuba."

94: **Baumes Rush.** Baumes Law was a 1926 New York state law that called for life imprisonment for any criminal convicted of a fourth felony. Professional criminals with a long record fled the state in a rush to avoid the penalty.

* page numbers keyed to the Black Lizard edition of *The Maltese Falcon*.

181

94: **Romeville.** A corruption of Rumville, referring to London from about the mid-sixteenth century. More generally, any large city with areas where unsavory people gather.

104: **Alexandria Hotel.** Modeled on either the Sir Francis Drake Hotel at Sutter and Powell Streets or the Clift at Geary and Taylor.

110: **Gunsel.** Hobo slang for young homosexual. Because of general misunderstanding of Hammett's use of the term, it came into general use to mean gunman after the novel was published.

112: **Palace Hotel.** A real hotel at the corner of Market and New Montgomery.

118: *The Call. The San Francisco Call and Post* newspaper.

119: **Ferry Building.** A real office building.

120: **Goose-berry lay.** Criminal slang that refers to stealing clothes hung out to dry on a clothesline.

140: **States Hof Brau.** A real restaurant in the Pacific Building on Market Street.

142: **Egan Mob.** A violent St. Louis mob organized about 1900 by Jellyroll Egan. Until 1920, the mob specialized in anti-union enforcement, then moved into bootlegging and jewel theft.

143: **Stuss-games.** A simplified form of faro designed for quick and easy betting in stuss parlors.

144: **Dixie Monahan.** Possibly a reference to Chicago lawyer and bootlegger J. K. Monahan, who was arrested attempting to bribe federal agents to allow withdrawals from whiskey warehouses in 1921 and who was apparently the J. Monahan arrested for rum-running on Lake Oswego, New York, in July 1926.

144: **Fallon.** William J. Fallon, New York criminal lawyer known as the Great Mouthpiece. He died in 1927 at the age of forty-one from heart disease and alcoholism.

144: **Joliet.** Illinois state prison.

144: **Nick the Greek.** The famous gambler in Chicago during the 1920s and in Las Vegas later. Born Nicholas Andrea Dandolos on Crete, he came to the United States in about 1911 at the age of eighteen, financed by his wealthy family.

144: **Newport Beach Boating Club.** Possibly a reference to the Newport Beach Boat House, which closed about 1927. Rum-running was common in the area.

145: **Arnold Rothstein.** A celebrated gambler and mobster, who reputedly fixed the 1919 World Series. He was murdered in 1928.

151: **Hotel Sutter.** A real hotel on the corner of Sutter and Kearny Streets.

161: **Pickwick Stage Terminal.** Bus depot in 1928, since torn down.

165: **John's Grill.** 63 Ellis Street. Present-day headquarters of the Dashiell Hammett Society.

181: **Heater.** Handgun.

181: **Fog.** Shoot.

203: **Dingus.** Thing.

204: **Rara avis.** Latin term meaning "rare bird."

NOTE

1. All place identifications are from Joe Gores, "A Foggy Night," *City of San Francisco Magazine,* 4 November 1975, pp. 29–32.

BIBLIOGRAPHY

WORKS BY HAMMETT

BOOKS: *Red Harvest* (New York & London: Knopf, 1929);

The Dain Curse (New York: Knopf, 1929; London: Knopf, 1930);

The Maltese Falcon (New York & London: Knopf, 1930);

The Glass Key (London & New York: Knopf, 1931);

The Thin Man (New York: Knopf, 1934; London: Barker, 1934);

Secret Agent X-9, books 1 and 2 (Philadelphia: McKay, 1934);

$106,000 Blood Money (New York: Spivak, 1943);

The Battle of the Aleutians, by Hammett and Robert Colodny (Adak, Alaska: U.S. Army Intelligence Section, Field Force Headquarters, Adak, 1944);

The Adventures of Sam Spade (New York: Spivak, 1944); republished as *They Can Only Hang You Once* (New York: The American Mercury / Spivak, 1949);

The Continental Op (New York: Spivak, 1945);

The Return of the Continental Op (New York: Spivak, 1945);

Hammett Homicides, edited by Ellery Queen (New York: Spivak, 1946);

Dead Yellow Women, edited by Queen (New York: Spivak, 1947);

Nightmare Town, edited by Queen (New York: The American Mercury / Spivak, 1948);

The Creeping Siamese, edited by Queen (New York: Spivak, 1950);

Woman in the Dark, edited by Queen (New York: Spivak, 1951);

A Man Named Thin, edited by Queen (New York: Ferman, 1962);

The Big Knockover, edited by Lillian Hellman (New York: Random House, 1966); reprinted as *The Dashiell Hammett Story Omnibus* (London: Cassell, 1966);

The Continental Op, edited by Steven Marcus (New York: Random House, 1974);

Woman in the Dark (New York: Knopf, 1988).

Nightmare Town, edited by Kirby McCauley, Martin Greenberg, and Ed Gorman (New York: Knopf, 1999).

Collection: *Complete Novels* (New York: Library of America, 1999).

OTHER: *Creeps by Night,* edited by Hammett (New York: Day, 1931; London: Gollancz, 1932);

After the Thin Man, in *New Black Mask 5 and 6,* edited by Matthew J. Bruccoli and Richard Layman (San Diego, New York & London: Harvest, 1986).

MOTION PICTURES: *City Streets,* original story by Hammett, Paramount, 1931;

Mister Dynamite, original story by Hammett, Universal, 1935;

After the Thin Man, original story by Hammett, M-G-M, 1936;

Another Thin Man, original story by Hammett, M-G-M, 1939;

Watch on the Rhine, screenplay by Hammett, Warner Bros., 1943.

BIBLIOGRAPHY

Layman, Richard. *Dashiell Hammett: A Descriptive Bibliography.* Pittsburgh: University of Pittsburgh Press, 1979. Lists primary and selected secondary works.

BIOGRAPHIES

Layman, Richard. *Shadow Man: The Life of Dashiell Hammett.* New York: Harcourt Brace Jovanovich, 1981. The first full biography of Hammett; stubbornly adheres to the facts of Hammett's life; all his published fiction is described.

Johnson, Diane. *Dashiell Hammett: A Life.* New York: Random House, 1983. The authorized biography, drawing on family materials unavailable to other biographers; a novelistic approach to Hammett's life.

Nolan, William F. *Hammett: A Life at the Edge.* New York: Cogdon & Weed, 1983. Biographical interpretation by the mystery writer and popular biographer who wrote the first book-length study of Hammett's life and career.

Symons, Julian. *Dashiell Hammett.* San Diego & New York: Harcourt Brace Jovanovich, 1985. An overview of Hammett's life and career by the noted literary critic and historian.

Mellen, Joan. *Hellman and Hammett: The Legendary Passion of Lillian Hellman and Dashiell Hammett.* New York: HarperCollins, 1996. The fullest account of the relationship between Hammett and Hellman. Supersedes previous biographies in the account of Hammett's life after 1931, though
the Hammett family disputes Mellen's assertion that Mary Jane Hammett was not the daughter of Dashiell Hammett.

REFERENCES

Bazelon, David T. "Dashiell Hammett's Private Eye," in *The Scene before You: A New Approach to American Culture,* edited by Chandler Brossard. New York & Toronto: Rinehart, 1955, pp. 180–190. Early critical essay arguing that Hammett is best at writing formula fiction in which motivation is not carefully analyzed.

Bentley, Christopher. "Radical Anger: Dashiell Hammett's *Red Harvest,*" in *American Crime Fiction: Studies in the Genre,* edited by Brian Docherty. New York: St. Martin's Press, 1988, pp. 54–70. A Marxist reading of Hammett's first novel.

Chandler, Raymond. "The Simple Art of Murder," *Atlantic Monthly* (December 1944): 53–59. Pioneering essay in which Hammett's writing is discussed in terms of tradition of American crime fiction.

Day, Gary. "Investigating the Investigator: Hammett's Continental Op," in *American Crime Fiction: Studies in the Genre,* edited by Brian Docherty. New York: St. Martin's Press, 1988, pp. 39–53. A discussion of the narrative strategies Hammett employed in the characterization of the unnamed detective hero of his first two novels and most of his short stories.

Dooley, Dennis. *Dashiell Hammett.* New York: Ungar, 1984. A general introduction to Hammett's works that discusses "only works that are readily available to the average reader." Half the book is given over to the short fiction.

Edenbaum, Robert I. "The Poetics of the Private-Eye: The Novels of Dashiell Hammett," in *Tough Guy Writers of the Thirties,* edited by David Madden. Carbondale: Southern Illinois University Press, 1968, pp. 80–103. Describes the code of toughness in Hammett's novels and points out that the mask of stoicism worn by Hammett's heroes is never lifted to show the reader their vulnerability.

Fechheimer, David, ed., Special issue of *City of San Francisco* magazine, 4 November 1975. Includes valuable resources for Hammett study, including the only published interview with Jose Hammett.

Gores, Joe. *Hammett: A Novel.* New York: Putnam, 1975. Novel based on careful research of Hammett's life. The author's note at the end provides biographical notes and information about Hammett in San Francisco and his use of the city in his fiction.

Gregory, Sinda. *Private Investigations: The Novels of Dashiell Hammett.* Carbondale & Edwardsville: Southern Illinois University Press, 1985. Critical and interpretive study of Hammett's fiction.

Hagemann, E. R. *A Comprehensive Index to Black Mask, 1920–1951.* Bowling Green, Ohio: Bowling Green State University Popular Press, 1982. A reliable inventory of all the stories in *Black Mask,* useful for understanding the publishing contexts of Hammett's work.

Hall, Jasmine Yong. "Jameson, Genre, and Gumshoes: *The Maltese Falcon* as Inverted Romance," in *The Cunning Craft: Original Essays on Detective Fiction,* edited by Ronald G. Walker. Macomb: Western Illinois University Press, 1990, pp. 109–119. A reading of *The Maltese Falcon* as a romance in the mode of the Grail legend.

Hamilton, Cynthia S. *Western and Hard-Boiled Detective Fiction in America: From High Noon to Midnight.* Iowa City: University of Iowa Press, 1987. An analysis of the works of Hammett, Zane Grey, Frederick Faust, and Raymond Chandler, based on "the dynamics of one generic tradition: the American adventure formula."

Herron, Don. *Dashiell Hammett Tour,* Herron's Literary Walks in San Francisco. San Francisco: Dawn Heron Press, 1979. Revised as *The Dashiell Hammett Tour.* San Francisco: City Lights Books, 1991.

Layman, Richard. "Dashiell Hammett" in *Dictionary of Literary Biography: Documentary Series,* volume 6: *Hardboiled Writers,* edited by Matthew J. Bruccoli and Layman. Detroit: Gale Research, 1989. A documentary record of Hammett's life and career, including much previously uncollected material.

Macdonald, Ross. "Homage to Dashiell Hammett," in *Self-Portrait: Ceaselessly in the Past.* Santa Barbara, Cal.: Capra, 1981, pp. 109–112. Essay by the crime writer describing Hammett's literary influence.

Malin, Irving. "Focus on 'The Maltese Falcon': The Metaphysical Falcon," in *Tough Guy Writers of the Thirties,* edited by David Madden. Carbondale: Southern Illinois University Press, 1968, pp. 104–109. Argues that *The Maltese Falcon* describes a mysterious world in which the falcon itself is the deity.

Marling, William. *Dashiell Hammett.* New York: Twayne, 1983. Biographical and critical study in the standard format of the Twayne United States Authors series.

Metress, Christopher, ed., *The Critical Response to Dashiell Hammett.* Westport, Conn.: Greenwood Press, 1994. Reprints excerpts from key works of criticism and includes a checklist of works about Hammett.

Nolan, William F. *Dashiell Hammett: A Casebook.* Santa Barbara: McNally & Loftin, 1969. Difficult-to-find first book about Hammett; the basis for Nolan's later biography.

Raubicheck, Walter. "Stirring It Up: Dashiell Hammett and the Tradition of the Detective Story," *Armchair Detective,* 20 (Winter 1987): 20–25. Examination of the innovations Hammett introduced to the detective story through irony and characterization.

Shulman, Robert. "Dashiell Hammett's Social Vision," *Centennial Review,* 29 (Fall 1985): 400–419. An attempt to reconcile the social views of *Red Harvest,* *The Maltese Falcon,* and *The Glass Key* with Hammett's later political views.

Thompson, George J. "The Problem of Moral Vision in Dashiell Hammett's Detective Novels," *Armchair Detective,* 6 (May 1973): 153–156; 6 (August 1973): 213–225; 7 (November 1973): 32–40; 7 (May 1974): 178–192; 7 (August 1974): 270–280; 8 (November 1974): 27–35; 8 (February 1975): 124–130. Long essay discussing Hammett's fiction in terms of the value system it advocates.

Wolfe, Peter. *Beams Falling: The Art of Dashiell Hammett.* Bowling Green, Ohio: Bowling Green University Popular Press, 1980. Critical discussion of Hammett's fiction.

PAPERS

The most important collection of Dashiell Hammett's papers is at the Harry Ransom Humanities Research Center, University of Texas, Austin. The Lillian Hellman archive includes letters from Hammett to Hellman and copies of her plays with his annotations. The Knopf archive there includes editorial correspondence and internal memos related to Hammett's novels.

WEBSITES

There are several websites devoted to Hammett and his works. In general, students should be wary of those sites that are unattributed or that do not provide an indication of sources. Use websites with extreme caution.

A Guide to Classic Mystery and Detection: <http://members.aol.com/mg4273/classics.htm> An educational site containing reading lists and essays on great mysteries, mainly of the pre-1960 era. It is designed and written by Michael E. Grost, a mystery fan who lives near Detroit, Michigan. It includes much information about Hammett's short stories in particular.

The Hammett Mailing List: <http://www.cigarsmokers.com/hammett/hammettmain.html> Hammett discussion list. Includes several links.

The Continental Op: <http://nanaimo.ark.com/~wilted/> An unattributed site dedicated to discussion of The Continental Op.

Continental Detective Agency: <http://www.transki.freeserve.co.uk/more.htm> Full, unattributed site from England. Includes links.

MASTER INDEX

W

Walton, Percy 151, 161
Warhol, Robyn 157
Warner Bros. 167
Watch on the Rhine (Hellman) 14
"Who Killed Bob Teal" (Hammett) 53
"The Whosis Kid" (Hammett) 49, 54
William, Warren 167
Williams, Race 130
Wilson, Edmund 82
The Wings of the Dove (James) 74
Wolfe, Peter 86
"Woman at Bay" (Coxe) 147
Women in Love (Lawrence) 87
Woolf, Virginia 87, 151

Woollcott, Alexander 10
World War I 4
Wright, Jimmy 6
Wright, Lee 123

X

Xenophile 83

Z

"Zigzags of Treachery" (Hammett) 133